The Ministry of the Word

The Ministry of the Word

A Handbook to the 1978 Lectionary

EDITED BY GEOFFREY CUMING

London
BIBLE READING FELLOWSHIP

Oxford   New York   Toronto   Melbourne
OXFORD UNIVERSITY PRESS · 1979

Oxford University Press, Walton Street, Oxford OX2 6DP

OXFORD LONDON GLASGOW
NEW YORK TORONTO MELBOURNE WELLINGTON
KUALA LUMPUR SINGAPORE JAKARTA HONG KONG TOKYO
DELHI BOMBAY CALCUTTA MADRAS KARACHI
NAIROBI DAR ES SALAAM CAPE TOWN

Bible Reading Fellowship, St Michael's House,
2 Elizabeth St., London SW1W 9RQ

© *Bible Reading Fellowship 1979*

British Library Cataloguing in Publication Data

The ministry of the word.
   1. Church of England. Liturgy and ritual
   2. Lectionaries
   I. Cuming, Geoffrey   II. Bible Reading
   Fellowship
   264'.032   BX5147.L4   79-40308

ISBN 0-19-213225-3
ISBN 0-19-213228-8 Pbk

Phototypeset in V.I.P. Plantin by
Western Printing Services Ltd, Bristol
Printed in Great Britain by
Billing & Sons Ltd Guildford, London and Worcester

Contents

Contributors

John Barton, Lecturer in Old Testament Theology, University of Oxford

F. V. A. Boyse, Chaplain of H.M. the Queen at Hampton Court Palace

R. J. Coggins, Lecturer in Old Testament Studies, King's College, London

G. J. Cuming, Tutor in Liturgy, Ripon College, Cuddesdon; Canon Theologian of Leicester

C. F. Evans, Emeritus Professor of New Testament Studies, King's College, London

J. C. Fenton, Canon of Christ Church, Oxford

Anthony Gelston, Senior Lecturer in Theology, University of Durham

J. E. Goldingay, Lecturer in Biblical Studies, St John's College, Nottingham

R. S. Good, Senior Lecturer in Religious Studies, Christ Church College, Canterbury

Gordon Hewitt, Chairman of Chelmsford Diocesan Liturgical Committee; Chaplain to H.M. the Queen

C. J. A. Hickling, Lecturer in New Testament Studies, King's College, London

J. L. Houlden, Lecturer in New Testament Studies, King's College, London

P. F. Johnson, Chaplain and Vice-Principal, St Chad's College, Durham

I. H. Jones, Lecturer in Biblical Studies, Wesley College, Bristol

S. S. S. C. Laws, Lecturer in New Testament Studies, King's College, London

G. Lloyd Jones, Lecturer in Hebrew and Old Testament, University College of North Wales, Bangor

A. L. Moore, Vice-Principal, Wycliffe Hall, Oxford

J. B. Muddiman, Tutor in New Testament Studies, St Stephen's House, Oxford

J. Mulrooney, Lecturer in Old Testament Studies, Heythrop College, University of London

Graham Neville, Lecturer in Religious Studies, Brighton Polytechnic

Anthony Phillips, Chaplain and Fellow, St John's College, Oxford

J. W. Rogerson, Professor of Biblical Studies, University of Sheffield

Michael Scott-Joynt, Vicar of Bicester, Oxfordshire

Leo Stephens-Hodge, formerly Lecturer in New Testament and Christian Worship, London College of Divinity

K. W. Stevenson, Lecturer of Boston Parish Church, Lincolnshire; Visiting Lecturer in Liturgy, Lincoln Theological College

David Thomas, Vice-Principal, St Stephen's House, Oxford

P.H.Vaughan, Principal, East Midlands Joint Ordination Training Scheme

E.C.Whitaker, Vicar of Plumpton Wall, Cumbria; Honorary Canon of Carlisle

Arthur Widdess, Canon Treasurer of York

David P. Wilcox, Principal, Ripon College, Cuddesdon

Wilf Wilkinson, Rector of St Mary's, Clifton, Nottinghamshire

Foreword by the Archbishop of Canterbury

William Temple's description of worship is well known, but it deserves repetition. He wrote of worship as:

the quickening of the conscience by the holiness of God; the nourishment of the mind by the truth of God; the purifying of the imagination by the beauty of God; the opening of the heart to the love of God, and the surrender of the will to the purpose of God—all gathered up in adoration, the chief remedy for self-centredness which is our original sin and the source of all actual sin.

That part of worship which calls on the worshipper to hear God's most holy word makes considerable demands on him. If his mind is to be nourished by the truth of God, that mind must be 'erect to God', alert, prepared. The value of worship to that individual may well depend in considerable measure on his *preparation* for it.

It is here, as I see it, that this book will come into its own. That it will be of help to preachers, I have no doubt. I sincerely hope it will. But most preachers—all, I would hope—have larger and more detailed aids to their preparation. I see this book, even more, as an aid to the man in the pew.

I see him, on Saturday night, spending a period of time in preparation for the worship of the following day. Before him he has open the passages which will be read at the eucharist. His aid, in his preparatory thinking and praying, may well be this book.

I have a further vision. The Jews have an ancient custom which we Christians would do well to emulate. On Friday night, in preparation for the worship of the ensuing Sabbath, the father gathers the members of the family round him, candles are lit, prayers are said, food is eaten. What a lovely thing it would be if more and more Christian families would engage in a like exercise—with the aid of this book! Family life would be stronger, and Sunday worship more meaningful.

I wish the book well.

Lambeth Palace,   Donald Cantuar:
London.

The 1978 Lectionary

On 9 July 1978 the General Synod of the Church of England authorized the use of a new table of readings at Holy Communion as an alternative to the epistles and gospels of the Book of Common Prayer, and this table of readings is related to a scheme for the Church's year which is not quite the same as that of the Prayer Book. This new provision was originally framed by the Joint Liturgical Group, a body which consists of representatives of eight Churches in the British Isles, including the Church of England, and was first published in *The Calendar and Lectionary* (ed. R. C. D. Jasper, Oxford University Press, 1967). In 1972 the Church of England adopted the lectionary proposals of this report almost exactly as they stood and approved them for experimental use. More recently, the proposals of the Joint Liturgical Group were finally approved by the General Synod, but not without considerable amendment of both the calendar and the lectionary. It is with this new calendar and lectionary that we are concerned here.

The Calendar

The most important new feature is that the presentation of the Church's year is shown to begin with a series of 'Sundays before Christmas', followed by the traditional Sundays of Advent. One small consequence of this arrangement is that the long series of Sundays after Trinity is correspondingly shorter, but the real reason for the new order is to provide a longer season of preparation for Christmas than the four Sundays of Advent. An explanation of this change is set out more fully below in our discussion of the lectionary. For the rest, the new features of the calendar are related to the names which we give to certain Sundays. Septuagesima and the two Sundays following are now called the Ninth, Eighth, and Seventh Sundays before Easter. To many people the old Latin names have been a source of confusion. The name Quinquagesima signifies to those skilled in Latin that this Sunday falls fifty days before Easter, and this is correct. But Septuagesima tells us that this Sunday is seventy days before Easter, which is plainly incorrect. The new designation of 'Sundays before Easter' performs the same function as the old Latin names in terms which everyone can understand, and with greater accuracy: it tells us that we now stop looking back to Christmas and begin to look forward to Easter. The Sunday after Ascension Day may now be called 'the Sixth Sunday after Easter'. This makes it more clear that the Great Fifty Days of the Easter season continue right up to Pentecost. These fifty days originated in the Jewish observance of the season from Passover to Pentecost, and are one of the earliest observances of the Church's calendar. Finally, Pentecost is the new designation of Whitsunday and, what perhaps is more important, the Sundays after Trinity are now renumbered as 'Sundays after Pentecost'. Trinity Sunday remains unaltered as a witness to the Church's faith in the Trinity. By calling the following Sundays 'Sundays after Pentecost' we remind ourselves that we live in the post-Pentecost era, the age of the Holy Spirit.

The Lectionary

The new series of 'Sundays before Christmas' prepares us for the celebration of the Incarnation at Christmas. We begin with creation, because the Incarnation inaugurated a new creation; we continue with the fall, because the Incarnation provided the remedy for the fall; the promise of redemption, the doctrine of the remnant, the progressive revelation of God, and the prophecies, all begin to find their fulfilment in the Incarnation. These matters sum up the Old Testament story. They provide us with the themes of the Ninth to the Fifth Sundays before Christmas, and are the context in which we understand the event which we celebrate at Christmas.

The first and second Sundays of Advent preserve the themes which are familiar to us from the Prayer Book. With the third and fourth Sundays of Advent we begin a series of readings of which the structure is determined by the life of Christ. It begins with the Forerunner (John the Baptist: this is logically if not chronologically correct), followed by the Annunciation. After Christmas it continues with the Baptism of Jesus and the call of the first disciples, and then through the ministry of Jesus to the Lent series which looks forward to the Passion and the Resurrection.

It may be seen that the Old Testament readings in Lent follow a course which in some respects is similar to the course of readings for the Sundays before Christmas. At both seasons the readings include the creation, the fall, the promises to faithful Abraham, and the Exodus. The tradition by which these readings were read to prepare for the celebration of redemption at Easter is a very ancient one, and they have therefore been preserved in this context. This tradition dates from a stage in the Church's life before there was any festival to celebrate the Incarnation. But since we now have the festivals of Christmas and the Epiphany, it seems appropriate to employ the same preparatory course at the beginning of the year also. It thus forms an introduction to the whole work of Christ, both in his Incarnation and in redemption.

In the past, such events as the Annunciation, the visit of the Magi, the Presentation, and the Transfiguration, have been celebrated on 'red-letter' days, which fall on Sunday only occasionally. It is therefore a useful consequence of the structure which follows the life of Christ that our attention is drawn to these events, not only on their appointed days but on Sundays as well. Thus for example the Annunciation is the theme of Advent 4, the Presentation of Christmas 1, the visit of the Magi of Christmas 2, and the Transfiguration of the Fourth Sunday in Lent.

After the celebration of the Resurrection, the Ascension, and the coming of the Holy Spirit, the Sundays after Pentecost focus our attention on the life of the Spirit-filled Church in the world. If 'Sundays after Trinity' are now replaced by 'Sundays after Pentecost', the Church's witness to its faith in the Trinity is not thereby diminished. On the contrary, the structure of the calendar and the lectionary is designed to testify to the Trinity, for the nine Sundays before Christmas direct our attention to God the Father and the world before the Incarnation, from Christmas onwards we celebrate the life of the incarnate Son, and the Sundays after Pentecost are concerned with the life of the Church in the Holy Spirit.

Although, as we have said, the Joint Liturgical Group's draft of the lectionary has been amended for use in the Church of England, the principles on which it was originally founded remain the same. An important consideration is to secure that a larger volume of scripture is read at the eucharist than is obtained by the ancient scheme preserved in the Prayer Book, according to which the same lessons are read year after year on any one Sunday. This has been achieved by framing a two-yearly, or biennial, scheme of readings so that where the Prayer Book provided, for example, fifty-two gospels for fifty-two Sundays, the new scheme provides one hundred and four. The modern Roman Catholic scheme goes further, for it is based on a three-year course, but a biennial scheme may have some advantage in so far as it better combines variety with familiarity.

The present century has seen sung Mattins very largely replaced by the celebration of the eucharist as the main act of Sunday worship. One consequence of this is that the many people who attend the Prayer Book service of Holy Communion only will scarcely ever hear the Old Testament. Yet this is the book which spoke to our Lord of his Father in Heaven, which he constantly quoted, and which he came not to destroy but to fulfil. So we may not destroy it either: it is a great improvement that readings from the Old Testament are now provided to be read at the eucharist, and there is no lack of ancient precedent for doing so.

The rubrics do not require that the Old Testament is always read, or that three readings must always be read. But if the time factor is important, it is better to give proper attention to the reading of scripture than to spend time on peripheral matters at the expense of the reading of scripture. When only two readings are read, the notes indicate that the gospel must always be one, and that we are free to choose whether to read the Old Testament reading or the New Testament one. However, the notes encourage us to give preference to the Old Testament on the nine Sundays before Christmas, and to the New Testament on the Sundays after Pentecost. These readings have been called 'the controlling reading'; they set the themes which give coherence to each group of three readings. It is important to recognize that the choice of readings has not been dictated by a pre-determined list of themes. Of course, in the main seasons of the Church's year the readings choose themselves, and follow themes which are indicated by the seasons. But for the Sundays after Pentecost, the procedure when the lectionary was originally framed was first to single out the passages of scripture which most deserved to be read, and only then to arrange them in coherent groups. Some people may find the themes helpful, others may not. The Joint Liturgical Group emphasized that 'the thematic titles provided are no more than *indications* of emphasis. They must not be allowed to give false rigidity to the hearing of scripture or to the preaching of the Word of God. The lections are, on the whole, rich in material. They may say different things to different people, and it is right that they should do so'.

'This is the Word of the Lord'

The practice of reading from Scripture during public worship goes back beyond Christianity to Jewish worship. Luke (4:16–20) tells us of Jesus reading from the prophecy of Isaiah in the synagogue, and Acts (13:14,15) of Paul and Barnabas reading from the Law and the Prophets at Antioch in Pisidia. The Christian Church carried on the Jewish practice. About A.D. 150 Justin Martyr describes the Sunday eucharist as beginning with the reading of 'the records of the apostles or the writings of the prophets', continued for as long as time allowed.

Some scholars indeed see such liturgical readings as having given the gospels their present form. Certainly the raw material of the gospels, in the form of stories leading up to a memorable saying, or of parables, must have been handed down from mouth to mouth, and especially at meetings for worship. If so, reading short extracts from the gospels as lessons is simply to return them to their original condition.

Certainly the epistles were written for reading aloud; again, probably during worship. Their use of the second person plural and the imperative makes them particularly suitable for the purpose; and the same is true of the Old Testament prophecies. Long narratives are less suited to reading at the eucharist under modern conditions. In the 1978 lectionary, for example, the story of David and Goliath has to be cut down to 14 verses out of 51 (1 Samuel 17). Consequently, the great majority of the Old Testament lessons are taken from the prophets.

In the fourth century it was the general practice to read three lessons, from the Prophets, the 'Apostle', and the Gospels. But in the early Middle Ages the number was reduced in most places to two, and it was the Old Testament lesson that usually disappeared, particularly in the West. At the Reformation Cranmer took over the medieval lessons of the Sunday Mass with very few changes. This somewhat haphazard selection of lessons thus lasted for something like a thousand years before being changed in the Roman Catholic

Church or in the Church of England. One consequence of its survival was that the Old Testament was heard at Holy Communion on only one Sunday in the year (and on six week-days); though, to be fair to Cranmer, it must be remembered that he expected the congregation to have heard an Old Testament lesson already at Mattins.

There are two ways of reading the Bible liturgically, which we may call 'serial' and 'thematic'. The serial method was widely used in the early Church. A great preacher would work steadily through a book of the Bible, taking the passage that had been read out; the biblical commentaries of such men as Origen and John Chrysostom were produced in this way. When Egeria, a nun from Spain or Southern France, visited Jerusalem during the years A.D. 381–4 she was specially impressed by the fact that the lessons were chosen to be apposite to the day. The Jews, however, had special lessons, at any rate for the great festivals, and these have been thought to underlie the vision of Revelation.

Neither method is adopted consistently in the Book of Common Prayer. The thematic approach is obviously used at the great festivals, in Advent and Lent, and on saints' days. Otherwise it is only found on the Second Sunday after Easter, where the word 'shepherd' links the epistle and gospel. Of serial reading there is even less: four Sundays after Epiphany work consecutively through Romans, chapter 12 and part of chapter 13; and the Sundays after Trinity from the 6th to the 24th provide readings from the Pauline epistles in biblical order (with one exception), but there is no connection between one Sunday and the next. So there was plenty of scope for a less random selection of readings.

The 1978 Lectionary is based on the thematic principle, though here and there a passage will continue where the previous Sunday left off, e.g., John chapter 15 on the Second, Third, and Fourth Sundays after Pentecost. Three lessons are provided for each Sunday communion service on a two-year basis. On the great feasts a choice of lessons is provided without allocating them to either year, to meet varying local conditions.

Even with the greatly increased number of readings it is impossible to do full justice to the Old Testament, at any rate in quantity: large parts of it remain unread on Sundays. As it is, some of the

handpicked passages are difficult for the man in the pew to relate to
what he believes in as a Christian and can accept as an ordinary
human being. The New Testament suggests more than one way in
which the Old Testament may be put to good use. 'Today this
scripture has been fulfilled in your hearing', says Jesus (Luke 4:21);
'These things were written for our example', says Paul (1 Corinthians 10:11). The point of reading the Old Testament in Christian
services is to show God at work in the world, operating already on
the same principles as in the life of Jesus. Furthermore, there are
important themes such as creation and social justice which are richly
treated in the Old Testament, and barely touched on in the New, not
because the Old Testament was wrong to deal with them, but
because it handled them well, and its teaching does not need re-
emphasizing.

Changing views in modern scholarship about the authority of the
Bible raise particular problems for the practice of reading portions of
Scripture aloud in the services, particularly when the reading is
followed by the formula 'This is the word of the Lord'. For some, of
course, this poses no problem: the Bible *is* the word of the Lord,
inspired in every syllable. For others, there will be no difficulty in
mentally demythologizing a lesson as it is read, and accepting, say,
the story of Adam and Eve as a dramatized discussion of human
nature. Others again will not want to go to either of these extremes.
For them the thematic method is a great help. Thematic lessons are
singled out because they speak to our condition. Elisha's axe-head
(2 Kings 6:1-7) and the Gadarene swine (Mark 5:1-13) do not
appear in the Sunday communion lessons. But there are still many
who find difficulty in saying 'This is the word of the Lord', even
after a lesson specially chosen for its relevance. For them, it is
necessary both to 'hear *and receive*' a passage before they can say that
it is 'God's holy word'. Their natural response would be 'May this be
the word of God to us', just as we pray later on in the service that the
bread and wine 'may be *to us*' the body and blood of Christ.

The function of the communion readings is to draw on the experience of God in the Old and New Testaments as a preparation for the
constantly renewed encounter with God in the communion. A link
may well be made explicitly during the sermon, and valuable hints

about the interpretation of the readings can often be found in the collect of the day. These are ways in which the Sunday readings may in fact be the word of God, speaking to us through prophet, apostle, or evangelist. The notes which make up this book have the same function, to enable these ancient writings, two or three thousand years old, to speak to us in contemporary words, and to communicate to us their permanently enduring message.

YEAR ONE

Ninth Sunday before Christmas
The Creation

Old Testament Reading **Genesis 1: 1–3, 24–31a**

New Testament Reading (Gospel) **John 1: 1–14**

At the heart of Christian worship is thanksgiving: we praise God for all that he is, for all that he has done, for all that he has given us.

For all that he is. He is the source of all. The immeasurable universe has sprung from his creative will. His purpose directs and sustains all things. We are because he is. Such was the fundamental belief of the Hebrew writer who, in the picture language and imagery natural to a pre-scientific age, expressed in Genesis the traditional wisdom of his people. It remains in every age the essential commitment of faith. To be a Christian is first of all to look beyond the seen to the unseen Creator.

For all that he has done. He has brought all things into being, but he is not some distant First Cause, detached from the universe which has sprung from his fiat. From the first he has been involved in a universe which, though complete and finished, nevertheless has not a static perfection but movement towards a final goal. The Fourth Gospel (John 1) sees the Word at work in Creation and finding fulfilment in the coming of the Christ. The Word emerges from the Being of God, whose outgoing purpose is expressed in communion with man, made 'in his image', capable of conscious response to his will. That communion of God and man is seen perfected as the Word himself becomes man.

For all that he has given us. Above all he has given to man the knowledge of himself, revealing himself through those who in response to his Word have been enabled to interpret his handiwork in creation and his ongoing purpose in human history. We acknowledge that all that we enjoy is his gift; if, under him, we are given the control and use of the world around us, it is as stewards, and we hold his gifts in trust.

Thanksgiving and worship are inseparably linked because the Creator's gifts are good. He saw what he had created to be good, and all points to his own goodness. Later the writer of Genesis is to wrestle with the spoiling of the creation through the bringing in of evil. The Fourth Gospel sets the coming of the Word to dwell among men against the background of man's failure and the rejection of his destiny. So the creation described in Genesis looked forward to the re-creation which is the theme of the Gospel.

New Testament Reading (Epistle)   **Colossians 1: 15–20**

Paul struggles to express the same inexpressible truth as does the prologue of the Fourth Gospel. Christ is the link between God's creative power and purpose and our present experience of communion with God. If man was made in God's image, Christ is in a special sense 'the image of the invisible God' (*v.* 15): in him true humanity is consummated, and in him the whole creative purpose of God is expressed. Creative purpose cannot be separated from the very being of God, for if God is, then he creates. So in Christ we come to know the wholeness of God himself.

Eighth Sunday before Christmas
The Fall

Old Testament Reading **Genesis 4: 1–10**

'Thanks be to God for his goodness'; those who come to worship and to praise God have always had this starting point. To believe in God is to trust him for the goodness of his design and purpose in creation, and in his continuing authority as he rules and directs the world which is his world. God is perfect in all his works and ways. Yet man has always been aware also that he lives in a very imperfect world. Is it possible both to thank God for his goodness and to come to terms with the manifest presence and power of evil and sin in human affairs and in the world of nature? In modern times we have seen this as a theological and philosophical problem and have attempted to state it in abstract language. The writers of Genesis thought no less profoundly, but drawing upon the ancient traditions of their people expressed themselves through myth and story.

Often the stories told overlap and indicate different aspects of human experience. So here the title in the lectionary, 'The Fall', is derived from and is usually associated with that other story (in Genesis 3) of Adam and Eve in the garden of Eden. There all that is evil and painful in our human lot is traced to rebellion against God's will, seen as an individual rejection of an arbitrary divine law, though with lasting consequences. By contrast in this story, in the earliest human society the power of sin was already *there*. It was indeed a rejection of the divine will (*v.* 6), but not rebellion against an external and arbitrary law, governing the relationship of the individual with God. Rather, from the first, sin against God had to do with the mutual relationships of brothers, and sprang from the innate jealousy and rivalry associated with differences of livelihood and all the resulting cultural divisions.

On one thing both stories are agreed: the continuing effects of sin. Adam and Eve are expelled from the garden: Cain is driven out from settled human society to become a vagrant and wanderer upon earth, bearing to the end the mark of his rejection and suffering. He becomes an exile not only from men but from the presence of God.

New Testament Reading (Epistle)   **1 John 3: 9–18**

The community which is the Christian Church becomes a symbol of redeemed society, marked not by jealousy leading to enmity and division but by mutual love, leading to forgiveness and reconciliation. The new relationship with God is incompatible with sin and failure (*v.* 9). This declaration is like the story of Cain and Abel: both interpret present experience by reference to an external goal; the Old Testament story looking to the goal from which we have come, the New Testament writer to the goal to which we move.

New Testament Reading (Gospel)   **Mark 7: 14–23**

Christ is involved in a debate about the nature of sin. The Pharisaic view, which he rejects, may be linked with the first of the two Genesis stories, that of Adam and Eve in the garden. Eve broke a law about touching and eating something external to herself, and the Pharisees tended to think of all sin like that. Cain was mastered by sin which crouching at the door came in and controlled the inner springs of motive and desire. So Christ spoke of what comes out of the heart, and saw the various manifestations of sin, fornication, theft, murder, adultery, and so on, as outward expressions of inner corruption. The cure of sin and evil must therefore lie not in the regimentation of man's outward actions but in an inner revolution.

Seventh Sunday before Christmas
The Election of God's People: Abraham

Old Testament Reading   **Genesis 12: 1–9**

Last week's Epistle (1 John 3:9–18) pointed to the community of brotherly love for which men yearn and which has now been given in Christ, a present experience and a future hope. Today's reading shows the beginning which many centuries later was to make possible the realization of that community. Like so many stories in Genesis, this narrative not only describes a past event but mirrors a constant pattern in the relationship of God and man. (Perhaps it is partly for this reason that it is often difficult to define precisely the setting of a narrative within a historical context: indeed at times one narrative may reflect more than one happening in history.) The way the biblical writer brings together and presents the stories and traditions which he uses shows that he saw particular importance in these constant factors.

1. God himself takes the initiative.
It was not just a good idea on Abraham's part to leave his old home in Mesopotamia. 'The Lord said to Abram' (*v.* 1) shows the divine initiative. God's nature as love did not allow him to stand aside from his creation or from man whom he had made in his own image, for personal converse with himself. If sin had marred human society, then God himself was ready to take the first steps which would lead to the righting of the wrong.

2. Man responds in faith.
We are here faced with the apparent contradictions which can only be resolved in experience. Abraham was in the language of later theology compelled by grace. Yet the essence of grace is that it evokes a free response and does not override man's liberty of choice: there is no compulsion. Here is one of the deepest of the mysteries of God's dealings with man. Looking back upon a particular decision a man may say, 'I had to decide, and the decision was mine alone': but on further reflection he adds, 'God was involved in that decision,

and without him I could not have made it'. Just such a decision is the act of faith whereby man commits himself in trust to God.

3. The universal comes through the particular.
God's ultimate concern is with all mankind, 'all the families on earth' (*v.* 3): but his purpose is worked out through the choice of a particular man and his descendants, and that purpose in the end finds its focus in the one man, Jesus Christ.

New Testament Reading (Epistle) **Romans 4: 13–end**

Paul sees Abraham's faith as the pattern of Christian faith. The contrast here is with the Law. The gospel is about personal trust in God, not about the keeping of the Law, however sacred.

New Testament Reading (Gospel) **John 8: 51–end**

These are the closing verses of a meditation upon the relationship of Christ and his own people. In reply to Christ's offer to his disciples of true freedom the Jews claim the freedom of the children of Abraham (*v.* 33). The evangelist shows that it is not physical descent from Abraham that is important but the doing of his work (*v.* 39). (Does this reflect the later expansion of the Church into the Gentile world?) Those who are linked as disciples to Christ (i.e. keep his word) will have the true freedom which is eternal life, and themselves will fulfil the destiny of Abraham. The character of God glimpsed with joy by Abraham was fully manifested in God's Word incarnate in Jesus Christ.

Sixth Sunday before Christmas
The Promise of Redemption: Moses

Old Testament Reading   **Exodus 3: 7–15**

To be redeemed is to be set free from slavery. In human experience slavery has taken many different forms, but the slave is essentially somebody who has been deprived of the freedom which is his due as a man or as a citizen or in some other capacity. The descendants of Abraham had lost their political freedom, and in Egypt had been reduced to serfs engaged in forced labour. They had been deprived of the opportunity, given to Abraham, to respond freely to God's grace and to acknowledge his sovereignty over their lives and destiny. God's sovereignty could only be vindicated by a restoration of that freedom.

Deliverance from the Egyptian bondage became symbolic of all redemption, and in the wider sweep of biblical history was seen to anticipate and to promise redemption from other enslavement. As biblical writers reflected upon the Exodus and the later history of Israel (and especially upon the Babylonian Exile and the Return, repeating something of the pattern of the Exodus), they came to realize that, important as it was that the Israelites should live in their own land under their own king, there were other slaveries to which they could and did become subject, all of them involving an infringement of God's sovereignty. These other slaveries were all in different ways manifestations of evil, which is that which is set against God's will. There was the worship of false gods, or the denial of covenant rights to fellow-Israelites, or the rejection of the message which the prophets spoke in God's name. Gradually the Israelites came to look for a final redemption by which the Kingdom of God would be realized in a new and all-inclusive way. The redemption under Moses looked forward to the deliverance of God's people from all the power of evil that they might enjoy to the full their freedom as God's sons.

New Testament Reading (Epistle) **Hebrews 3: 1–6**

The heart of the Christian gospel is the declaration that in Jesus Christ the final triumph of God's sovereignty has taken place, God's Kingdom is present, and so man is delivered from all slavery and bondage to evil. The Epistle to the Hebrews, addressed to readers familiar with the heritage of the old Israel, is an elaborate exposition of the fulfilment in Christ of the partial and fragmentary patterns of redemption in the Old Testament.

In this passage the writer emphasizes both the full humanity of Jesus, who is our 'Apostle and High Priest', and is able to represent mankind whose sufferings he has shared, and the distinction between his work and that of other men. The contrast between Moses and Jesus is as great as that between a servant and the builder and master of a house. So also is the contrast between the redemption under Moses and that gained by Christ.

New Testament Reading (Gospel) **John 6: 25–35**

In John's Gospel we enter a world of different picture language, but the theme is the same. 'They' (who are the speakers in *v.* 25) represent the people of the old Israel in their failure to respond to God's redemptive grace. They make the fundamental mistake of supposing that they will earn eternal life (i.e. life redeemed from the power of evil and its limitations) by their deeds. In the end all that is required is to accept God's gift in faith, and his supreme gift is Christ, who brings redemption, i.e. eternal life, as bread sustains and nourishes our ordinary life.

Fifth Sunday before Christmas
The Remnant of Israel

Old Testament Reading 1 Kings 19: 9–18

God called Abraham and chose that the people descended from him should through many vicissitudes prepare for the coming of Christ. Time and again the divine purpose must have seemed to be frustrated or brought to nothing. The slavery of the people in Egypt appeared to bring to an end their independent life: yet under Moses they were redeemed and led out from their bondage. Even when they had entered the land of Israel their survival was precarious. Later writers reflecting on their history interpreted their weakness and their defeats as the result of their rejection of God's will made known through lawgiver and prophet. The royal house of David and the city of Jerusalem were invested with special significance in the working-out of the divine purpose. Yet most of the tribes of Israel revolted from David's dynasty, and both dynasty and city were eventually to be destroyed by foreign invaders and the people carried into exile. A new exodus brought the people back to their own land and Jerusalem was restored, but they frequently fell under the domination of the great imperial powers and eventually under the rule of the Romans, as in the time of Christ.

This passage records the despair of the prophet Elijah, who had fled from the threat of retribution from queen Jezebel. It seemed to him that the national apostasy was total and that the divine cause for which he had made a courageous stand (ch. 18) was lost. In his desert retreat he was made aware that despite all appearances God's purpose was being carried forward: there were still seven thousand in Israel who were loyal to the LORD, and he himself would still be used to bring about God's purpose in the political mêlée of the times.

Through the centuries it became more and more apparent that the full response to God's will would not be by the people as such, but through a 'remnant'. Christians believe that in the end both the divine purpose and human response were focused in Christ himself; through him Israel has been brought to newness of life.

New Testament Reading (Epistle)   **Romans 11: 13–24**

This passage carries the double theme of redemption and judgement still further. Paul to his infinite sorrow saw in the course of his own ministry how his own people, through their rejection of Christ, fell under judgement and were themselves rejected as the instruments of God's redemptive purpose for the world. That purpose would not and could not fail: others took their place and Gentiles assumed the vocation of God's people. While we praise God for the depth of his wisdom and knowledge, we pray that we too may be delivered in the day of judgement.

New Testament Reading (Gospel)   **Matthew 24: 37–44**

The final realization of God's purposes through his people would be a day of redemption: but redemption necessarily involves divine judgement. Some would be found ready and able to enter into the joy of the full manifestation of the divine sovereignty, 'when the Son of Man comes' (*v.* 39). Some would be rejected, and would have no part in it. There was undoubtedly in Jesus's proclamation of good news a stern note of warning.

First Sunday in Advent
The Advent Hope

Old Testament Reading   **Isaiah 52: 7–10**

The prophet speaks a word of comfort to his fellow-exiles in Babylon; God has taken pity, he is now rescuing his people, restoring them to '*Shalom*', which means life with God and the peace and well-being that flow from him. He calls them to put their trust in this God, rather than fall into despair and the immoral behaviour of those among whom they were living.

New Testament Reading (Epistle)   **1 Thessalonians 5: 1–11**

Christians have taken his words, with others like them, as finding their ultimate meaning in Jesus; in him, God has offered life to all, acting in the character that the prophets trusted him to have. And so Paul, like the prophets long before, encourages his fellow-Christians to 'live with him'.

New Testament Reading (Gospel)   **Luke 21: 25–35**

But Christians have also continued to look forward, to what God is doing and to what he will do; and they have found, in these same prophecies, the imagery with which to do so. And this tension—looking back, but also looking forward, to God's deliverance in Jesus—specially marked the earliest decades of the Church's life. Christians believed that they were in the middle of the great drama of salvation (as if in the interval, someone has aptly said, between the whirring of a grandfather-clock's mechanism, and its striking the hour); what God had started in the life, death and resurrection of Jesus, he would soon bring to a grand completion—'the present generation will live to see it all'.

All this can seem very foreign to us, who know that this interval has extended for nearly 2,000 years; but it is a vision, a hope, well worth the prayerful effort necessary if we are to share it. God calls us still to recognize in Jesus of Nazareth the Coming for which Jews had

longed, and through which he still offers Life to all; he calls us to
keep alert for the Coming of this Lord in the people and events of
daily living, to judge, forgive, call and enable us to serve him; and he
calls us to look forward ('Thy Kingdom come . . .') to that completion of God's will for his world, for which one traditional description
is the 'Second Coming' of Christ.

Second Sunday in Advent
The Word of God in the Old Testament

Old Testament Reading   **Isaiah 55: 1-11**

Chapters 40–55 of Isaiah are a collection of the utterances of a
prophet in exile with his people in Babylon, probably in the years
after 550 B.C.; of this collection, this Sunday's reading stands as the
tailpiece, gathering together and underlining the themes of the
prophet's preaching.

Throughout these chapters, God is revealed as offering, to an
exiled and dispirited people, forgiveness, a fresh start and a new
hope; he will rebuild their old relationship with him, and renew their
old commission, if they will only listen, and trust him, and worship
him and live for him again. And in this passage, the prophet speaks
of God's way of making all this known—the prophets' preaching,
the prophetic Word in which God reveals his own character, his
continuing commitment to his people, and the response he looks for
from them. And this Word is effective; in it men encounter God, and
are changed and renewed by him; through it, God is active not just
in, but upon, his world.

New Testament Reading (Epistle)   **2 Timothy 3: 14–4:5**

Paul and his colleagues and assistants, like other Jews of their
generation, were 'from boyhood' steeped in the Jewish scriptures
(our Old Testament); but they had learnt to read them through the
spectacles, as it were, of the conviction that everywhere these
writings pointed to and shed light upon, and were in turn illuminated
by, what God had done in Jesus of Nazareth. They saw him implicitly
as John saw him explicitly, as the summary, the incarnation, of the
prophetic Word of God. Through the study of the Word of God, his
address to and action for mankind kept for them in the scriptures,
they found that God opened their eyes to what he had done in Jesus,
and trained them to recognize and to obey his will and his lead,
shown them as insistently in their own day as it had been in the days
of the exile.

New Testament Reading (Gospel)   **John 5: 36—end**

But even in the early days of the Church, men and women could misuse the Scriptures; in Paul's letter to the Galatians, as well as in today's Gospel, there are signs that people were treating the scriptures more as oracles, final and authoritative in their own right, like the instruction for some complicated electrical appliance. This, Jesus implies, is idolatry; and it is an idolatry that has often been very tempting for Christians. The Word of God is still active, still working to make all things new, and to give us fresh insights, and a fresh discipleship; and the more seriously and expectantly we read the scriptures, the more we must remember that God has given them as pointers to himself, their Lord as well as ours.

Third Sunday in Advent
The Forerunner

Old Testament Reading   **Isaiah 40: 1–11**

To anyone brought up on Handel's *Messiah*, today's reading comes singing out of the page, and seems tame, a vital dimension missing, if it is only read in church. It asks to be sung, and to set us singing too. And there is a profound rightness about this feeling; as Methodism, especially, has taught us, one of the ways in which we can most surely make the Church's faith part of our own thoughts and lives, so that we can share it with others, is through singing it, in the form of a finely worded hymn. So it can be with Isaiah 40, the opening, as Isaiah 55 was the close, of a collection of prophecies. The prophet's call to his original hearers still stands—'Comfort my people, speak tenderly. . . . "Your God is here"'; and so does his description of God's character, of what God is doing.

New Testament Reading (Epistle)   **1 Corinthians 4: 1–5**

Paul speaks of himself, and of his colleagues in the support and leadership of the Churches, as 'stewards of the secrets of God'; that is to say, of the fact that this message about God was true, because it had been confirmed and made available to all in Jesus, who died on a cross and whom God raised. Paul sees himself and the others caught up in the song the prophet called men to sing, made pointers to God's activity.

New Testament Reading (Gospel)   **John 1: 19–28**

In the Gospel, John the Baptist refuses the starring roles in the divine drama, offered him by the deputation; instead he takes the role of pointer, forerunner of the One whose life will enact, and give fresh meaning to, the ancient claim 'Your God is here' (see Isaiah 7:14 with Matthew 1:23).

   It was a constant wonder to Paul, as it should be to us, that he, or we, have been caught up by God into his activity, and enrolled as pointers to his Son. See Romans 14: 4, written out of his own hard-won Christian experience.

Fourth Sunday in Advent
The Annunciation

Old Testament Reading   **Isaiah 11: 1-9**

In the disaster that threatens Jerusalem from the Assyrians, Isaiah has seen God's judgement on Judah and her king (see Isaiah 10: 33–34); but he trusts God to remain consistent in character ('Thou art the same Lord, whose property is always to have mercy'), and looks forward to a time when God will raise a second David, a king who will actually practise the ideals expressed at every coronation in Jerusalem (see, for example, Psalm 72). Such a king will involve his people in his own obedience to God, and so his time will see a restoration of the internal harmony of all creation.

Christians have seen Isaiah's hope fulfilled in Jesus, and in the life of the Church—yet not fully; and so, though we do not pray, as the Jew still prays, for the coming of the Messiah, he himself taught us to pray 'Thy Kingdom come'. We look to God, with the full confidence that life in Christ gives, yet still 'through a glass darkly', for the future that God is shaping for his creation; and Isaiah 11, read with Romans 8: 18–25, can help us realise how all-embracing is the Christian hope for the world.

New Testament Reading (Epistle)   **1 Corinthians 1: 26–end**

Just as David was the least likely choice (1 Samuel 16: 11f), so are we; whatever we are in his service, the fact that we are in it at all is God's doing and God's business; he calls us neither to boast of our gifts, nor to try to escape serving him by pleading that we are weak or unsuitable. God has chosen to present himself to men and women in a crucified man; beside that ultimate contradiction, his choice of us in our weakness or ordinariness is unimportant, yet characteristic.

New Testament Reading (Gospel)   **Luke 1: 26–38a**

The question for us, as for Mary in the Gospel, is not our suitability, in our own or anyone else's eyes; it is whether we will trust God's presence and his power, and say in each of the demanding situations and relationships in which he places us, 'Here I am; I am the Lord's servant'.

Christmas Eve

Old Testament Reading   **Isaiah 62: 1–5**

There are many today, young as well as older people, in whom the
state of the world induces only gloom and despair. It was to people
who felt like that (see Haggai 1: 5–6!) in Jerusalem in the last quarter
of the sixth century (from about 525 B.C.) that the prophets, whose
work we find in Isaiah 56–66, probably spoke. In today's passage,
the prophet responsible for Isaiah 60–62 allies himself with those
who said (Zechariah 1: 12) 'How long, O Lord of Hosts, will you
withhold your compassion from Jerusalem and the cities of Judah';
but his message is still one of hope; he trusts that God has still in
store for Jerusalem a splendid future, which he sees in thoroughly
worldly terms. Another contemporary, however, saw differently.
'In those days . . . they shall pluck the robe of a Jew and say "We will
go with you, because we have heard that God is with you"' (Zechariah 8: 23).

New Testament Reading (Epistle)   **Acts 13: 16–26**

Luke's summary of Paul's preaching boldly repeats the Church's
conviction, that the whole history of God's dealing with Israel, and
of Israel's with God, finds its goal in Jesus. And the lovely song, built
out of phrases from Old Testament prophets, which Luke gives to
Zechariah, gracefully sums up the Church's claim that the insights
of those prophets are both confirmed by Jesus, and illuminate his
person and his role. Yet how strangely, if we stop to think about
them and then about him, he also turns them upside down and
corrects them; to take an example from today's passage, it is more
the desolation and forsaken-ness, and God's presence among them,
than the prophet's hope of their reversal, that Jesus confirms in the
place of his birth, the place and manner of his death, and many of the
actions of his life.

New Testament Reading (Gospel) **Luke 1: 67–79**

Zechariah's song follows immediately, in Luke, his act of obedience; it is his first use of his restored powers of speech; and it is itself followed by Luke's account of Jesus's birth. We read it today as the climax, not only of Luke's first chapter, but of all our Advent preparation for Christmas. Like the rest of Luke's first chapter, it paints a picture of men and women faithfully practising their religion, steeped in its scriptures, and praising God according to their tradition; and because of all this—not, as we often think today, in spite of it—they look forward expectantly to the new things that God will show them.

Christmas Day

Old Testament Reading   **Isaiah 9: 2,6,7**

The experience of joy, for the child and the adult alike, is especially the experience of the arrival of a moment long looked forward to with more and more eager excitement. So it is in this reading. The time of victory and peace for Israel, so ardently longed-for while 'the rod of his oppressor' was still being wielded, had arrived. The great light of freedom had arrived. The great light of freedom from political instability and fear had broken forth upon those hitherto in despairing darkness. At the centre is the young ruler, the king newly enthroned, whose reign the prophet hails: it will be marked by just administration and by a strong foreign policy by which he would 'establish the kingdom' of David. For Christians, the time of a peace and order that are to be, in a finally lasting way, God's gift lies in the future. The kingship of Jesus, which the Church finds foretold in Isaiah's words, is not yet a visible one. Yet there is joy for us, joy even for those who 'dwell in a land of deep darkness' in loneliness and suffering. The reign of justice and peace, which is the visible reign of Christ, may be served even now. It must, indeed, be worked for by those willing to sacrifice themselves for their ideals. Ours, then, is not so much the 'joy at the harvest' as the joy of those who labour in the sowing, confident that a harvest will come.

New Testament Reading (Epistle)   **Titus 2: 11–14; 3: 3–7**

The words 'salvation' and 'Saviour' occur four times in these verses. They focus for us the meaning of Christmas both for our present and for our future. We are urged to look forward to the future 'appearing in glory' of the Lord whose coming among us in humility we celebrate today. The future was nearly always more important for the first Christians than the present. They believed that God would shortly bring all present experience to an end when the glory of Christ was manifested at the coming of God's kingdom. For us, it is necessary to grow in our inward conviction that not only our ultimate future—about that, we dare do little more than believe and guess—but also our immediate future is in the hands of One who will make himself known to us as a Saviour. And now already, through Christ's coming on the first Christmas Day, God has acted 'for the salvation of all mankind'. All that Jesus both is and will be comes about because God has shown that he himself is the Saviour of men, in his kindness and—to translate the Greek term literally—his 'friendship towards mankind'.

New Testament Reading (Gospel)　　　　　**Luke 2: 1-20**

Humility and glory go hand in hand in the faith and hope of Christians. God's glory is bestowed upon us as we wait upon him in joyful humility. For 'the glory as of the only-begotten of the Father' was revealed in the humility of an obscure human setting, of birth in poverty-stricken surroundings. So we read in this passage both of glory and of humility. The angelic annunciation tells us that Jesus's birth was the long-awaited fulfilment of all that we thought of in the first reading. As Saviour, he is to be the bringer of visible and glorious deliverance. It is indeed 'news of great joy', and the host of angels acclaims its announcement with a cry of 'Glory to God!' Yet the 'sign'—the proof—that all this has truly come is one that unmistakably speaks of Jesus's humility. He was to be identified through being found 'wrapped in swaddling clothes' like any other child born in humble surroundings. He would be lying in a manger intended for the provender for cattle. We, too, shall not find God's glory until we have learned to seek out and deeply to reverence his humility.

Alternative Readings

Old Testament Reading   **Isaiah 62: 10–12**

We probably take it for granted more often than we realize, in our private assumptions about life, that God has left us on our own to manage as best we can. Our own individual lives seem to us to be a struggle—whether more successful, most of the time, or less so—in which our own unaided efforts are all we have. We feel, too, despite all that is said to the contrary, that the Church must survive as best she can. What we may believe, in our heart of hearts, to be her gradual but inevitable decline continues with no supporting hand to check or reverse it. This failure to hope, whether for ourselves or for the Church, is condemned by the message of Christmas. The prophet, in this first reading, saw Jerusalem desolate after being sacked by the invader. Yet he proclaimed that a road must be prepared for its exiled people to return. Jerusalem, he cried, is 'a city not forsaken'. What God did once for Jerusalem, he will do for us individually and for his Church. 'Behold, your salvation comes!' The birth of Jesus, and, with him, of a new and immeasurably potent way of being human, promises that God's saving and victorious action is at hand for us, too.

New Testament Reading (Epistle)   **1 John 4: 7–14**

Love means sacrifice. God, who is himself love, demonstrated what love means when he sent Jesus to be the sacrifice by which sin's power over us might be destroyed. Love is not, in the first place, any capacity of ours. It is not a choice on our part to enter into relationships as we will and in the measure we prefer. It is the sublime generosity of God, a generosity that is ready to suffer. Anything that we can give to other people springs from this love with which God loves us. So the Christmas message speaks of something both more splendid and more demanding than 'goodwill'. We *'ought* to love one another'. We owe other people a duty to show in our behaviour towards them that complete commitment to their good which we have known, as Christians, to be the very nature of God himself. So a

24

great and joyful fulfilment of all that is best in ourselves awaits us. As we learn this hard lesson of love, the promise of Christmas is made true again, and 'God dwells in us'. Should we doubt this, the presence of his Spirit, whom we feel impelling us to love, is all the proof we need. So we use no mere hallowed form of words when we testify that God sent his Son to be the Saviour of the world. We speak out of our experience of trying to love sacrificially, and of knowing that, with the Spirit's help, we sometimes begin to succeed.

New Testament Reading (Gospel)   **Luke 2: 8–20**

Luke describes for us two greatly contrasted scenes through which the truth about Jesus was communicated to men. First, the open fields and the sky, a splendour of light and the terrifying manifestation of the heavenly army of angels; then, the homely decision of the shepherds to walk to Bethlehem, and their discovery in the little town of Joseph and Mary and the Child. It is the manger, symbol of lowliness, that links these two scenes. In the solemn and joyful declaration of truth made by the angel, the prophecy that Jesus would be found in a manger offered the guarantee of the heavenly promise. So, when the shepherds saw Jesus in exactly the circumstances that had been prophesied, they knew that they had been given all the confirmation they needed. They, in their turn, were now able to pass on to those standing by the truth which they had heard spoken by the angel and had now verified for themselves. So the promise of God comes to us in the solemnity of the Church's worship, or, it may be, in the stillness—which is no less solemn—of our private prayer. It is verified in our most ordinary day-to-day experience, in order that we, in our turn, may communicate it to those around us.

Alternative Readings

Old Testament Reading   **Micah 5: 2–4**

We habitually think at Christmas of the Christ-child in his weakness and poverty. Nothing, in any case, is more vulnerable than a newly born baby. And the familiar carols and gospel readings combine to impress on our minds the simplicity of the stable at Bethlehem. Micah's prophecy about the One who was to come forth from Bethlehem—a prophecy which the Church could not fail to apply to Christ—strikes a very different note. This 'Man born to be King' is glorious and powerful. He is of ancient royal lineage—his 'origin is from of old'—and, indeed, as Christians hear these words, they think of Jesus as 'begotten of the Father before all worlds'. His coming, Micah prophesies, will mean the reversal of the misery of those 'given up' to hardship until the moment of his birth; and here, too, we think of a redemption brought, not merely to Israel, but to all mankind. Like the ideal ruler of the old Israel, then, but through a far deeper communion with 'the majesty of the name of the Lord his God', Jesus is presented as One destined to exercise authority over men so as to bring them to a peace in which they will 'dwell secure'. Indeed, the words immediately following this reading tell us—as translated in the older English Bibles—that 'this Man shall be the peace'. Few words could more splendidly sum up the message of Christmas.

New Testament Reading (Epistle)   **Hebrews 1: 1–12**

The universe, for most of us, is an unimaginably vast machine. We may know a little about its structure and movement as they are understood at present, or we may know practically nothing. In either case, it is our natural habit of thought—twentieth-century citizens as we are—to regard space and all it contains as a neutral and purposeless stage on which we live the best lives we can. The faith of the writer of this reading is different. For him, the entire universe is destined to be the possession of Jesus, for he is 'heir of all things'. More than that, the universe owes its very existence to the creative work of the Son of God before all time. Its continuation in being, day by day, is brought about 'by the word of his power'. So there is no room for fear or loneliness, for any sense that anyone's life has become altogether too 'private' and has lost all serious purpose. As the fullest completion of his obedience to the Father's will, Jesus brought about that 'purification of sins' that believers like ourselves have known in our own experience again and again. It is this same Jesus, says this writer, who is Creator and Lord of every part of our environment, just as he is Creator and Lord of all that makes us, as individuals, what we are. So often, just as 'our God is too small', so our thought about Christ makes him too small. It is indeed a mighty Lord, whose power sustains the whole universe, whom we trustfully receive as 'Redeemer, Friend, and Brother' in our Christmas Communion.

New Testament Reading (Gospel)   **John 1: 1–14**

This great proclamation of the universal reach of Christ's creative power, and of his humility in becoming man, continues the thought of the second reading. No member of the human race escapes being illuminated by the true Light, we are told, any more than the remotest galaxies could owe their existence to anyone but Christ. Yet all are free to reject the Light that has touched them, and most do. How great, then, is our responsibility. In receiving the Light, we have been given authority to become God's children. Sharing as we do—even at a distance—in what the Church's earliest members saw with their own eyes, we have 'beheld the glory' of the Word made flesh. We must never forget the many who may one day be brought to realize that in the Light they have rejected, true life is to be found, and nowhere else.

Sunday after Christmas Day
The Incarnation

Old Testament Reading   **Isaiah 7: 10–14**

Ahaz declined the invitation to ask for a sign in the depth or in the height, yet it was given him. For the name given to the child whose birth Isaiah foretells—Immanuel—means 'God is with us': it was, perhaps, a war-cry, and conveys the certainty that God will not leave us on our own, either in the most abject humiliation or in the highest triumph. It is very fitting, then, that Matthew should apply this prophecy to the birth of Jesus. For he who 'descended into hell' and rose again to ascend 'far above all heavens' has bound us to himself so that, in him, God might be with us both 'in the time of our tribulation' and in our moments of greatest joy. Psalm 139 expresses the meaning for Christian readers of God's answer to Ahaz's refusal to ask for a sign: 'Even the darkness is not dark to thee, the night is as bright as the day; for darkness is as light to thee'. This has been the experience of countless Christians, and it may yet be ours.

New Testament Reading (Epistle)   **Galatians 4: 1–7**

It is not easy for most of us to enter into the experience behind this reading. If we may think of a frontier established between the Christian life in all its fullness and a life from which God and grace are absent, most of us might admit that we have lived most of our lives near this frontier; at any rate, we are not conscious of having once crossed it and now of having left it far behind. So it is difficult for us to appreciate the sense of liberation felt by Paul and his converts (unless indeed we are among those converted ourselves in adolescence or as adults). For Paul, the contrast between the old and the new was absolute. Entry into the new, Christian life meant—as this reading puts it—acceptance of the privileges of adulthood and of being acknowledged as a son of God. It was for this that God sent Jesus to share the conditions of slavery (slavery to the Law, that is, for Paul is thinking primarily of Jewish Christians) which consti-tuted the old life. The proof, says Paul, that all this has really

28

happened is our possession of the Holy Spirit, through whom we address God as 'Father' in the word, 'Abba', which Jesus himself had used. These certainties go further, it may be, than anything of which we may be sure in our own lives. We ask that the Spirit, making his work in us ever more clearly felt, may enable us to know more decisively and encouragingly the truth of our liberation into a new life of sonship to God.

New Testament Reading (Gospel)   **John 1: 14–18**

John expounds in four statements much that is essential in our relationship with Jesus. The first and the last display its fundamental meaning. Jesus himself communicates to us the nature of God. He 'explains' (this is nearer the meaning of the Greek than 'made known') the full truth of what God is like. For 'God is love'. He is, in his own inmost being, the sacrificial willingness to give to the utmost which is what love means. This truth we have made our own in gazing by faith at the glory of Jesus. All that the gospels tell us of his humility, his compassion, his readiness for sacrifice, are the varied refractions of the 'glory as of the only Son from the Father'. It is John himself who has shown us the true meaning of glory, as he has the real force of love (and the two are closely related). The crucifixion of Jesus was the climax of his being 'glorified' by the Father. But the knowledge given through Jesus and received by us is only the beginning. In relationship with him, we receive from his fullness 'grace upon grace', as one stage in our capacity to accept the creative mercy of God is continually succeeded by another and deeper one. Finally, this is not for our benefit only. John 'bore witness concerning him', and we are to do the same, both by what we say and, still more, by what we are.

Second Sunday after Christmas
'My Father's House'

Old Testament Reading   **Exodus 12: 21–27**

Jesus was born for sacrifice, and Christmas points on towards Good
Friday and Easter. So it is fitting that we should hear today the
description of the ancient ritual of the Passover. This was the festival
during which Jesus was put to death, and its symbolism helped the
Church to interpret that death. 'Select lambs for yourselves', the
Israelites of old were instructed. But, as with Abraham on Mount
Moriah, it was God himself who, in the birth of Jesus, provided a
lamb for the sacrifice. So the death of Jesus, the destiny for which he
came into the world, was the true 'sacrifice of the Lord's Passover'
by which he delivered us all.

or   **Ecclesiasticus 3: 2–7**

We sometimes forget that, when the Bible speaks of both Jesus and
ourselves as God's sons, it is an older idea of family relationships
than our own which is in mind. When, therefore, this reading lays all
its stress on the respect and honour which a son ought to show to his
father, we sense what is to us a somewhat alien note. Yet the writer's
words comment tellingly on what John's gospel, above all, holds to
be the essential relationship between Jesus and God. Jesus, as Son,
honours his Father and gives glory to him. His obedience is
rewarded; yet in ways which sometimes fulfil, sometimes contradict
what this reading tells us. Jesus indeed finds joy in us, the children
whom God has given him. In a far deeper way than Ecclesiasticus
could understand, he has made atonement for our sins and has been
heard in his intercession for us. 'Length of days', however, was not
to be his. It was by his death while still a young man that Jesus
redeemed us and made us children of God.

New Testament Reading (Epistle) **Romans 8: 11–17**

We live in two worlds at once. We think and feel and make our decisions, to a greater extent than we realize, in accord with the standards of the world around us. Yet we know that we have been summoned to decide and think and feel in all respects as the Spirit impels us. So we are presented with a continual daily choice. It is the Spirit himself who enables us to make this choice as we should. For the Spirit was given to us to dwell within us. He is our strength, sent from God, who brought about Jesus's resurrection and will bring about our own daily resurrection. For this is the Spirit through whom we know ourselves to be God's sons. Like true sons, we are to be heirs of all that he has to give—provided we are willing, in our own measure, to 'suffer with' Jesus so that we may share his glory.

New Testament Reading (Gospel) **Luke 2: 41–end**

The life-long process of growing up means growing away from one's own past. Almost certainly this will mean some growing away from one's family. Luke believed that this was so for Jesus, too. Mary and Joseph, Jesus's reputed father, did not understand what was happening. Luke also shows us the consequence of the desire to serve God. Jesus was in the Temple, the place of sacrifice. He was occupied there—so we must understand the scene—with the true understanding of God's law. For us, too, as we grow up into an ever-deepening discovery of the person God means us to be, there can be no substitute for continual return to the presence of God in adoration and the offering of self, or for unceasing reflective enquiry into God's will for us and for the world we live in.

The Epiphany

Old Testament Reading   **Isaiah 49: 1–6**

All of us are summoned to the exacting job of Christian evangelism in a world for which the beliefs of Christians have often ceased to mean anything. It is a daunting situation. We may well feel as unsure of ourselves as did the servant of the Lord who speaks in this reading. But God's reply to him, and to us, is to present us with an even greater challenge. The Lord's servant is told that to have God's people, Israel, as his only mission-field is too easy. He must bring knowledge of salvation to the Gentiles too. We also must expect to find God's call inviting us to look further afield than we have done hitherto. Both as individuals—at work or in our home neighbourhood—and as members of our local church, we must seek out new people to serve, new opportunities for making ourselves and our faith known. If we feel discouraged, as God's servant did, we must trust in our Master. Through our resolute determination to communicate God's truth as widely as we can, he will carry out his promise to make us 'a light to the nations'.

New Testament Reading (Epistle)   **Ephesians 3: 1–12**

Once the presence of God in the midst of this world and his promises for its future were reserved for Jews alone. But since the coming of Jesus, Gentiles have been able to become at one with them. This is the supreme message of Paul, today's reading says, and it is one of the themes we celebrate at Epiphany. What does this mean for us? It means that we are to be 'spiritually Jewish'. The one God's sovereignty as Creator, and the absolute authority of his will for men, are fundamental for us. So is much else that God revealed to Israel about his justice and his mercy. But the gathering-in that happened once is to take place again. The Church, heir to God's promises to Israel, carries the mystery of God's universal mercy to those who do not yet believe. So all of us have the 'many-sided wisdom of God' as a precious trust. We shall not be able to 'make 'known' this wisdom until we have gone some way in the life-long endeavour to enter into its riches for ourselves. This is partly why we devote ourselves to the reading of the scriptures with prayer. In this way the Epiphany ('shining forth') of God's glory and mercy continually goes on through our thoughtful readiness to impart to others whatever we have learned of the wisdom of God.

New Testament Reading (Gospel)   **Matthew 2: 1–12**

Most of us feel that we have a long distance to travel through our own partial agnosticism before our knowledge of God and of Jesus can be more than indistinct and second-hand. So we, too, are pilgrims, like the eastern magicians guided towards Judea by their astrological calculations, as we have been through so many aspects of our own experience. Our journeying is done, as theirs was, in faith and in hope. In all that really matters, we have already, like them, arrived at our journey's end. We have rejoiced in the knowledge that, in Jesus, God is truly among men. We have made our offering—'ourselves, our souls and bodies'—in the place where we found him. 'Thou wouldst not seek me if thou hadst not already found me'—the words are said to us as well as to Pascal. Continually searching and in pilgrimage, we are yet already possessors of the treasure of relationship with God. We ask for patience when we still feel we have far to go, and for ever-deepening appreciation of what God has already given us.

33

First Sunday after Epiphany
Revelation: The Baptism of Jesus

Old Testament Reading   1 Samuel 16: 1–13a

As Samuel anoints David to be king, 'the spirit of the Lord' comes
upon him, and remains with him 'from that day onwards' (*v.* 13).
Our Lord, anointed with the Spirit at his baptism was to fulfil both
Samuel's role as prophet and spokesman and David's role as king of
'ransomed Israel.'

New Testament Reading (Epistle)   Acts 10: 34–38a

This links the baptism of Jesus—'how God anointed him with Holy
Spirit and with power' (*v.* 38)—with his universal mission as 'lord of
all' (*v.* 36).

New Testament Reading (Gospel)   Matthew 3: 13–end

All four gospels give our Lord's baptism prominence as a prelude to
his public ministry, and it was the central theme of the Epiphany
festival in the eastern church. Early Christian writers interpreted its
meaning through images familiar to them from the Old Testament.
Jesus, as he comes to be baptized by John, is a new Noah, carrying
God's people through the waters of destruction; a new Moses,
bringing them beyond reach of their enemies through the waters of
the Red Sea; a new Joshua leading them over Jordan to the Promised
Land. The descent of the Spirit upon Jesus, 'like a dove' (*v.* 16),
recalled the spirit hovering over the waters of chaos to produce life
and order (Genesis 1:2). The baptism of Jesus thus came to be seen
as the sign of the new creation under which his followers would enter
his kingdom, share his mission, and receive the enlightenment of the
Spirit.

Vv. 14–15 have no parallel in other gospels and can best be read as
Matthew's way of explaining how 'the sinless one' (2 Corinthians
5:21; Hebrews 4:15) could submit himself to John's baptism 'for

repentance' (*v.* 11). It was 'to fulfil God's purpose' that he stood with sinners whom he had come to save.

V. 17 'This is my Son, my Beloved' (see Isaiah 42: 1 and Psalm 2: 7). 'We might say that from that time he knew he was in the grasp of the Spirit. God was taking him into his service, equipping him and authorizing him to be his messenger and the inaugurator of the time of salvation. At his baptism Jesus experienced his call' (J. Jeremias). But this call was to lead him inexorably forward to suffering and death, also to be spoken of as his 'baptism' (Luke 12: 50). Thus, from the first, the baptism of Christians was thought of as (*a*) adoption into sonship with Christ; (*b*) following Christ in the power of the Spirit; (*c*) dying with Christ and being raised with him to new life (Romans 6: 1–4).

For thought or discussion   Does the meaning of our own baptism become clearer if we relate it to the baptism of Jesus—that is not as an event in our distant past, but as God's call in the present to become 'like Christ' in sonship, mission, and dying into newness of life?

Second Sunday after Epiphany
Revelation: The First Disciples

Old Testament Reading   **Jeremiah 1: 4–10**

New Testament Reading (Epistle)   **Acts 26: 1,9–20**

Both readings see God's call as a lifelong commission which over-
rides feelings of unworthiness and provides the authority and conviction to carry it through. Paul's proud words before king Herod
Agrippa (Acts 26:19) challenge us still to remain loyal to the vision
we have received.

New Testament Reading (Gospel)   **Mark 1: 14–20**

After his baptism, followed by forty days of withdrawal into solitude, Jesus reappears in Galilee proclaiming the good news from
God. God, he says, has drawn near, and his nearness calls for
repentance (that is, a radical change in outlook and way of living); and
faith in the goodness of the news, which will make this change
possible.

God's call, and the response of trustful obedience to the call, are
exemplified in the way two pairs of brothers, all fishermen from
Galilee, go off to follow Jesus, leaving their homes and livelihood
without looking back. The story (*vv.* 16–20) is told in barest outline,
but Mark's earliest readers would not expect more detail: they had
heard the call in similar terms; and for some of them, at least, the
response would have been no less costly than for Peter, Andrew,
James, and John. 'The call of God in Christ comes with a divine
power which does not need to wait upon accidental human circumstances: it can create the response it demands. And that response
must be one of unconditional obedience' (D. E. Nineham).

V. 17 'fishers of men'. Jewish rabbis and Greek philosophers also
used to speak of 'catching' men. But the call here is not simply to
accept a place among a select group of followers and admirers: it is to
share responsibility for the mission of Jesus and to draw men into the
net of new life which he throws out.

V. 18 'at once'—a favourite expression of Mark's gospel, expressing the urgency of decision because God himself is now acting swiftly to bring in his kingdom, or reign.

The apostles—chosen, called, obedient to our Lord's summons—formed the original nucleus of the Church. In one sense his call to them was unique and unrepeatable. Yet for countless men and women ever since, the call of Jesus has been seen as a total commitment of life to him; and a readiness, at the least, to go anywhere and to part with everything to his sake (Mark 8:34 'Anyone who wishes to be a follower of mine must leave self behind').

For thought or discussion   What does it mean for me, now, to be drawn into the net of new life with Christ; to draw others in? What is special and unrepeatable in the call of the first disciples, and what still holds true for the Christian disciple anywhere, at any time?

Third Sunday after Epiphany
Revelation: Signs of Glory

Old Testament Reading   **Exodus 33: 12–end**

Moses, needing assurance that the Lord himself will travel with his people through the desert, asks to be shown his 'glory'. His prayer is granted in part only, but enough for God's glory to be reflected in his face when he returns to the camp (Exodus 34:29). Paul uses this story to encourage Christians in Corinth (2 Corinthians 3:7–18).

New Testament Reading (Epistle)   **1 John 1: 1–7**

God, who is eternal life and light, is 'made visible' in Jesus, and Christians are called to leave the darkness behind and to walk in God's light with him, sharing a common life and cleansed from sin.

New Testament Reading (Gospel)   **John 2: 1–11**

In the calendar used by eastern provinces of the Roman Empire, 6 January was the winter solstice, and with it were associated nature-myths of gods who appeared at woodland springs, turning them into cascades of wine. This may account in part for the early choice of this story as an Epiphany reading, either on the festival itself or a few days later, as the Christian answer to pagan superstition. *V.* 11 describes the transformation of water into wine at a wedding-feast as 'the first of the signs by which Jesus revealed his glory'. In John's account of our Lord's ministry these signs provide a series of moments of insight, revealing his unique relationship with the Father, and the transforming power of faith in those who respond to him.

In this first sign John's purpose is to show that the old way of communion with God—through obedience to the Law of Moses—has been superseded. The glory of God is now unveiled in the life and actions of the incarnate Word. A lavish use of word-signals and forward-pointing allusions lie beneath the surface of his story-telling. For example, *v.* 1 'the third day' points forward to the

38

resurrection. *V.* 3 'no wine left' underlines the inadequacy of the old supply of contact with God and the lavish abundance of the new supply in the Word made flesh (cf. John 1:16, 'Out of his full store we have all received grace upon grace').

V. 6 'six stone jars'. The imperfect number indicates the failure of the purificatory rites of the Old Testament.

V. 9 'the servants knew'. The ignorance of the master of ceremonies is contrasted with the knowledge of the servants ('deacons') who obey the command of Jesus, and thus become partners in his action.

V. 10 'the best wine till now'. This is the key to the whole sign-story. In Jesus the new age has arrived. The disciples recognize this, and respond to him (*v.* 11) with complete obedience and trust.

For thought or discussion 'You have kept the best wine till now.' Think of ways in which this is true in your own experience of life and worship—and give thanks.

Fourth Sunday after Epiphany
Revelation: The New Temple

Old Testament Reading   **1 Kings 8: 22–30**

This beautiful prayer, in its present form at least, is of later date than king Solomon's reign. It reflects the agony and ecstasy of loving the temple at a distance—from exile in Babylon. But this experience helped the exiles to recognize the temporary and provisional character of all temples made with human hands.

New Testament Reading (Epistle)   **1 Corinthians 3: 10–17**

Note especially *v.* 16: 'You are God's temple, where the Spirit of God dwells'. Paul is exasperated by the way church members in Corinth use the names of great leaders—Paul, Apollos, Cephas—as party labels, and so are held back from reaching the full height of their own calling as Christians.

New Testament Reading (Gospel)   **John 2: 13–22**

In the first three gospels the cleansing of the temple by Jesus serves as the immediate prelude to his arrest, trial, and death. John also sees it as pointing forward to his passion; but he introduces it in his gospel immediately after the story of the wedding-feast at Cana to reinforce the 'sign' of water turned into wine. With Christ's coming not only the purificatory rites of the old covenant, but the whole system of animal sacrifices will be superseded by his own self-offering.

V. 16 'a market'. Whereas Mark relates Jesus's action to Isaiah 56:7 ('my house of prayer') and Jeremiah 7:11 ('a robber's cave'), John finds the key to its meaning in Zechariah 14:21 ('when that day comes, no traders shall be seen in the house of the Lord').

V. 17 'Zeal for thy house will destroy me' (Psalm 69: 9). Verses from Psalm 69 are used extensively in the New Testament to interpret the passion of Christ. 'Just as the righteous sufferer in the Psalm paid the price of his loyalty to the temple, so the action of Jesus in cleansing the temple will bring him to grief' (C. H. Dodd).

V. 19 'destroy this temple'. Mark (14:58) and Matthew (26:61) record similar reported words of Jesus being used in the case for the prosecution at his trial before the Council.

V. 20 'It has taken forty-six years to build'. Herod's temple was started about 20 B.C. and was not finished until A.D. 63, only seven years before its demolition by the Romans.

V. 21 'the temple. . . .his body'. The transition from the old way to the new way of worship is to be achieved through Christ's death and resurrection. Instructed readers of John's gospel would understand this underlying meaning, and would also be familiar with the use of 'temple' and 'Christ's body' as signifying the Church (cf. Ephesians 2:21, 4:12).

For thought or discussion 'The Church is not a building, not the clergy, but God's new people anywhere, at any time.' That's easy to accept in theory, but hard to live up to when a much-loved church building is declared redundant, or a village is deprived of a resident pastor. Does the idea of 'the new temple' help in such a situation?

Fifth Sunday after Epiphany
Revelation: The Wisdom of God

Christians of the eastern Roman Empire, who were the first to celebrate the Epiphany, venerated Christ as the Wisdom of God. The dedication *Sancta Sophia* for the great church in Constantinople, and the use of the acclamation 'Wisdom!' in eastern liturgies bear witness to this emphasis. But it was already present in the New Testament. Both Paul and John identify Jesus with the pre-existent 'Logos' or 'Wisdom' of God; and in this way they relate the revelation of God in Christ to his continuing work as Creator and Sustainer of the universe.

Old Testament Reading **Proverbs 2: 1–9** *or* **Ecclesiasticus 42: 15–end**

The reading from Proverbs emphasizes the practical and moral aspects of wisdom, leading to an integrated life and a concern for justice. The reading from Ecclesiasticus is a hymn of praise for the beauty and wonder of God's creation. For both writers wisdom is not an intellectual exercise. It is the heart-felt response to God who is active in creation and in human affairs—a response which expresses itself in faithfulness, trust, wonder, and worship.

New Testament Reading (Epistle) **1 Corinthians 3: 18–end**

'Every possible experience of life, and even the experience of death itself *belongs* to Christians in the sense that in the end it will turn out to be for their good. Every experience which a Christian may undergo is therefore his servant; but he himself is a servant to Christ, and Christ is servant to God' (Margaret Thrall).

New Testament Reading (Gospel) **Matthew 12: 38–42**

Vv. 41, 42 'What is here'. What was the prophet Jonah as a preacher of repentance; what was Solomon as the outstanding example of a wise king, compared with 'what is here' in Jesus?

V. 42 'from the ends of the earth'. Sheba was, in fact, southern Arabia: but the contrast is made between the long journey taken by its queen to learn wisdom from Solomon, and the people of Palestine. They had no long journey to make in order to hear the wisdom of 'David's greater Son', yet they failed to respond to him. Those who ask for a sign will receive one when for them it is too late.

V. 39 'the sign of Jonah'. Luke interprets it as his preaching to the people of Nineveh; Matthew sees it as referring to Jonah's imprisonment in the belly of the sea-monster. The difference of interpretation may relate to the fact that the whole of the book of Jonah was read on the Jewish Day of Atonement. For Jewish Christians its first half would be taken as a prophecy of Christ's death, burial, and resurrection; and its second half as foreshadowing his call for repentance and faith in those who heard his teaching.

For thought or discussion　What is the heart of Christian wisdom for daily living? 'As having nothing, yet possessing all things' (2 Corinthians 6:10).

Sixth Sunday after Epiphany
Revelation: Parables

God's purpose was disclosed by our Lord partly through the use of parables, a device common among Jewish teachers of his time. Before the parables of Jesus were written down, they were 'lived' in the early Christian Church; and many of them were given an 'allegorical' interpretation in which each detail was given a specific meaning. Christian readers today should feel free to concentrate on the parables themselves in the search for a message to the Church in the world of today.

Old Testament Reading   **2 Samuel 12: 1–10**

The parable with which the prophet Nathan confronted David moved him to repent. The gospel-writers would no doubt have preferred to claim a similar success for the parables of Jesus; but they knew that his parables were angrily rejected by the religious leaders in Palestine, and contributed to his arrest, trial, and death. They saw what he was getting at, but could not accept the message.

New Testament Reading (Epistle)   **Romans 1: 18–25**

The passage was chosen in relation to the theme of the gospel. How is the presence of badness or evil in the world to be explained? God, says Paul, has disclosed himself 'in the things he has made' (*v.* 20); but men have 'bartered away the true God for a false one', and have worshipped not the Creator, but his creatures. It is not difficult to identify examples of this 'creature-worship' in western materialism today.

New Testament Reading (Gospel)   **Matthew 13: 24–30**

In this chapter Matthew collects seven parables to make up one of his extended sections of our Lord's teaching. This parable of the true and false wheat may have been prompted by an actual event in which a farmer played a dirty trick on a neighbour. The darnel often bred a poisonous fungus, but was so like the wheat in its early stages of growth that weeding it out was far from easy. Unlike the earlier Parable of the Sower (Matthew 13:4–8), the contrast here is between seeds, not soils. The church for which Matthew wrote his gospel may well have interpreted the parable to mean that God intended to leave Christian church and Jewish synagogue side by side until the end of the age. Our Lord may have intended it rather as a warning against premature judgement of people who responded to his message at different levels of commitment. The first organized Christian communities had to make a difficult choice between the ideal of a 'pure' church, safeguarded by a rigid discipline; or a 'mixed' church, in which judgement of the sincerity of its members had to be left to God (cf. 1 Corinthians 4:5).

For thought or discussion   Throughout Christian history there has been tension between those who advocate rigorist policies in order to keep the Church pure, and those who conscientiously believe that 'judgement' belongs to God and not to man. How can high standards be maintained in church membership without making premature, and possibly mistaken, judgement of individuals and of groups?

Ninth Sunday before Easter
Christ the Teacher

Whilst the populace generally seems to have thought of Jesus as a prophet (see e.g. Mark 8:28), the disciples referred to him often as 'Rabbi', i.e. Teacher—a title which, according to the Fourth Gospel, Jesus accepted ('you call me Teacher and Lord; and you are right, for so I am', John 13:13). That is why the followers of this teacher are themselves called 'disciples', i.e. learners. Even some who apparently remained uncommitted to him recognized in Jesus's words and works a 'new teaching' (Mark 1:27) characterized by a note of authority which was frequently lacking in the teaching of their own religious leaders (Mark 1:22). In this role of teacher, Jesus fulfils the longing for understanding which every man feels who grapples with the problems of living and dying in a strange and difficult world. This longing, running through Israel's religious consciousness, is nowhere more explicit than in today's Old Testament reading.

Old Testament Reading   **Isaiah 30: 18–21**

The over-riding and ever-present question is, why do people suffer, why is life so hard? Is it because after all there is no God? Or is it because, though there is a God, he does not care? Isaiah here affirms both these suggestions to be utterly wrong. God *is* real and he *does* care. Certainly he allows his creatures to wander as though lost in a dark place, bearing all the loneliness, anguish, pain, and death that this entails. But his ultimate purpose is light and life. The prophet looks forward eagerly to the time when this purpose will find fulfilment, and man will be no longer lost or afraid. Isaiah does not suppose that man needs merely intellectual enlightenment; rather, he needs moral guidance and the wisdom to live meaningfully. It is this that the awaited teacher will give.

New Testament Reading (Epistle)   **1 Corinthians 4: 8–13**

Here is a teacher of quite a different order from the one envisaged by
Isaiah. Quite different, indeed, is this teacher from most teachers
and academics, who are generally held in some esteem (certainly this
was the case in the world of Paul's time). The Christian apostle,
however, stands in a position not of honour but of shame and
ridicule; in the world's eyes he is something of a joke! The reason for
this strange phenomenon is found only when we turn to our Gospel
reading and see the Teacher himself, him for whom Isaiah hoped
and to whom Paul bore witness.

New Testament Reading (Gospel)   **Matthew 5: 1–12**

In the fullness of time (cp. Mark 1:15), the Teacher came, the new
Moses who issued his new 'law' from the mount. But what paradoxical teachings he gave! No wonder that 'outsiders' were astonished
(see Matthew 7:28f.). Here, in the Beatitudes, we find a reversal of
values which was characteristic of Jesus's entire teaching and which
might be summarized in the short saying of Mark 8:35. To man who
through self-assertion seeks life (and, tragically, finds only death),
these congratulations seem almost absurd. Yet in the cross and
resurrection of Jesus we discover that the self-loss of which the
Beatitudes speak does in fact lead to life. The Teacher guides along a
strange path indeed, one that leads himself and his followers to
Calvary. But this same path leads also *through* death and beyond it
into life and fulfilment.

Lord, teach us to walk in your way so that we may find true life.

47

Eighth Sunday before Easter
Christ the Healer

One of the most striking features of Jesus's ministry, particularly of the early period in Galilee, is his healing of sickness (with which we should associate also exorcism and the restoration of harmony to disordered nature). Indeed, the summary statement of Mark 1:32–34 gives almost the impression of a travelling dispensary to which everyone might come with ailments of every kind, and find help and healing. Mark concludes the Galilean ministry with a comment of the astonished crowds, 'He has done all things well; he makes even the deaf to hear and the dumb to speak' (Mark 7:37, cp. Isaiah 35:5f.). In this role of healer, Jesus fulfils Israel's longings and authenticates his own declaration that God's kingly rule was dawning.

Old Testament Reading   **Zephaniah 3: 14–end**

The prophet Zephaniah lived in the latter part of the seventh century and generally forecast doom for the apostate people of Israel. So pessimistic, indeed, is his message that many scholars think the prophecy of ultimate hope in our passage is by a later hand. It is, however, entirely proper that God should be depicted here as one who, having punished his wayward people for their rebellion and faithlessness, should then show them mercy, should heal and forgive them. For God remains faithful to himself and to his determination to bless his people with wholeness and life. This wholeness and this life flow from his own sovereign and caring presence with them.

New Testament Reading (Epistle)   **James 5: 13–16a**

The Christian neither pretends that pain is not real (so, when he suffers, he cannot lightly claim that he does not!), nor is he ashamed of times of health and happiness (so, when he prospers, he does not feel guilty about it!). He rejoices and weeps as appropriate; he sighs for help in times of need and sings God's praise in times of well-being (*v*. 13). James then gives an important reminder (*v*. 14), that the Church (always concerned for wholeness and health) should not scorn the contemporary vehicles of soothing and healing. Anointing with oil was a common remedy for a variety of ills, and James commends its use. Yet he adds—since medicine alone is never enough truly to heal the whole man—that with anointing must come the 'prayer of faith'. Christians who long for healing for themselves or for some other will thankfully accept every benefit of medical and psychiatric skill that is available, seeing in them God's good gifts to his disordered creation; but they will also turn to prayer, recognizing that all healing comes from the loving hands of God himself.

New Testament Reading (Gospel) **Mark 2: 1–12**

But why do we suffer sickness in the first place? Job's 'comforters' tried to convince him that he was suffering because he had sinned more than most—in their view there was a direct and proportionate connection between sin and sickness. This heartless and unrealistic doctrine must, surely, be rejected (see Luke 13:2ff. and John 9:2–3). And yet there is some connection: both sin and sickness are manifestations of man's broken relationship with God. Jesus heals this relationship ('making peace by the blood of his cross', Colossians 1:20); therefore from him come both pardon and healing. God is concerned for the whole man, and that man might become whole. Of course, not every illness can be cured. But where sin is forgiven, the sick man even in his sickness will discover a wholeness which not even death can destroy.

'I came that they may have life, and have it abundantly' (John 10:10).

Seventh Sunday before Easter
Christ the Friend of Sinners

Matthew records that the Magi not unnaturally went to Herod's palace expecting there to greet the one born 'king of the Jews'. Presumably they were as surprised as any to find this king in a lowly place, pushed almost onto the edge of human affairs because there was no room in any place more central or more respectable. But God does not despise such a lowly place—Christ 'being found in fashion as a man humbled himself' (Philippians 2:8). And as the lowly one, he is not ashamed to call other lowly folk to himself—indeed, he makes it a condition of association with himself that we should embrace the simple sense of inadequacy and dependence of a child, and that we should not be too proud to belong to the fellowship of the lowly (cp. 1 Corinthians 1:26ff.). Our readings today explore the thought of God's friendship and how that friendship is extended specifically to the ordinary, to the insignificant, and even to the downright despised in society.

Old Testament Reading   **Hosea 14: 1–7**

Behind man's sense of being lost in a strange world and behind the sickness that assails both man and his world, there lies (according to the Old Testament prophets) rebellion against God. This rebellion was represented dramatically in the story of the Fall, but it was also to be seen in the corporate history of Israel and in the lives of every individual. In this passage Hosea looks forward with longing to the end of this rebellion. He sighs for the day when men will no longer look to false friends, whether fickle political allies (such as Assyria) or useless spiritual devices such as man-made idols. *God* is the only true friend to whom man may look with utter confidence, secure that he will pardon, that he will remain true despite every act of treachery and rebellion on man's side, certain that he will fulfil his purposes of love.

New Testament Reading (Epistle) **Philemon 1–16**

Such were the bonds of friendship and love within the early Christian community that Paul was not ashamed to take up Onesimus's case and to plead his cause. What he was asking was no small thing, for the slave had absconded, apparently taking with him some money or property belonging to his owner, and was now hoping to return to Philemon pardoned and re-instated. Here is a picture of concern and friendship in action. The real friend stands by to help, even where a brother does what is patently wrong; he accepts the man although not necessarily approving the action.

New Testament Reading (Gospel) **Mark 2: 13–17**

The Roman occupation forces left it to nationals to procure from their fellows the taxes levied by central government. They recognized that such tax-collectors would only do the job because they could, in the process, inflate what was demanded and cream off the extra as their own profit. These collectors were not unnaturally despised by their fellows both as lackeys of a hated occupying power and also as extortioners. 'Tax-collector' was, therefore, practically synonymous with 'sinner', and the expression 'tax-collectors and sinners' (*vv.* 15–16) simply means 'all manner of socially and morally despicable characters'. What was so distinctive and, to many, so offensive about Jesus was that he was generally found in the company of such people. He did not condone their behaviour (cp. 'go, and do not sin again', John 8:11), but he showed them God's pardon and concern, extending to them the right hand of friendship. God is always found where human self-satisfaction crumbles, where pride no longer keeps him out.

'What a friend we have in Jesus!'

Ash Wednesday

The Christian church inherited from Judaism the custom of fasting on certain days of the week and at certain seasons of the year. Although Jesus saw the inappropriateness of such a custom amongst his own followers so long as he was with them, he seems to have envisaged that they would fast after his death (see Mark 2:19–20). Ash Wednesday reminds us of this ancient practice and summons us to a special period of intense self-discipline and penitence; and it adds point to this call by associating it with Jesus's own period of fasting at the outset of his public ministry, a period during which he committed himself afresh to obedient trust of his Father and to humble service of mankind.

Old Testament Reading   **Isaiah 58: 1–8**

This passage might be headed 'religion and morality'. Religious people sometimes make professions of faith or perform religious acts whilst at the same time turning a blind eye to the obvious needs of fellow men around them—as though the service of God might excuse neglect of one's fellows. Isaiah makes it quite clear that God cannot delight in religious words or works when these mask cold lovelessness. No amount of religious observances can atone for indifference to the various needs of people. *True* fasting, however (which, far from cloaking indifference either to God or to one's fellows, actually expresses a genuine contriteness and concern), encounters God's compassionate forgiveness and the wholeness that a restored relationship with God brings (*v.* 8).

or   **Joel 2: 12–17**

Certain calamities have befallen the people of God; they have been plagued by locusts, bad harvests, and prairie fires. The prophet interprets these as expressions, not simply of the unpredictableness of nature, but of the sovereign hand of God who chastises his people for their fickleness in turning away from true worship and service of him. Therefore, Joel sees that Israel's only hope is repentance; a genuine turning back, heart and will, to humble obedience to God. He does not mean that through repentance Israel can prevail on an angry God and cause him to become well-disposed towards them! He simply means that it is only as men learn to live trustingly and obediently out of God's hand that they find in whatever befalls them (whether good or bad) occasions of thankfulness and contentment. But this humble, trusting stance towards God must come from the heart; mere outward religious show will only add to Israel's sin.

or   **Amos 5: 6–15**

The burden of this passage is that repentance is a matter of a deep change of heart and will, and not simply of the performance of certain prescribed religious ceremonies. But whereas Joel simply called the people to a day of national repentance and mourning, Amos stresses the social aspects of penitence. Real sorrow for sin, like every genuine religious sentiment, must express itself in concern for the well-being of others, for justice and social equity. God, after all, is the Creator who himself takes responsibility for every man and for the society in which men live. He cares, therefore, for each man and for the ways in which societies live. Because of this, Amos inveighs against those who think only of their own prosperity and security, and who, though leaders in society, shrug off their responsibilities. It is inevitable that God's gracious presence meets such folk only in the form of judgement.

New Testament Reading (Epistle)   **1 Corinthians 9: 24–end**

Christian discipleship is like a race for which we must prepare with rigorous training and self-discipline. Whatever might detract from fitness for this race must be strenuously resisted. The reason why discipleship is such a struggle is this: we are all by nature self-centred and self-seeking, whereas Jesus shows us a new pattern of living which is wholly self-forgetful. If we are to follow his new way (which looks as though it must lead to defeat but actually leads to fulfilment and life!), then it will inevitably mean resolute rejection of the old policy that is so much a part of us. To 'pommel the body' (*v.* 27) therefore means not simply to control our physical body but rather to have control of that entire old, self-centred nature. The Christian, engaged on these exercises, may not pride himself on any progress he might make, because that very pride would be a denial of any progress at all! For this 'race' is simply a movement towards Christ-likeness and so towards greater self-forgetfulness.

or   **James 4: 1–10**

It is perhaps easy to imagine that God should be like any other powerful and important being; one, that is, who takes note of the successful but who ignores the ordinary. But the God who disclosed himself to Israel and who, supremely, disclosed himself to the world in Jesus is, in fact, quite different. It is indeed as though he took special note of some and not of others; but it is the lowly rather than the powerful, the ordinary rather the important, the downright despised in society rather than the successful, to whom he first turns and of whom he takes special note. As the *Magnificat* reminds us (Luke 1:53), 'he has filled the hungry with good things, and the rich he has sent empty away'. Almost inevitably, therefore, anyone whose first concern is for a fine reputation amongst his fellows, or for personal success and security, will find himself out of harmony with this God (*v*. 4). Conversely, submission to God is the secret of true success and of true importance—for *God exalts* the lowly (*v*. 10). This strange policy of self-abasement is also the key to harmony within disordered society and to contentment within the restless spirit of the individual (*vv*. 1–3).

New Testament Reading (Gospel)   **Matthew 6: 16–21**

We read first of a reward that is transitory and unworthy (though it has proved a strong attraction to religious people through the ages): it is the reward of other people's admiration of us. Those who themselves may not necessarily be religious or self-disciplined can, and sometimes do, admire those who are. But real discipleship, real religion looks not to such admiration but rather to him who is the object of worship, the 'Father who sees in secret'. Our reading then speaks of a true reward. Here we should think not so much of a future situation in which compensation will be meted out in return for any sacrifice we may have made in our earthly life; rather, the real treasure in heaven is the Lord himself upon whom we concentrate our gaze, towards whom we direct all our living, in whom we trust for our forgiveness. He is the treasure that never fails us, and 'laying up treasure' (cp. the expression 'lay hold of eternal life' in 1 Timothy 6:12) simply means increasing our hold on him.

or   **Luke 18: 9–14**

The point of this story is not that the good man was really not very good after all; we have no reason to doubt the accuracy of his self-assessment that he was sincere and morally upright. Nor is the point of the story that the bad man was, after all, not really so very bad—the tax-collector was beyond doubt both quisling and extortionist. The point simply is that what puts a man right with God is not moral effort nor moral achievement; it is simply God who justifies the ungodly. Therefore the only appropriate stance before God is the modest recognition that even when we have done our very best, we are still entirely dependent on the gracious forgiveness of God (cp. Luke 17:10). This is what we see in Jesus; one who though morally beyond reproach nevertheless made no claims upon his Father, but committed himself humbly into his hands in trust and obedience. This sense of trust and dependence (the opposite of any desire to argue our case before God or to make any claims upon him) is precisely the quality which Jesus commends in calling us to become like little children if we would enter God's kingdom. The question is not 'are we splendid enough', only 'are we small enough' to know God!

'God be merciful to me, a sinner.'

First Sunday in Lent
The King and the Kingdom: Temptation

Because God has given us free will, we are all bound to be tempted to disobey him. Even Jesus was no exception. We only commit sin when we give in to the temptation. Billy Graham has given a good example: temptation is seeing the dirty book on the stall; sin is going back for a second look.

Old Testament Reading   **Genesis 2: 7–9; 3: 1–7**

The Hebrew phrase 'good and evil' means everything. By eating from the fruit of the tree Adam and Eve hoped to know as only God can know, and so be able to do without him. This is always man's basic temptation—to forget that he is dependent on God and instead act as if he is master of creation.

New Testament Reading (Epistle)   **Hebrews 2: 14–end**

Christians believe that in every respect Jesus was like us—fully man. He too knew what it was to be tempted, but he did not sin, for in all things he put God first, and so triumphed even over death. The incarnation and the resurrection are therefore the fundamental doctrines of Christianity. But because Jesus has endured the power of temptation, he can both help us when tempted and make us acceptable to God even when we have failed him.

New Testament Reading (Gospel)   **Matthew 4: 1–11**

The Gospel presents in dramatic form the three basic temptations which faced Jesus throughout his ministry. But there is a particular irony about these temptations—they could all have been justified in the short term.

The first temptation concerns physical need. Had Jesus been able to satisfy his own hunger by turning stones into bread, then he could

56

also have satisfied the physical needs of all who were suffering in Palestine. But Jesus was not just a humanist concerned with alleviating the sufferings of this world. His mission was to point men to God in whose image they were made, and with whom they were to have a relationship which would outlast this world. When the time came, he would feed his people with the spiritual food of his own body —but that could only be from beyond the cross.

Secondly, Jesus is asked to give proof that he is Messiah. If he had done so, men would undoubtedly have flocked to his cause. But what God wants is faith, and faith by its very nature means that there can be no proof. To give men proof takes away their freedom of choice, makes them less than human. But God in creating man in his image gave him the glorious liberty of the children of God. This is his most sacred possession.

Finally, Jesus is tempted with full temporal power. But his kingdom is not of this world, and it can only be inaugurated through the defeat of the devil by Jesus's death on the cross. Men would not see the true nature of God in the exploits of a triumphant monarch; they could see him in the crumpled figure on the cross. While the devil could give Jesus the kingdoms of the world, only God could give him the kingdom of heaven. And it is for that kingdom that man is destined. But the way to it is not through worldly satisfaction, proof, and power, but suffering, doubt, and rejection.

In meeting all three temptations, Jesus quoted from the book of Deuteronomy. We too can face the temptation to avoid the way of the cross to which we have been called, if we also rely on God's word.

Second Sunday in Lent
The King and the Kingdom: Conflict

From primeval times man has rebelled against God and rejected his love. As a result man still does not enjoy that peace and harmony which remains God's will for him.

Old Testament Reading   **Genesis 6: 11–end**

Man's rebellion now embraces the whole world in violence. This can only lead to total chaos. While the flood is presented as God's direct judgement on sinful man, in effect man had brought it upon himself by his own chaotic misuse of God's creation. But because of his love, God will not let man go: he saves Noah and his family.

New Testament Reading (Epistle)   **1 John 4: 1–6**

False prophecy was a live issue throughout the biblical period (Deuteronomy 13:1–5, 18:22). While for the Christians at Corinth it was enough to confess Jesus as Lord (1 Corinthians 12:3), in this passage the confession must include an explicit acknowledgement that he was really man. This requirement is specifically aimed at those who regarded matter as evil, and so argued that Jesus only seemed to be man (the docetists). But to deny the humanity of Jesus challenges the two basic Christian doctrines of the incarnation and resurrection, for if he was not really man then he could not have died, and so have risen from the dead. The doctrine of the incarnation, like the doctrine of creation, indicates that matter is of itself good, but that it is man's misuse of it that leads to chaos. To reject the humanity of Christ is to rebel against the full measure of God's love.

New Testament Reading (Gospel)   **Luke 19: 41–end**

Jesus foresees that the chaotic state of Judaism could only lead to its collapse. The enormity of the tragedy which would engulf his people hurts the really human Jesus to the full. It was not easy to watch such self-destruction, and remain powerless to stop it. Yet in God's law Judaism had been given the means to bring about *shalom*, peace and harmony for all men. So the eighth century prophets Isaiah and Micah picture the nations of the world going up to Jerusalem for instruction in God's ways (Isaiah 2:2–4; Micah 4:1–4). Israel is to be a light to the nations (Isaiah 49:6) and so re-establish that divine order which God willed for his world at its creation, in which even wild and domestic animals will lie down together and children play in safety by snakes' nests (Isaiah 11:6–9). Instead Jerusalem had become a centre of religious hypocrisy, and the Gentiles in whose court the trading took place were treated solely as a source for worldly gain. So Jesus takes action against this perversion of his Father's will for those whom he has created, and the final conflict begins. It is a conflict with love, and since the way of love is sacrifice and self-giving, the immediate outcome is certain. The Jewish authorities will succeed in destroying their Messiah in a vain attempt to preserve their own position. Yet the good news of the Gospel is that the love which weeps over the coming destruction of Jerusalem and is prepared to face its own destruction cannot in the end be annihilated, no matter what men may do.

Third Sunday in Lent
The King and the Kingdom: Suffering

Suffering does not merely put faith to the test: it is part of the believer's vocation through which alone God's kingdom can be inaugurated.

Old Testament Reading   **Genesis 22: 1–13**

Abraham is ordered by God to sacrifice his only son through whom he had been promised that he would be the father of God's people. Although incapable of understanding God's apparent contradiction of himself, he obeys his command. Abraham has been brought to the supreme test, the test of self-destruction. Yet he is prepared to take the knife which will nullify the promise. He thereby demonstrates that he has no legal claims over Isaac; that the boy is the gift of promise; that that promise is not dependent on Isaac himself, but on God alone, who, once Abraham has acted, provides the sacrificial ram. For at no time does the promise become automatic: faith had continually to be lived out, continually reaffirmed, even when to do so seems illogical, for even God appears to be one's enemy.

New Testament Reading (Epistle)   **Colossians 1: 24–end**

Paul regards his sufferings on behalf of the Colossians as parallel to, though dependent upon, Christ's suffering for man. In other words for Paul, suffering for those for whom he was responsible was the natural pastoral role and one over which he could justifiably rejoice. It is to this suffering on behalf of others that Christ's disciples are called. For Paul suffering and the proclamation of the gospels are inseparable. Discipleship can only be costly.

New Testament Reading (Gospel)   **Luke 9: 18–27**

Anyone of Jesus's authority and independence was bound to become the focus of public attention: the Gospels confirm the widespread speculation as to his possible identity. In discussion with his disciples, Peter acknowledges Jesus as Messiah. Jesus does not deny this confession, but in order to avoid misunderstanding, makes the nature of his messiahship plain. He is no triumphal Davidic prince who will defeat the Romans and restore Jewish independence. Rather he must suffer and die. It is clear that Jesus' choice of the 'son of man' of Daniel 7:13f. as the model best fitted to describe his ministry was deliberate. In Daniel this figure is identified with 'the saints most high'—that is those faithful Israelites who were enduring persecution probably at the time of the Maccabean revolt (166 B.C.). In this some would die, though later they would know resurrection (Daniel 12), and the saints most high would be vindicated and their authority acknowledged by all nations. What Jesus does is to take this plural concept of the son of man in Daniel and apply it to himself alone. He is *the* Son of Man. His authority is being rejected, he must suffer even unto death, but he will rise from the dead, and all nations will acknowledge his sovereignty.

But until his rule is acknowledged everywhere, Christ's disciples are called to share his vocation with him. It is probable that originally Jesus may have expected that some of them would actually die with him, and that thereby they would together inaugurate the coming of his kingdom which others would live to see. Even Paul thought that he was living in the last days, though he had to modify his theology when Christians began to die before Christ's kingdom came (cp. I and 2 Thessalonians). Indeed it is still left to his followers to bring about its realization. But that will only be achieved through that costly sacrifice which, like the Maccabean martyrs, Christ, and Paul, is prepared to face not only suffering, but even self-annihilation.

Fourth Sunday in Lent
The King and the Kingdom: Transfiguration

As a result of Jesus's ministry, God is no longer hidden from man. Instead he is readily to be approached in order that he can transfigure man with his divine glory.

Old Testament Reading　　　　　　　　　　　　**Exodus 34: 29–end**

The original meaning of this story is now no longer clear. In its present form it describes the first occasion on which after speaking with God, Moses's face took on a divine glow, and then points out that this continued to occur whenever Moses had been in God's presence. The purpose of the mask which was apparently only worn when Moses was neither speaking to God nor the people is unclear. But it is possible that an ancient practice of wearing a mask when giving oracles has here been modified in the light of subsequent reforms, when such cult objects were found to be unacceptable.

New Testament Reading (Epistle)　　　　　　**2 Corinthians 3: 7–end**

Paul's use of the incident of Moses's shining face is extremely complex and difficult to interpret. His argument depends on the idea that the divine light on Moses's face was soon to fade. Yet there is no indication of this in the Old Testament account. But since Moses's shining face is nowhere else mentioned in the Old Testament, it is possible that the idea of its temporary nature already formed part of current Jewish interpretation.

Paul uses the incident both to contrast the temporary nature of the old covenant with the permanency of the new, and to indicate the obstinate nature of Judaism in failing to see that the Old Testament itself pointed forward to the New. There, the fearfulness of Moses who veiled his face is replaced by the boldness of Christians who through the work of the Spirit are gradually being changed into an ever deeper reflection of divine glory. Each Christian ought then to be engaged in a spriritual journey, the progress of which should be visually apparent. It is not God's intention that even in this world man should remain in his natural state, but rather to begin his transfiguration here. But this can only happen in so far as a man is prepared to allow God's Spirit to work in him.

New Testament Reading (Gospel) **Luke 9: 28–36**

The Transfiguration confirms both Peter's confession of Jesus as Messiah and Jesus's own interpretation of that role as one of suffering and death, but which would ultimately lead to his vindication and glory. And the appearance of Moses and Elijah—the representatives of the law and the prophets—indicates that in Jesus the hopes and aspirations of the Old Testament reach their fulfilment.

In the excitement of the moment, Peter unthinkingly tries to perpetuate the vision. But it is only a vision, and its actualization could only be accomplished by Jesus in Jerusalem, where in Gethsemane, with the same three disciples, he finally submitted himself to his vocation. In this way he fully revealed to man the true nature of the God with whom he has to deal. No longer can there be any veil between God and man. And to confirm this, the evangelists record that at the moment of Jesus's death the curtain of the temple separating the worshippers from the Holy of Holies was torn in two. No more was the invisible God to be curtained off from men (cp. Hebrews 10:19ff.).

Fifth Sunday in Lent
The King and the Kingdom: The Victory of the Cross

The Bible is the story of how God set about restoring man's relationship with him. This could only be achieved through God disclosing his full nature. This meant he had both to live and die as man among men.

Old Testament Reading   **Exodus 6: 2–13**

The foundation of Israel's faith was her deliverance from Egypt. She believed that God of his own free choice, and through no merit on her part, had miraculously delivered a band of Hebrew slaves, led them through the desert, and given them the rich land of Canaan promised long ago to their ancestors. Her very existence then depended solely on God's grace. She had not earned her salvation: he had willed it. Further, both in Egypt and during the desert wandering she had often doubted God: yet he had remained faithful to his promise. In spite of disobedience he could not let her go (Hosea 11:8–9). Such was his nature.

New Testament Reading (Epistle)   **Colossians 2: 8–15**

Paul is fearful that the Colossians will be subverted from their basic faith which rests on the incarnation and resurrection. Through the former, men had been able to see and handle the 'fullness of deity', and the latter had confirmed Jesus's victory over every power ranged against him. While circumcision was the rite through which a man entered Israel, and acted from the days of Abraham, the father of Israel, as a sign of God's continued blessing on his people (Genesis 17), baptism far exceeded this. For through this sacrament Christians were not only made members of the church, the new Israel, but were also enabled to share in all the benefits of Christ's victory on the cross. Not only were their sins forgiven, but already in this world they began to experience the resurrection life.

New Testament Reading (Gospel)   **John 12: 20–32**

John depicts Jesus throughout his ministry as waiting for the moment at which he should perform the work for which he had been destined, the hour which would change all history. The work was to enable all men—this is the significance of the Gentile Greeks—to see in him his divine glory. But paradoxically that glory could only be recognized through the self-annihilation of the man Jesus. Through his death alone could men understand the God who could not spare himself for man. Thus his lifting up on the cross to die is also his exaltation in glory. And once men recognize this twofold aspect of the cross, the Prince of this world has no more power over them. It is then not force which drives him out, but self-sacrificing love. Triumphalism has no place in the gospel of peace: rather, Christianity depends on the powerlessness of love. But the call to hate oneself in this world should not be misunderstood. 'Hate' here carries its Hebrew meaning of 'not prefer'. Like his Master, the Christian is to prefer others to himself, and so sacrifice himself for them. While Jesus has defeated the Prince of this world, it is left to his followers to realize the fullness of that victory. And in their own sacrificial love for others they will find Christ with them and so share in his glory.

Palm Sunday
The Way of the Cross

Old Testament Reading **Isaiah 50: 4–9a**

The Suffering Servant

The prophet Isaiah preached to people living in exile. By the waters of Babylon the Jews longed for the time when they would be able to return to Jerusalem and worship the Lord in his temple. To this dejected group of people Isaiah brought a message of comfort and hope. Under the protection of God they would go back to Zion and restore the stricken city to its former glory. Embedded in the prophecy are four (so-called) Servant Songs, passages which refer either to some specific individual, or, in a collective sense, to the people of Israel. Although the writer seems to leave the identity of the Servant intentionally vague, in this song God's chosen spokesman has all the marks of a prophet. In particular, he treads the path of martyrdom. He accepts with patience the inevitable suffering that follows the courageous preaching of God's word in a hostile environment. But in spite of humiliation and rejection the Servant expresses his determination to carry out his task in the confidence that the Lord will vindicate him. With God on his side his adversaries will not have the last word.

New Testament Reading (Epistle) **Philippians 2: 5–11**

The Obedient Son

Although this poetic passage is full of important doctrinal statements about the person of Christ, its primary purpose was not theological speculation. Paul is addressing himself to the feuds that have arisen in the church at Philippi, and in doing so emphasizes the moral significance of what may have been an early Christian hymn. The stress here is not on credal statements and orthodox beliefs, but on a particular disposition or attitude of mind. The Philippians, who are guilty of selfishness and conceit (see 2:3–4), are bidden to follow the example of their risen Lord, who is presented to them in three ways: first, in his original status; second, as he chose to be; and third, as Lord of all. In his original glory Christ was the possessor of the divine nature. He was 'true God'. But he did not try to cling tooth and nail to his equality with his heavenly Father. Through humility and obedience he allowed himself to become subject to the weaknesses and limitations of a human being. This same Jesus who was humiliated and crucified, the humble and obedient Son, now sits at the right hand of God and receives homage from men. 'Jesus Christ is Lord' became the one and only article of faith for the early Christians.

New Testament Reading (Gospel)   **Mark 14: 32–15: 41**

The Lonely Messiah

From the moment that he went to Gethsemane with his three friends Jesus became more and more isolated. While he prayed the disciples slept. When he was betrayed with a kiss, 'they all forsook him, and fled'. Peter denied him three times. As he died on the cross passers-by abused him, the priests and the lawyers made fun of him, and the two robbers crucified with him taunted him. His last spoken word, according to Mark, expresses his feeling of alienation from God caused by human sin. But as he died tragedy turned into triumph. His 'loud cry' (*v.* 37) was not a cry of despair or a sigh of relief, but the triumphant shout of the victor. On hearing the cry, even the pagan soldier recognized the presence of the divine, 'Truly this man was a son of God'.

Alternative Readings
The Triumphal Entry

Old Testament Reading   **Zechariah 9: 9–12**

Power and Peace

Important moments in the history of Israel were often the occasion
of prophecy. Some commentators claim that this prophetic oracle is
linked to the fall of the Persian Empire in the fourth century B.C. and
the emergence of Greece as the dominant world power under Alex-
ander the Great. In verses 1–8 of this chapter the prophet interprets
the signs of the times by proclaiming Judah's triumph over her
enemies and emphasizing that God's rule extends over all nations.
Verses 9–12 announce the appointment of the agent through whom
God will rule in Jerusalem, and make three claims about the nature
of his Kingdom. First, victory is linked with humility. The conquer-
ing King gains his victory not by his own might, but by divine help.
Second, the King defends Jerusalem and extends his sway over all
peoples by 'commanding peace'. The keynote of his reign will be
disarmament. He will use his power to promote peace, to ensure the
welfare and well-being of all men. Finally, the prophet sees the King
as a liberator who will deliver those in bondage and offer hope to the
depressed.

New Testament Reading (Epistle)   **1 Corinthians 1: 18–25**

The Paradox of the Gospel

To the majority of Jews in Paul's day Jesus Christ was a 'stumbling-
block', they found it impossible to believe that he was the expected
Messiah. They stumbled against his method. He was a popular and
respected teacher, yet he disregarded the authority of tradition. He
claimed to be of God, yet consorted with sinners and lepers. He
acted like a king, but did nothing to save his people from their
oppressors. They stumbled against his murder. According to the
Law (Deuteronomy 21:23), crucifixion was the punishment meted
out for the most serious crimes, and the offender was considered to

be accursed in the eyes of God. A crucified Messiah was a contradiction in terms. To the Greeks the Christian gospel did not present religious problems, they simply regarded it as foolish. Because they approached it from the standards of this world, they could see neither rhyme nor reason in it. But for the Christian the weak and foolish things of this world had become a source of strength and wisdom. Through them God made himself known as Lord and Saviour.

New Testament Reading (Gospel)   **Matthew 21: 1–13**

The King of Peace

None of those lining the road into Jerusalem on the first Palm Sunday could have been in any doubt that Jesus claimed to be a king, or that his triumphal entry was to be regarded as a sacred occasion. He came mounted on a colt, on which, according to Mark (11:2), no man had ever ridden. This fact alone points to the sacredness of the event. The cart which carried the ark of the covenant (1 Samuel 6:7), the symbol of God's presence with his people, was to be drawn by two cows which had never before been yoked. Furthermore, the ass was the beast on which kings rode when they came in peace; only in war did they ride on horseback. In his entry into Jerusalem, Jesus claimed to be King of peace. He deliberately refused the role of warrior, and sought for a throne in the hearts of men. In this last symbolic drama, in which actions were meant to speak louder than words, he made one last appeal to men to accept him as Lord of their lives.

Monday in Holy Week

Old Testament Reading   **Isaiah 42: 1–7**

The Royal Servant

This Servant Song, in which God addresses the listeners, opens with
a reference to the Servant's *election* to service. God has an agent on
earth with whom he is 'well pleased', and whom he has designated as
his emissary. Apart from God himself, the Servant is the most
important figure in the whole prophecy; he is indispensable to the
divine plan of salvation. The passage refers also to the *task* which
faces the Servant. Initially his mission is to comfort Israel pining in
exile, but through her he is to bring forth (i.e. announce, bring out of
the mouth) justice to the non-Jewish nations. His ministry is to be
one of enlightenment and liberation in which he will seek to make
God's will known to all men. Finally, the *way* in which the task is to
be accomplished is mentioned. Equipped with the spirit of the Lord,
'the spirit of wisdom and understanding, the spirit of counsel and
might' (Isaiah 11:2), the Servant will not be deterred. But he is not to
conceive of his mission in terms of the ecstatic frenzy of the early
prophets, or of a noisy procession through the streets in the fashion
of a new king proclaiming and re-enacting laws. His missionary
method is to be the still small voice of persuasion.

New Testament Reading (Epistle)   **Hebrews 2: 9–18**

The Bridge-Builder

The Epistle to the Hebrews was originally written to a depressed and
pessimistic group of Christians. The recipients had grown weary of
trying to resist the might and corruption of the Roman Empire; they
were ready to abandon the fight and to sink without trace. This letter
is a rope thrown out to the struggling swimmers to pull them to the
safety of the shore. After showing that man, though in a privileged
position within the created order, has failed to respond to God's
grace (verses 1–8), the writer directs the attention of his readers to

Jesus. The 'but' with which verse 9 opens is emphatic. Amid the human dilemma the Christian is bidden to keep his attention fixed on Jesus, to look beyond this world to the one who has access to God as high priest. He is the *Pontifex*, the builder of bridges, the one who makes communication possible. Jesus is uniquely qualified to effect this communication, and thereby save man from his predicament, on two counts: his divinity and his humanity. As the one who 'reflects the glory of God and bears the very stamp of his nature' (1:3), he is true God. As the one who suffered and was tempted 'like his brethren in every respect', he is true man.

New Testament Reading (Gospel)   **Matthew 26: 1–30**

Preparing for the Passion

While Jesus was visiting a leper at Bethany an unknown woman anointed him with precious oil. We are not told why she did it. In ancient Israel kings were anointed before they took office. The inclusion of this story within the Passion narrative may indicate that the common people expected Jesus to be a political figure who would lead an insurrection against the Romans. If this was the intention, Jesus rejects it and regards the act as part of the preparation that must be made for his burial. This picture of a Messiah who is in command of the situation and predicts with confidence what is going to happen, is a marked feature of Matthew's version of the Passion. Jesus is aware that his 'time is at hand'. He realizes that he must fulfil what has been written about him. The chosen servant must suffer.

Tuesday in Holy Week

Old Testament Reading   **Isaiah 49: 1–6**

The Discouraged Servant

The words of this song are addressed by the Servant to the Gentiles, to foreign peoples of distant lands to whom he has already been commissioned (42:4). Here again the Servant's election is emphasized. In language reminiscent of the call of Jeremiah, he describes how he was chosen before he was born to serve God. The service of a human agent was central to God's plan. His message to his contemporaries was to be 'like a sharp sword', capable of piercing the hard shell of indifference and apathy. But he becomes despondent; all effort seems futile and nothing comes of his work. He fails to bring Israel back to God. The answer to his despondency is not release from service but additional duties. His mission is to be extended beyond the borders of Israel and he is to be 'a light to the nations'. His consolation (*v.*7) will be that kings and princes will come to recognize the hand of God in the promised restoration of Israel. They will realize that the Holy One keeps faith despite his people's stubbornness.

New Testament Reading (Epistle)   **Hebrews 8: 1–6**

The Superiority of Christ

As the opening verse indicates, this passage sums up the argument of the previous chapter about the nature of the priesthood. The function of the priest in Israel was to represent the people before God. The sacrifices which he offered atoned for the sins of the nation. In Jesus the Christian has a high priest who is superior in at least three ways to the priests who ministered in the temple. The first token of Christ's superiority is the permanent nature of his priesthood. Unlike the levitical priests who died and therefore could not continue in office, Jesus has conquered death and is unceasingly available to intercede for men before God. Secondly, the sacrifice offered by Christ is perfect and unrepeatable. The Jerusalem priests had to maintain a daily round of sacrifices, but Christ's oblation of himself for man's redemption was made once, and once for all. Thirdly, Jesus's priesthood is linked to the 'true tent', the heavenly sanctuary of which the temple of Solomon is simply a pale and imperfect copy or shadow. Because he stands at the right hand of the Father, it is only Jesus who can give man access to the ultimate reality which is God, and lead him to his true home in heaven.

New Testament Reading (Gospel)   **Matthew 26: 31–end**

The Power of Prayer

The story of Gethsemane forms a part of the Passion narrative in Matthew, Mark, and Luke. To this garden Jesus came with his disciples to pray. The evangelists do not often describe Jesus's emotions; they prefer to allow the reader to make his own deductions. But here we are told explicitly that he was sad and troubled, 'my soul is very sorrowful, even to death'. He was despondent not only at the prospect of suffering, but also at the realization that he had been finally rejected by his own people. His experience in Gethsemane enabled him to overcome his sorrow, for in his prayer he committed himself entirely into his Father's hands. This trust in the divine protection and the readiness to accept God's will sustained him to the bitter end. 'Rise, let us be going' are the words of one who is able to face the future with confidence. Jesus does not allow disaster to overcome him, but goes out to meet it and masters it through the power of prayer.

Wednesday in Holy Week

Old Testament Reading   **Isaiah 50: 4–9a**

The Trusting Servant

We noted on Palm Sunday that the Servant in this chapter has the characteristics of a prophet. In common with some of his fellow exiles he is listening to the voice of God and seeking his will for the nation. He has the gift of oratory and is summoned to preach to his sorrowing compatriots, 'to sustain with a word' those who are weary and downhearted. But before he can be used by God he must know God. As a disciple, as one 'of those who are taught', he communes with God daily. As a preacher he is open to harassment and criticism, but when called to speak, he does not refuse; he bears the taunts and insults of his listeners with patience. His trust in God's justice enables him to endure the torments to which he is subjected 'with a face like flint'. His certainty that his prayer will be answered gives him the confidence to challenge his opponents and to proclaim his faith in a saving God. Whoever this Servant was as the prophet intended to portray him, for the Christian reader only Jesus, crucified and risen, responds adequately to his person and work.

New Testament Reading (Epistle)   **1 Peter 2: 19–end**

Patient in Tribulation

The writer of this letter seeks to encourage a particular Christian community to stand fast in the face of persecution. The readers, like those addressed in the Letter to the Hebrews, were in danger of apostasy and of abandoning their faith because they lived in fear of the cruelty to which they were subjected. In order to help them face such continuous hostility the author stresses the example of Christ in his sufferings. Slaves who are ill-treated by their master for no apparent reason should remember how Jesus suffered unto death, though he had committed no sin. The language in which the suffering is described is borrowed, to a very large extent, from the fourth

Servant Song in Isaiah 53, which suggests that the writer deliberately set the passion of Christ within the context of Old Testament
prophecy. But Jesus's death was more than an example for his
followers. By dying on the cross he took the sins of mankind with
him and blotted them out, so that men 'might die to sin and live to
righteousness'.

New Testament Reading (Gospel)   **Matthew 27: 1–56**

Whose Fault?

According to the Gospels it was the custom in Judea under Roman
rule to offer amnesty to a prisoner at Passover. When Pilate offered
to release either Barabbas or Jesus, the crowd chose the former and
called for the death of Christ. The governor was not happy with the
choice, for Barabbas was a notorious murderer and rebel (Mark
15:7), but Jesus was innocent. Matthew seems to have made deliberate additions to the Marcan narrative to emphasize Pilate's innocence and to put the blame for the crucifixion on the Jewish nation in
its entirety. The apparent readiness of 'all the people' to accept
responsibility and guilt for his death (*v.*25) represents the anti-
Jewish feelings of later Christians who regarded the destruction of
Jerusalem in A.D. 70 as punishment for taking Christ to the cross. In
subsequent centuries this particular verse was adopted as the basis of
Christian antisemitism and of the charge of deicide against the Jews
in general. Whose fault was it? Certainly not that of the people as a
whole. The Jewish leaders who incited the crowds must take some of
the blame. But in the last analysis Pilate bears the responsibility for
handing Jesus over in the first place and for washing his hands of the
whole affair.

Maundy Thursday

Old Testament Reading   **Exodus 12: 1–14**

A Nation's Birthday

The Exodus event was so crucial to the religion of Israel that it was used to inaugurate a new calendar (*v.* 2) and was commemorated with an annual festival (*v.* 14). The Passover was originally a family festival which required no priest, no altar, and no shrine. It was celebrated in the home, and the head of the household was the officiant. Later, under the influence of religious reformers, it became a pilgrimage feast during which every family was expected to make the journey to Jerusalem and keep the Passover at the temple. But whether it was celebrated at home or in Jerusalem, the significance of the festival was the same. It commemorated an event which marked the birth of the nation. By the gracious action of God an enslaved people was set free and led through the wilderness to the promised land. The memory of this deliverance has upheld the Jewish people in every major crisis from that day to this.

New Testament Reading (Epistle)   **1 Corinthians 11: 23–29**

Do this

The earliest account of the institution of the Holy Communion is part of a discussion of specific problems connected with public worship. After criticizing the irreverent attitude of the Corinthian Christians towards the celebration of the Lord's Supper, Paul records the tradition handed on to him by the apostolic Church about the nature and significance of the Eucharist. There is an unmistakable emphasis on action. Those who gather in the name of Christ are not told to say something, but to *do* something. They are to imitate the Lord Jesus's action of taking, blessing, breaking, and giving, and in so doing to remember him. Whenever such a remembrance is made, the Lord uses the act as a means of being present with his followers to grant pardon and power. Those who participate in the service should do so only when they are capable of 'discerning the body', i.e. of seeing in their fellow communicants the presence of the risen Christ. The sacrament is a bond which binds those who partake of it to one another in love. The 'one bread' makes those who eat it into 'one body'.

New Testament Reading (Gospel) **John 13: 1-15**

Preparation for Service

Instead of the story of the institution of the Eucharist, the Fourth Gospel includes an account of the foot-washing, the symbolism of which may be understood in several ways. Verses 12–15 indicate that the episode is to be taken as an ethical example. The disciples are to observe the self-sacrificial humility of Christ, and to imitate, not necessarily the act of foot-washing itself, but the spirit in which it is done. Jesus's action could also be interpreted as an expression of his love for his friends. Guests would have bathed before attending a feast, but as they walked to the appointed place in sandals their feet would become dusty. It was the duty of the junior slave to bring a bowl of water and wash their feet on their arrival. Jesus undertook this most menial of tasks to show how devoted he was to his disciples. Verses 6–11, however, suggest that more is implied in the story than ethical example or a demonstration of love. It may also be understood as a cleansing from sin. All the disciples save one are clean, i.e. fitted for Christ's service through their faith and loyalty. But even they who are already bathed must allow their feet to be washed. The forgiveness of sins must be more than a doctrine; it must be realized in forgiveness and repentance.

Good Friday
He bore our sufferings

Old Testament Reading   **Isaiah 52: 13–53: end**

What the prophet says about suffering is new and surprising to his
contemporaries. He perceives, beyond its humiliation and apparent
pointlessness, a purpose and intention that nobody had expected.
God's suffering and degraded servant is the one through whom God
reaches others, and they are enabled to see that their sin has been
borne for them, and their transgressions have been wiped out, by the
servant's disgrace and death.

New Testament Reading (Epistle)   **Hebrews 10: 1–25 *or* 10: 12–22**

The death of Jesus is the one, final, and complete sacrifice for sins;
all that the Israelites hoped to receive through the offerings com-
manded in the Old Testament is now available through what Christ
has done. He has fulfilled Psalm 40 by doing God's will; and the
prophecy of Jeremiah (ch. 31) has now become true: there is a new
covenant between God and man, and God will never again recall
their failures and rebellions, but always see them through eyes of
love and approval.

or   **Hebrews 4: 14–end; 5: 7–9**

The one who once suffered is now alive, and with God. He knows
from experience what it is like to be human, and what desperation
and despair really are. Moreover, his sinlessness makes him even
more sympathetic to others, because there is no self-centredness or
impatience in him. He is thus qualified in every way to be our
representative with God. And the consequence of this is that we can
approach God, with him, in complete confidence that we shall be
accepted and receive all that we require.

New Testament Reading (Gospel)　　　**John 18: 1–19: 37** *or* **19: 1–37**

One of the titles of Jesus that appears with increased frequency in all four accounts of the crucifixion is King. In John's Gospel, the evangelist helps us to see what this title, which could easily be misunderstood, really means when it is used of Jesus. First of all, Old Testament prophecies are fulfilled: therefore Jesus has God's complete approval and authority; he is acting for him, with the Father's entire goodwill. Nevertheless he is rejected by his own, and the evangelist exposes their reason for doing so: they would rather acknowledge Caesar as their King, than Jesus; they prefer somebody like themselves, another creature, to the Word of God, by whom they were made. Their sin, which is also our sin, is to deny creatureliness, and pretend that we are independent beings. Jesus has come to bear witness to the truth, and the truth is that he is our Maker. His way of showing his authority over us is not by overwhelming us with power, or forcing himself upon us against our wills: he makes his claim upon us by dying, enduring our rejection of him; and he does this in love. He is King over those whom he makes free by his death, free to accept him freely; and he adopts them, not as servants, but as brethren. All this he does liberally, royally, and with complete efficacy, so that he can say, It is accomplished! We need have no hesitation or fear.

Easter Eve
If a man dies, can he live again?

Old Testament Reading   **Job 14: 1–14**

Almost all the writers of the Old Testament lived without hope for a life after death. The author of Job here begins by stating the usual view at the time, that there is no future beyond the grave; he expects the answer 'No' to the question, 'If a man dies, can he live again?' But then he dares to ask God that there may be something further, and that death be not the end. We read this passage, because we believe that Job's prayer for life after death has been answered: Jesus is alive, and has conquered the grave and death.

New Testament Reading (Epistle)   **1 Peter 3: 17–end**

From the early days of Christianity, new members of the Church have been baptized on Easter Eve, and it is not difficult to see why: in baptism we die with Christ, and in baptism we are raised with him.

> With Christ we share a mystic grave,
> With Christ we buried lie.

The water of baptism recalls the story of the flood in the Old Testament (Genesis chs. 6–8), and of the ark in which Noah and his family were brought to safety. The resurrection of Jesus means that his family, similarly, can be confident that, in spite of everything, he will bring them safely to God.

New Testament Reading (Gospel)   **Matthew 27: 57–end**

The death of Jesus provokes two different reactions, one in Joseph of Arimathaea, and the other in the Jewish leaders. Joseph is moved to fulfil the normal obligation concerning the burial of the dead, regarded as of great importance in the ancient world. The Jewish leaders, still thinking Jesus to be a false, heretical teacher, try to ensure that his disciples do not compound the fraud by pretending that he has been raised from the dead. What will in fact happen on the following morning will take both parties by surprise: neither Joseph's stone nor Pilate's guard will restrain God's power and glory.

or   **John 2: 18–22**

The sign for which the Jews were asking was the evidence by means of a miracle, that Jesus had authority to cleanse the temple. He replied that the resurrection would be his authentication. His zeal for God and his house has brought him now to his death, and has brought the temple to its end (it is soon to be destroyed by the Romans); but through the resurrection of Jesus there is a new temple, the body of Christ, the Church, of which we are part, and where God dwells with us and is worshipped.

Easter Day
The Firstborn among many brethren

Old Testament Reading   Isaiah 12

What the prophets said about the day of the Lord, Christians now apply to Easter Day. God the Father has delivered Jesus his Son from death, and turned his anger from us. This is the reason for our joy today. Therefore we thank God, and we make his deeds known in the world around. God has triumphed over sin and death; the Holy One, Emmanuel, is indeed among us in majesty.

New Testament Reading (Epistle)   **Revelation 1: 10–18**

On a Sunday, the Lord's day, John sees Christ as he is now, risen and glorified; he is among the golden lamps, that is to say, among the churches, which are also seen as the stars held in his right hand. He is the living one who was dead; he has power over death, and he will bring everything to its proper goal.

New Testament Reading (Gospel)   **Matthew 28: 1–10**

The two Marys came to look at the grave of the crucified Jesus, but instead they saw an empty tomb and an angel of the Lord, from whom they heard the good news that Jesus was alive, raised up from the dead by God, as he had said. They are given the message to pass on to the disciples of Jesus, first by the angel, and then by the Lord himself. He, however, does not call them disciples, but uses the more familiar term, My brothers.

Only a few days ago the disciples had failed, and Peter had denied Jesus; but now, the past is forgotten; it is dead and buried, never to be remembered again. Instead of it, there is new life from the grave, the living Lord who calls us his brothers and sisters, and commands us what we are to do, and reveals himself to us as we obey him.

Alternative Readings

The New and Final Exodus

Old Testament Reading   **Exodus 14: 15–22**

Parallels and similarities between the resurrection of Christ and the
exodus of Israel from Egypt were seen in the earliest days of Christianity: hence the reading of this passage today. Both when Jesus had
died, and when the Israelites saw the Egyptians pursuing them,
the situation seemed impossible, and it looked as though nothing
could be done. But in both cases, God acted so as to save his
people and reveal his glory. We shall understand our own situation best if we think of ourselves as in the same position as the
Israelites who could do nothing to protect themselves from the
might of Egypt: we cannot withstand evil on our own. The resurrection assures us that we are not alone: God is with us, to
help.

New Testament Reading (Epistle)   **1 Corinthians 15: 12–20**

Resurrection is the heart of the good news. Without resurrection,
there would be no point to the preaching and no point to the
believing: we should be where we were before we were baptized—still in the power of sin. Only God could deal with our
situation, and the resurrection of Christ is the evidence that he can,
and does.

New Testament Reading (Gospel)   **John 20: 1–10 (11–18)**

The evidence was ambiguous and could be interpreted in more than
one way: to Mary of Magdala, the explanation that first suggested
itself was that people had removed the body of Jesus from the grave;
to the disciple whom Jesus loved, the sight of the tomb and the
burial-cloths pointed, not to the robbery of a grave, but to resurrection; and this was also, he realized, the meaning of the prophecies in
the Old Testament.

We cannot make other people believe (though we can make it
harder for them to do so); we cannot even make ourselves believe. If

83

we do believe in the resurrection of Jesus, this is a present that we have received; and all presents should be acknowledged.

Therefore we thank God today that he has given us faith to believe in the resurrection of his Son from the dead—Jesus who is alive for evermore.

Alternative Readings

I will do a New Thing

Old Testament Reading   **Isaiah 43: 16–21**

The prophet recalls the exodus of Israel and the destruction of the Egyptian army in the Red Sea, only to point away from the past to the future, to a new act of God which is to come. We read this passage in the light of Easter Day, and see it as a prophecy of Christ's resurrection from the dead; and of the Church which was created thereby, the people whom God has formed for himself, who proclaim his praises.

New Testament Reading (Epistle)   **Colossians 3: 1–11**

The believer has both died with Christ, and been raised to life with him. We must live out both death to evil, and life to God; we must be what we really are. This will mean a continual putting-off and putting-on: off with the old life of sin, and on with the new life of holiness, love and union with all.

New Testament Reading (Gospel)   **Mark 16: 1–8**

This account (perhaps the earliest we have) of the visit of the women to the tomb brings out the element of surprise and unexpectedness; God is doing a new thing, and it leaves the women speechless. They had set out early to anoint the corpse of Jesus, but not before sunrise, so they could not have been mistaken as to the place, or what they saw there. Their minds were on the stone and how to move it in order to enter the tomb. The first shock was when they saw that the great stone was rolled back already; the second was the sight of the youth dressed in white; the third was what he said to them: 'He has been raised. . . .He is going on before you into Galilee; there you will see him'. They were completely overcome.

Easter is always a surprise; it is always unexpected: there is more to it than we had thought. It is about God, and God's power: his vindication of Jesus, and his incredible and indescribable mercy towards us.

Monday in Easter Week

The three passages to be read on the day following Easter Sunday, with its proclamation of the glorious resurrection of Jesus Christ, have as their common theme the prophetic hope of God's salvation; a hope held out by the prophet of Israel's exile, and seen by Christians as fulfilled in God's act of deliverance through Christ.

Old Testament Reading   **Isaiah 42: 10–16**

The prophet addresses Israel in her exile in Babylon, and proclaims the mighty act of God that will release her. For a long time it must have seemed that God was out of sight, and that he had forsaken her, for he has 'held his peace'. In picturing Israel's return to her own land, the prophet visualizes God as making a smooth and easy path for blind walkers, guiding their steps, and giving them light in their darkness. He also sets the deliverance of Israel in the context of the wider world, whose inhabitants will witness God's act and sing his praise, though they are not themselves the recipients of his salvation.

New Testament Reading (Epistle)   **1 Peter 1: 1–12**

For Peter, the wider world is now fully involved in the saving act of God, since it is clear from his letter that the Christian converts in Asia Minor to whom he writes have come from the Gentile and not the Jewish world. They have come to believe and rejoice in the resurrection of Jesus Christ from the dead as the means of their salvation, and in this he tells them they have found what the prophets of old were looking for. But hope now fulfilled has produced a new hope for the future. They do not now see the Christ whom they have come to love, and they therefore look for his future revelation and for their heavenly inheritance. It is this hope which carries them through the trials which they have to face in the present. These believers from among the nations do not see their saviour, but yet they can rejoice, both in what they have received and in what they have to come.

New Testament Reading (Gospel)   **Luke 24: 13-35**

In Luke's story of Jesus's meeting with the two disciples on the road
to Emmaus, the theme of hope fulfilled again appears. It is the Risen
Lord himself who interprets his suffering and glory as the realization
of all prophetic hopes, from Moses onwards. The two disciples
whom he joins do not at first know whom they are seeing, and they
walk on their way as if blind. At the very moment of their recognition, he vanishes from their sight. So, like Peter's Gentile converts,
these two witnesses of the resurrection become Christians for whom
their Lord is not now available to sight. Yet they had recognized him
in the breaking of bread, and for them and for all subsequent
generations of Christians there remains a special point at which they
proclaim their experience of salvation, meeting together in the
eucharist in the unseen presence of their Risen Lord.

Tuesday in Easter Week

In these three passages, the salvation of God is seen in terms of the forgiveness of sins. Only if man's inadequacy, indeed alienation, is acknowledged, will the act of God be understood for what it is: an act of love that is also a demand.

Old Testament Reading   **Micah 7: 7–end**

The prophet speaks in the character of defeated Jerusalem, looking confidently to God for her restoration. Her present suffering is accepted as the just consequence of her sin. She has sinned against her God; yet it is precisely this God whom she has sinned against who will vindicate her. His deliverance is a token of his forgiveness; indeed, *is* forgiveness. God forgives Israel because of what he is in himself; he is a God faithful to his promises of old, and a God of 'steadfast love'. Yet in seeing God's deliverance as the forgiveness of Israel's sin, the prophet also sees it as the vindication of Israel over against her enemies: the nations will see and be ashamed; and if they turn to Israel's God, it is in dread and fear.

New Testament Reading (Epistle)   **1 Peter 1: 13–end**

From Peter, too, there is an expression of confidence in God as the deliverer and redeemer. But for him too the experience of God's present salvation involves a recognition of former life as under God's judgement. There must be no return to the former way of life. The God who is known as Father is also the judge who calls his newly-begotten children to a holiness that is an imitation of his own. There is still a place for fear, for these believers who have come to God from among the nations. Yet their first response is love. They are the new-born children of God, whose word they have received, and this issues in love for one another.

New Testament Reading (Gospel)　　　　　　　　**Luke 24: 36–49**

Jerusalem is once again the place where God's saving act is proclaimed. There, remaining in the city, the eleven disciples are joined
by the Risen Lord, whose suffering and resurrection fulfil everything that has been looked for in the law, the prophets, and the
psalms. The response of the disciples to this encounter is quite
inadequate: it is first fear and questioning, then 'disbelief from joy'.
They need Jesus's own demonstration of his reality. It is to be their
task to take to the nations of the world the message of what they have
witnessed, and they are in themselves hardly ready for this task.
They will need 'power from on high', and when they go out to the
nations it will be in the power of the Holy Spirit, and the message
they will take is what Peter describes as 'the living and abiding word
of God'. The message is of forgiveness of sins, and with this goes
repentance, for only in the acknowledgement of sin can there be the
knowledge that it is forgiven.

Wednesday in Easter Week

These three readings suggest further exploration of the nature of resurrection faith. The Jesus of the resurrection is the Jesus of the past, but now present in a way that is decisively new. This faith is not easy to accept or understand, but once accepted it opens up for the believer also the experience of new life.

Old Testament Reading   **1 Kings 17: 17–24**

The Old Testament story is of the death and raising to life of an only son, by a miracle of God's power; and this would seem an appropriate story to read when we are thinking of the death and raising to life of the only-begotten Son of God. This son's raising to life is a restoration to the life that he had left: his soul came back into him again and he was restored to his mother. No doubt he subsequently grew up to live out the normal span of an ordinary human life. The experience of this death had been unacceptable and divisive: the woman who had sheltered Elijah and experienced God's power in a miraculous supply of food now cries out against the man of God. Elijah in his turn cries out against God himself. Yet Elijah turns to God in prayer, and the woman who thus receives her son alive comes to belief in the true word of God.

New Testament Reading (Epistle)   **1 Peter 2: 1–10**

For those who have come to belief in the resurrection of Christ, and who 'declare the wonderful deeds of God', the experience is of a break with the past. They have been re-born, and are growing up in their new life. Formerly 'no people', they are now the new people of God. Yet belief does not come easily. The image of Christ as the 'stone' is a many-sided one. For some he may be the keystone of God's building, in which they are incorporated; for others he is the obstacle that lies in their path, unavoidable but unacceptable.

New Testament Reading (Gospel)   **John 20: 24—end**

For Thomas, too, belief did not come easily, and he is initially divided from the rest of the eleven by his inability to accept that Jesus is risen indeed. Jesus shows himself to Thomas as the Jesus whom Thomas has known: there is in the resurrection this element of restoration, for the Risen Jesus is the same Jesus who taught in Galilee and died on the cross. But Thomas's response to this demonstration is essentially a new response: he now knows Jesus not just as his former master restored to him, but as 'my Lord and my God'. This is the acceptance of a wholly new and transforming relationship, and is available to all without the need of confirmation by sight such as Thomas had. This is the acceptance that the gospel calls belief, which brings with it the experience of life 'in his name': a new life, understood in the light of Jesus's own.

Thursday in Easter Week

The three passages explore the theme of exile and restoration or
return. Jeremiah looks for the return of Israel from exile and her
restoration to the life she had formerly enjoyed. Peter interprets the
Christian life as a continuing exile; and in the gospel the Risen Jesus
calls his disciples again from their former way of life.

Old Testament Reading   **Jeremiah 31: 1–14**

Jeremiah assures defeated and scattered Israel of her eventual restoration. He sees the people as gathered by God like a scattered flock
brought together again by its shepherd. They will return to their
land, and can look forward to life becoming again what it had once
been: once again the planting of crops and the gathering of harvest,
and once again singing, dancing, and merriment among young and
old alike. This glorious hope is offered at a time of deepest despair;
and the prophet is able to offer it out of his conviction of the
everlasting love and faithfulness of God.

New Testament Reading (Epistle)   **1 Peter 2: 11–end**

Peter also pictures his readers as strayed sheep who have been
gathered by God, their true shepherd. Yet, gathered as they have
been, they are still to regard themselves as 'aliens and exiles', as the
people of God out in the world and away from their true home, their
'citizenship in heaven'. But for Peter this exile is not a matter for
despair, but of opportunity. As the people of God out in the world,
they have the opportunity to bring the world to God, by demonstrat-
ing to those outside what it means to be his people. Peter is confident
that the unbeliever can recognize standards of moral goodness and
respond to them. Indeed, pagan society establishes laws and institutions of government precisely to maintain such standards. It is
important that Christians should respect these, and it is no part of
Christian freedom to reject what is good even in a non-Christian
society. The outside world does not, however, always live up even to

its own standards. Yet here again the Christian exile has opportunity: in his life in an unjust society he can live out the pattern of the life of Christ himself, suffering for righteousness' sake. The call to the Christian life in the world is a call to all: the Christian servant, enduring in his humdrum life the treatment meted out by a harsh master, is as much the imitator of Christ as the most shining martyr among his saints.

New Testament Reading (Gospel)   **John 21: 1–14**

In this story of the third meeting of Jesus with his disciples, the group of seven has apparently returned to its old life. They are back in Galilee, and back at their former work as fishermen. But it is not possible for things to be as they once were. All the disciples know that the one who waits for them is 'the Lord'. His appearance is marked by a miraculous catch of fish, as in Luke's account the first call of Peter had been (5:1–11). This is a meeting which represents a new call: the disciples are to go out into the world as 'fishers of men'. But before they go out, they eat with Jesus; a meal of fellowship that recalls the feeding of the five thousand, and looks forward to the continuing meals of fellowship with Christ in his Church. In the eucharist we are 'at home' with Christ; but in it we also pray, 'Send us out into the world'.

Friday in Easter Week

The theme that can be seen to link these three passages together is the theme of renewal. For the prophet it is the renewal of national life; for the author of the epistle a renewed understanding of human relationships; and in the gospel there is the renewal of the relationship between the disciple and his Lord.

Old Testament Reading   **Ezekiel 37: 1–14**

In Ezekiel's vision of the valley of dry bones, resurrection is an image of restoration. Scattered, hopeless Israel is like a great heap of dry, lifeless bones. The message of the vision is that she will be gathered and brought home, and her national life will be revived. But as just putting the bones together, and covering them with sinews and skin, did not make them live, so it will need more than simply the return home to bring Israel to life. What is needed for her renewal is what only God can give her: the indwelling of his spirit.

New Testament Reading (Epistle)   **1 Peter 3: 1–12**

The advice to wives to be submissive to their husbands, and to husbands to treat their wives as 'the weaker sex' may seem to strike an uneasy and archaic note in these days of sexual equality. But Peter's advice is not merely the convention of his day. The marriage relationship is given a new understanding. In the marriage of Christian partners there is a true equality: an equality that comes from their response to the gospel, for they are 'joint heirs of the grace of life'. The consideration that believing husband shows to believing wife is one manifestation of the unity and mutual love that should inform the whole Christian community. A mixed marriage, of believing wife and unbelieving husband (and no doubt there were many such in Peter's day, as in our own), could be seen as a source of strain and unhappiness. Peter rather sees it as giving a special opportunity for the wife, since by her behaviour her husband may be won to her faith. Christians, conscious of the blessings they have received from God, can take any opportunity in their daily lives for extending this blessing to those they love who stand outside the faith, for this mission is not the province of the specialist.

New Testament Reading (Gospel)   **John 21: 15–17**

The brief conversation between Jesus and Peter also has undertones of renewal, blessing, and opportunity. Peter is hurt by Jesus's three-fold questioning of his love, and feels their relationship is threatened. We can see it as the counterpart of his three-fold denial of Jesus. In this meeting Peter is fully restored in his relationship with Jesus, but it is also given a new direction. Peter's love for Jesus is now directed to caring for his sheep: both those that are, and those that are not yet, of the fold.

Saturday in Easter Week

The Christian proclamation of the resurrection of Jesus Christ from the dead raises the question of the possibility of human survival, and the hope of a future life. This hope has been a part of Christian belief, but the Christian hope for life after death is based on the resurrection of Christ and not on any inherent quality of man. In the three passages we see the Old Testament poet striving for such a hope; and the Christian perspective on it.

Old Testament Reading   **Job 14: 1–14**

The poet paints a desolate picture of human life in this world: brief, unhappy, and ending in nothingness. He sees a pattern of renewal and revival in nature, but can see no such hope for man. He seems to be longing for a hope for a future life, but unable to allow himself to accept it. 'Would that it were so'—but it is not so. What lies ahead of him is Sheol, the place of shadows and of less than half-life. The poet would be content to think of himself as waiting there, waiting to be re-called by God's remembering him; but he has nothing on which to base such a hope, and it remains beyond his grasp.

New Testament Reading (Epistle)   **1 Peter 4: 1–11**

For Peter, by contrast, there is a confident expectation of a future life. There are those who have received the gospel, and subsequently died, but the preaching of the gospel to them was not a waste of time, since they will 'live in the spirit'. More importantly, though, he looks for 'the end of all things' in which both living and dead will be involved. There is much in the way of a Christian expectation for the future. However, this does not mean that the present should be seen as a time of inactive waiting, like Job's supposed sojourn in Sheol. For the Christian there is no clear-cut contrast between this life and the next, for in union with the dead and risen Christ he has already entered into a new life. There is no going back to the dead past, but a demand to live the new life to the full.

New Testament Reading (Gospel)   **John 21: 20–25**

Peter, in his conversation with the Risen Lord, is similarly told not to be preoccupied with questions of survival and the idea of waiting for the return of Christ. Peter has his own duty to perform now in working out the call of Jesus to 'follow me'. The notion that the beloved disciple might live to wait for Jesus's return, however it arose, no doubt intrigued many, but in the conclusion to his gospel the evangelist draws attention to the disciple's true rôle. He bore witness to Jesus, and that witness is inexhaustible. It is for every Christian disciple to bear witness in his own life; 'we are God's children now; it does not yet appear what we shall be' (1 John 3:2).

First Sunday after Easter
The Upper Room

Old Testament Reading   **Exodus 15: 1–11**

One aspect of the meaning of Jesus's death and resurrection is that it was God's great act of judgement on the powers of evil. They tried to assert themselves against Christ, but were totally defeated. At the Exodus, these powers of evil were embodied in the oppressive forces of Pharaoh with their arrogance and greed. Then, too, God won a mighty victory which turned apparent defeat into triumph. Thus Christians at Easter can echo the song of Moses and Israel.

The song expresses itself poetically, so that we cannot be sure what the singers had literally seen, and historians are diffident about reconstructing precisely what happened. Nevertheless the song is clearly celebrating a real objective event which actually happened. And yet the important thing about the song is that it adds human response to the factuality of the event. It declares that God's act of deliverance is true for *me*. The resurrection, too, reaches its full meaning when it is not only an objective event, but something I respond to by acknowledging Jesus as my Lord in worship and life.

New Testament Reading (Epistle)   **1 Peter 1: 3–9**

But what difference does Jesus's resurrection make? Peter here emphasizes that the resurrection is the basis of a believer's hope. Men do not inevitably go to heaven; life's afflictions do not inevitably give way to blessings. Jesus rose from the dead to a new life, and this is the advance proof of the resurrection of others. He then entered into his inheritance in heaven, and this is the proof that others can. So because of the resurrection we can be 'born again'—begin life all over again, begin a totally new life that is now characterized by hope instead of the hopelessness appropriate to a man without Christ. This hope of a new world to come then transforms our attitude to this world. It enables us to face the difficulties and afflictions of this life with a new confidence, believing that they play some part in preparing for that new world. Blessed be the God and Father of our Lord Jesus Christ for the hope he has given us through Jesus's resurrection!

New Testament Reading (Gospel)   **John 20: 19–29**

Three times Jesus says, 'Peace be with you'. The words are here much more than a conventional greeting. First, Jesus speaks of peace to men paralysed by fear. The marks of crucifixion prove who he is, and the presence of the crucified one with them removes all reason for fear.

'Peace', he says again, but he has not come merely to reassure the fearful. He bestows on them the Spirit who had operated in him: now, instead of locking their doors to keep the world out, they are to walk through them into the world. His time in the world is over, and now they are to live (and to die) for the world to bring it God's forgiveness. Its forgiveness depends on them as once it depended on him.

'Peace', he says a third time a week later, just to Thomas. Thomas was a pessimist by character; furthermore, he knew that seeing is believing, and that dead men don't walk. But the Lord in his mercy appears to him, and Thomas by his response shows that he was not unworthy of the special sign. He was willing to make Jesus his Lord.

Experiences like Thomas's do not come to many. We are called to believe on the testimony of others, as Thomas was supposed to do. After all, that is why this gospel was written (see verses 30–31).

Second Sunday after Easter
The Emmaus Road

Old Testament Reading   **Isaiah 25: 6–9**

Here is the final blessing God intends for all peoples, blessing in what he takes away and in what he gives. In Israel, to cover one's head was a sign of being distraught: God will take away such distress, and will put an end to death itself. The sovereign Lord will himself wipe the tears from the faces of those who weep, like a father consoling his children or a friend consoling one he loves. He will also take away the particular sadness of his own people, her continual discrediting before the world, which so contrasts with the destiny he intended for her.

All such sadness is replaced by the unrestrained happiness of the ultimate party, overflowing with the choicest meat and the best vintage wines. People will rejoice in it as the great day to which they have long looked forward. 'At last the waiting is over, he is here': it will be a day of enjoyment of the Lord himself.

When Jesus came, he declared that this feast was now beginning.

New Testament Reading (Epistle)   **Revelation 19: 6–9**

In John's vision, the last great party has become a wedding celebration (as it is in Jesus's parables). The bride is the church: she has got herself ready, though her wedding dress is one she has been given (her righteousness stems from God's grace). The groom is a lamb!—because it is the Christ who was willing to be sacrificed to save his bride. But the final focus in this extraordinary wedding is the groom's father: 'Hallelujah! For the Lord our God the Almighty reigns!'

Each experience of the joy of a wedding can bring home to us in anticipation the joy of that marriage feast to which we all have our invitation. And every time we join the other guests at Holy Communion, we share in a supper which looks forward to that last great celebration.

New Testament Reading (Gospel)   **Luke 24: 13–35**

Like Thomas, the two disciples walking to Emmaus did not make much of the stories about Jesus being alive again. Like Thomas, they met Jesus. At first, however, this takes them no further forward: so much for the idea that seeing Christ in the flesh for oneself would be the key to finding a living faith in him. This had not been true before his death, and it was not true after his resurrection.

These two came to recognize Jesus as the risen Messiah in an entirely different way. As Jews, they knew their Bible well already, but they had not grasped its real message. The stranger looked at the scriptures with them: and now the penny dropped and the pieces of the jigsaw fitted together. The scriptures provided the clue to understanding the enigmas of the events they had been involved in.

Then the stranger broke bread. And this was one of the last things Jesus had done, when he had said that the broken bread stood for the breaking of his body. For the two disciples, this was the equivalent to Thomas's look at Jesus's wounded hands and side, the moment of recognition.

It is also the moment of disappearance. They cannot hold on to his physical presence. But they do have continuing access to the truth about Christ in the scriptures and to the presence of Christ in the breaking of the bread. And that we all have in common.

Third Sunday after Easter
The Lakeside

Old Testament Reading   **Isaiah 61: 1–7**

Here a prophet speaks of the calling God has given him. He does so because the object of his calling is so relevant to those he is to minister to. Their neediness is portrayed in many vivid ways: they are downtrodden, broken, in bondage, defeated, grief-stricken, hopeless. But this is the moment when God takes the side of the downtrodden, supports the broken, frees the prisoners, gives victory to the defeated, and replaces the pain of bereavement by the joy of a wedding, and the silence of hopelessness by the enthusiastic praise of the righteous glorifying God.

What this implied at the time is described in more liberal terms in the second half of the passage. But as a portrait of the caring action of God it is not limited to that context. It constitutes God's invitation to his people to hope in him in any experience of oppression or suffering, of exile or defeat, of sorrow or the loss of faith and hope. Whatever is their literal need at that moment, he promises to meet it: that he may have praise (*v.* 3) and they may have joy (*v.* 7).

New Testament Reading (Epistle)   **1 Corinthians 15: 1–11**

Paul's gospel focuses on the Easter message. It begins from Jesus and his first disciples, and his appearing to them. As if to anticipate questions as to whether the resurrection really happened, Paul emphasizes the sheer fact of it. The evidence, he points out, is overwhelming. Christ died and was buried (that proves he was really dead). Christ was raised and appeared on all those occasions (that proves he really came back to life).

But Paul cannot resist the temptation to go on to talk about Jesus and himself. Paul was a living proof of the grace and power of the risen Christ, which had turned persecutor into preacher. He had an awful past, but grace had dealt with it by bringing forgiveness and transformation.

The passage's challenge, however, concerns Jesus and the readers (see the opening and closing verses). Do they take seriously the testimony of those who saw Jesus? Do they still affirm their response to the preaching of the apostle? Everything depends on this.

New Testament Reading (Gospel) **John 21: 1–14**

The miracle may also be a parable, in which ordinary fishing stands for fishing men. Such work is futile without the Lord's direction; but when the fishermen have his word to follow, failure becomes success and the whole world can be won (according to one of the Church Fathers, 153 was the total number of species of fish in the world) without the receptacle, the Church, being unable to cope.

More straightforwardly, the story portrays the wonder of God's grace shown in the resurrection appearances. Most of the twelve return to their old job—what else were they to do? But it wasn't the same. They had lost their touch. Then suddenly frustration and failure become the joy of achievement, and Jesus is there again, once more the host at one of those fellowship meals together, when time stood still in his presence.

It is not strange if our periodic felt experiences of the living Christ are very precious to us; we are not generally granted to live every day that way. Yet no moment is one which the risen Christ cannot suddenly enter, turning emptiness and frustration into the joy of his presence.

Fourth Sunday after Easter
The Charge to Peter

Old Testament Reading   **Isaiah 62: 1-5**

Promises like the ones declared in last Sunday's Old Testament
lesson are all very well, but sometimes they appear not to come true.
God seems silent and inactive in response to his people's prayers.
Here the prophet ministers to the temptation to disillusion by declar-
ing that God will not remain apparently silent and inactive, and by
reaffirming the promises. Israel, his people, *will* lose her shame
before the world, and come to be acknowledged by the new name
appropriate to a new city. She *will* be transformed into a beauty for
God himself to be proud of. The relationship which seems broken is
not over: the marriage between God and his people *will* be experienced as living reality again.

   The uncomfortable calling of the people of God is to keep faith in
such promises even when (especially when) God seems not to fulfil
them.

New Testament Reading (Epistle)   **Revelation 3: 14-end**

Laodicea, in Turkey, was proud of its wealth, of its medical school,
and of the cloth produced in its area. The Laodicean church shared
that pride, and could not see that it was spiritually bankrupt, blind,
and exposed. But the Lord could see this, and it sickened him. Near
Laodicea water from hot springs flowed across a plateau and (now
lukewarm) down a waterfall near the city: the Lord felt about the
church the way a man from Laodicea would feel if he drank from
those streams.

   Although the letter is cutting in its condemnation, it is also tender
in its affection. The harsh words stem from love. The Lord wants to
come back into the Laodicean church's life. Holman Hunt's portrait
of him knocking at its door has helped many people to see their
need to open their lives to Christ. But the letter is addressed
to the Church. A church, too, can carry on living its outward

life, keeping its services and functions going, but be without Christ.

It has been suggested that none of the letters to the churches in Revelation is more appropriate to the twentieth-century Church than this one.

New Testament Reading (Gospel)   John 21: 15–22

Throughout the scene at the lake, Peter has been the one with the drive and energy. In Jesus's conversation with this man with all his potential as a leader, three verbs play a key role. 'Do you *love* me?' I can see you're more energetic than them, but do you love me more than them? You once claimed to be more committed to me than anyone—then you denied knowing me. So do you love me?

If you love me, take care of me: so we might expect the conversation to go. But no, the good shepherd is not concerned about himself being taken care of, but about the sheep. 'If you love me, direct that energy of yours into *taking care* of the ones I care about.'

And in taking care of my sheep, '*Follow* me'. Following is a costly matter. Peter is called to follow one who went to a cross, and he will find that his calling leads the same way. Love leads to a cross; caring for the sheep leads to a cross. Following is also an individual matter. Peter, with his drive and energy, is to be the front man in the Christian mission, and will pay the price for that. The beloved disciple, with his insight, is to bear witness by writing more than by preaching. That is a calling from Christ, too, and one disciple is not to ask questions about the calling of another.

Fifth Sunday after Easter
Going to the Father

Old Testament Reading   **Hosea 6: 1–6**

Prayer is no substitute for obedience, and prayer meetings are no substitute for the people of God changing their way of life.

Hosea is speaking at a time when Israel is threatened with enemy attack, and her moment of need draws her back to her God. She acknowledges that it is he who has been chastising her, that her future lies only with him, and that he can speedily restore her.

All this is moving and true. One is then surprised to discover God's response, in the second half of the passage. Her prayer moves him only to sadness and despair. It is not a true and authentic turning to God. It does not last long enough, and it does not have the right characteristics—a real turning to God manifests itself in commitment to God in one's life ('steadfast love') and in recognizing that God is God and must be treated as such ('knowledge of God'). Compared with that, prayer is nothing. It is meaningless.

New Testament Reading (Epistle)   **1 Corinthians 15: 21–28**

The Feast of the Ascension celebrates Christ's reigning as Lord of his Kingdom, a reign that began with the resurrection. That resurrection, Paul declares, was the firstfruits of the resurrection of all those who belong to him. As men give God the firstfruits of the harvest as the pledge that they will subsequently give the whole of it to him, so God gave men in Christ the firstfruits of new life as the pledge and guarantee that all who are in Christ will rise again.

On that basis, faith in Christ as Lord thus looks forward as well as back, forward to the abolition of death and the enjoyment of resurrection life, to the reversal of the curse of death which has hung over men since Adam, to the fulfilment of God's purpose in Christ, and to Christ's new freedom then to lay down the authority he received in order to fulfil this purpose.

But then in the present, faith in Christ as Lord also looks up and around and within, and affirms by faith that Christ is even now overwhelming all resistance to his Lordship. It also recognizes that our own lives are part of the battle for the victory of Christ's Kingdom. Acknowledging Jesus as Lord is a matter of the stance of my life, not merely the words on my lips.

New Testament Reading (Gospel)   **John 16: 25–end**

Jesus's disciples present rather a gloomy picture. They grasp rather little of the truth about him (they don't even acknowledge their own incomprehension!). They are not able to approach God for themselves; Jesus has to negotiate for them. Their faith is shallow; despite their protests Jesus knows that it will soon dissolve, and they will give up. Their future is bound to include suffering, and they do not have the resources to cope with the experience.

But Jesus is to die for them, to rise again for them, and to give them his Holy Spirit. And that will mean incomprehension can be replaced by insight; fickleness and unbelief can be replaced by faith and commitment; distance from God can be replaced by the direct access to him which is the privilege of members of his family; and fear can be replaced by peace, confidence, and victory.

Ascension Day

Old Testament Reading   **Daniel 7: 9–14**

A vision of judgement in the heavenly court, where God (the 'one ancient in years') accepts and gives authority to an angelic-human figure ('one like a man'), who is the protector and representative of his people on earth. The 'ascension' of this representative of the old Israel to the throne of God is seen by Christians as a symbolic foreshadowing of Christ's ascension, in which Christian believers are taken up into the glory he shares with the Father and enabled to dwell continually with him.

New Testament Reading (Epistle)   **Acts 1: 1–11**

In Luke's account of the Ascension the risen Christ inaugurates the period of his disciples' wider mission, branching out from Jerusalem to all the world, by empowering them with his Holy Spirit; and the necessary precondition of this is that he should no longer be limited to one place or time, but should ascend to God the Father and so, like the Father, be present with them at all times and in all places. The disciples are not to gaze after him, but to begin their work of preaching in readiness for his second coming in glory to judge the whole world, which it is their task to evangelize. The universality of Christ's dominion is not to be understood in merely political or national terms, as they still seem to think (*v.* 6) in spite of the many hints in the gospels that it has a wider, more cosmic scope; and the way in which it will be established is not revealed to men. God takes the initiative, as he had done in raising Jesus from the dead, and as he now does in raising him to his right hand in glory. Resurrection, Ascension, and Pentecost are different aspects of the one saving work of God, who glorifies the Jesus who suffered on the cross, and so transforms the world through the Spirit which is the bond between Father and Son: the Church is the earthly instrument of that transformation, the channel through which Christ's risen power extends and embraces all mankind.

New Testament Reading (Gospel)   **Matthew 28: 16–end**

Unlike Luke, Matthew records that the risen Jesus appeared to his disciples in Galilee, the scene of much of his ministry, as predicted by the angel at the tomb (Matthew 28:7, compare Mark 16:7). Although Matthew does not say that Jesus ascended into heaven, this passage makes it clear that this is a 'farewell' address like that in Acts 1, and the same themes are present—Jesus has 'full authority in heaven and earth'; he is with his disciples 'until the end of time', that is, until the completion of all God's plans in the final events when, according to Acts, Jesus will 'come' again 'in the same way that you have seen him go'; and the whole world is to be evangelized and all nations made his disciples (*v.* 12). Verse 19 is the most explicit reference to the Holy Trinity in the New Testament, summing up in a brief formula what is implied in the Ascension, that the Holy Spirit comes from God through the risen and ascended Christ, and that it is into this mysterious working of the one God that Christians are baptized.

Sunday after Ascension Day
The Ascension of Christ

Old Testament Reading   **Daniel 7: 9–14**

As above for Ascension Day (p. 108).

New Testament Reading (Epistle)   **Ephesians 1: 15–end**

On Ascension Day we read the historical account of Christ's ascension; now on the following Sunday we turn to meditate on the meaning of the event described in Acts. A characteristic feature of the Epistle to the Ephesians is that it does not divide up the mystery of Christ into birth, crucifixion, resurrection, ascension, and the coming of the Spirit, but regards all these as aspects of the indivisible plan of God which redeems, sanctifies, and transforms the world. Already in 1: 7–10 the death of Jesus is said to have had as its goal the bringing of all created things 'into a unity in Christ', and this theme of cosmic triumph and renewal is developed in this passage in connection with Christ's resurrection and ascension (seen as one action, the 'enthronement' of Christ at God's right hand, *v.* 20) and the establishment of the Church of which he is the head. Verses 22–23 probably mean that the Church, which is seen as a centre from which God's salvation flows out to all mankind (compare Acts 1:8), is 'filled' with Christ just as Christ is filled with the being of God himself, so that Christian believers—and, through them, all mankind—are taken up into the life of heaven. The practical consequences of this are spiritual insight and vision (*vv.* 17–18) which enable the Christian, in the words of the Epistle to the Hebrews (12:1–2), to 'run with resolution the race for which we are entered, our eyes fixed on Jesus . . . who, for the sake of the joy that lay ahead of him, endured the cross, making light of its disgrace, and has taken his seat at the right hand of the throne of God.'

New Testament Reading (Gospel)   **Luke 24: 45-end**

Luke is to begin his second volume, *The Acts of the Apostles*, with a detailed account of the Ascension, but he ends the gospel with a briefer summary of its main features, leaving the disciples praising God in the temple and awaiting the coming of the Holy Spirit, of which we are to think next week. Before the work of evangelism can begin and the period of the Church (living in readiness for the second coming) can be inaugurated by the gift of the Spirit, there is a short period of joyful expectation, not unlike that with which Luke's gospel begins—a time for reflection on the plan of God which has brought the history of Israel and of the world to this new stage (compare Luke 1:39–80). As Mary and Zechariah reflected on the great things God had done and foretold, so the disciples are instructed by Jesus in the way his suffering, death, and resurrection fitted into the plan of God predicted in the Old Testament scriptures, and were to lead to a new beginning in the world's history, by which not just Israel but all nations are to be brought into the loving purposes of the Father (*vv.* 46–48)—the process that today's epistle describes in more cosmic language as the filling of all things by God through Christ and his Church.

Pentecost (Whit-Sunday)

Old Testament Reading   **Genesis 11: 1–9**

The story of the Tower of Babel provides the background for understanding the events of the day of Pentecost as told in Acts 2. The fact that human beings are divided by language barriers is here presented as a punishment for their pride in trying to scale the heavens—that is, trying to get control over God himself—by building a tower that would give them access to his dwelling-place (compare the desire for divine knowledge that is beyond men's reach in Genesis 3). Babel is a symbol of the confusion and misunderstanding among men that result from human arrogance, as Pentecost shows the mutual understanding and harmony that prevail where God's Holy Spirit is at work.

or   **Exodus 19: 16–25**

The story of the law-giving on Sinai was one of the lessons read at the Jewish feast of Pentecost in New Testament times. When God comes down on the mountain to speak to Moses, he is wrapped in fire, and it is too dangerous for any but Moses and Aaron to approach him; and in the passage that follows his laws are revealed to Israel, his chosen people. In the Christian Pentecost, by contrast, the fire of the Spirit empowers the disciples to make God freely available to all mankind.

New Testament Reading (Epistle)   **Acts 2: 1–11 (or 1–21)**

In Luke's account of the day of Pentecost the mission of the Church to preach the gospel to all nations is inaugurated in a spectacular way by the outpouring of the Holy Spirit. The Spirit appears in wind and fire, as in God's appearance on Mount Sinai (Exodus 19), and it fills the apostles with a miraculous gift of speech by which they can communicate the good news to all men, reversing the effects of sin which brought about the confusion of Babel (Genesis 11). This does not seem to be the same as the gift of 'tongues' referred to by Paul, which involves speaking in an *unknown* language, though (as *v.* 13 shows) speech in a foreign language could sound like drunken raving to those who did not speak it themselves. Perhaps the comprehensibility of what the apostles said depended on the receptiveness of the hearer as well as on the language spoken. The list of countries from which the hearers came reminds us how cosmopolitan Jerusalem was, especially at festival time, and how natural it was as a centre from which the gospel could spread to both Jews and Gentiles.

(The extension of God's rule to the whole world, and of his gifts of prophecy and discernment to all his people, had already been foreseen in some parts of the Old Testament, as the quotation from Joel 2:28–32 in *vv.* 16–21 shows. All mankind is to have free access to the Holy Spirit of God; no one who 'calls on the name of the Lord' is excluded from his promises.)

New Testament Reading (Gospel)   **John 14: 15–26**

A passage from Jesus's last discourse to his disciples, at the Last Supper, in which we see another aspect of the Holy Spirit whom the Lord's glorification will make it possible for his followers to receive. The Spirit is to be the Christian's 'advocate', that is, one who intercedes with God on his behalf and empowers him to obey God's commands and so to enjoy the fullness of life which God has to offer (compare Romans 8:9–28). Whereas in Acts 2 the emphasis is on the Spirit as the one who enables the disciples to preach and bear witness to all mankind of the salvation brought by Jesus, here the Spirit's power is seen in the inner transformation of the Christian into one who 'receives' Jesus's 'commands and obeys them', and so finds that the Father and the Son make their dwelling with him, incorporating him into their own divine life. Both aspects are essential parts of the Christian experience of God the Holy Spirit.

or   **John 20: 19–23**

The alternative gospel for today brings out a striking feature of John's gospel, that it sees the resurrection and the gift of the Holy Spirit to the disciples as more or less simultaneous events, two aspects of the glorification of Jesus on Easter Sunday. But this only

113

stresses more clearly what is plain in Luke's account, that the pouring out of the Spirit on the day of Pentecost was not a fresh beginning in God's work of salvation, but the completion of Christ's resurrection and ascension. It is because Christ is glorified that Christians are raised with him to eternal life with God, and so participate in the Holy Spirit of God who empowers them to preach the gospel of forgiveness and salvation to all mankind. The power to forgive which is given to the apostles is essentially the power to bring people within the ambit of God's salvation by preaching and baptism, but the Church has also understood it as authority to pronounce or withhold the absolution of particular sins within the Christian community.

Trinity Sunday

Old Testament Reading   **Isaiah 6: 1–8**

Eight centuries before Christ Isaiah went into the temple in Jerusalem to 'see God', as the conventional phrase ran, and was overcome with awe to find that he actually did see him. As with all the visions of God in the Old Testament, the stress lies on the mystery that surrounds him, with seraphim (probably angels clothed in flame) in attendance, and clouds of incense hiding his face from the sight of mere mortals. But the purpose of the vision is not to destroy Isaiah, as he fears, but to purify him and give him his commission as a prophet. The awesomeness of God the Father does not lie in his being unknowable, but precisely in the fact that he allows himself to be known, through Christ and in the action of the Holy Spirit in the Church, in the world, and in the hearts of Christians, forgiving their sin and giving them a personal task to carry out.

New Testament Reading (Epistle)   **Ephesians 1: 3–14**

On the face of it, this passage seems to be an abstract discussion designed to show that the Christian mystery is the key to understanding the universe: the world makes sense because all events in it are part of a fixed plan of God which binds all things into a unity, and both this plan and the resulting unity can be in some way identified with 'Christ'—the human Jesus, the Messiah, but seen as existing from all eternity with God the Father (compare John 1: 1). This is therefore a basic text for understanding how the doctrine of the Trinity came to be understood and expressed in the early church. But the weight of the passage does not lie in abstract speculation, but in Christian experience of salvation (*v.* 13): 'when you had heard the message of the truth, the good news of your salvation, . . . [you] became incorporate in Christ and received the seal of the promised Holy Spirit' (*NEB*). Because Christ has a universal, cosmic significance, Christians are really in touch with—indeed, share in—the life of the true God himself; and their experience of the Spirit directing and guiding their actions is a genuine experience of participating in God's plan for the world, not an illusion. The doctrine of the Trinity is here a ground of assurance that Christian experience is *authentic*, that the God revealed in Christ and known through the Spirit is the real and the only God. It is not a warning that God is unknown, but an assurance that he is well known, revealed, not hidden, in the Christian mystery.

New Testament Reading (Gospel)   **John 14: 8–17**

In his last conversation with the disciples before his passion, Jesus (in John's gospel) clearly discloses the truth of his unity with God the Father: to know him is to know the Father, since his human nature reveals God himself—he is transparent to the glory of God. And this (*v.* 11) is not just an unsubstantiated claim, but is supported by his 'deeds'. The immediate reference here will be to the miracles or 'signs' performed by Jesus in his ministry, but in the context of the whole gospel these 'deeds' include his death and resurrection, the actions by which the world is redeemed, and which reveal him to be none other than God incarnate. Recognizing this, the disciples can also recognize, as the world in general cannot, the power of God that lives in them through their acceptance of Jesus; and this power is the Holy Spirit, the bond between Father and Son.

Second Sunday after Pentecost
The People of God

Old Testament Reading   **Exodus 19: 1–6**

'Holy' in the Old Testament carries the sense of 'belonging to God'. As creator, God owns the whole world, but he has made a special bond with Israel and given the whole people a unique intimacy with himself: it is as if they were all kings and priests within God's entourage. This status is entirely the result of God's gift, as the vivid and beautiful image of the eagle's wings makes plain. The creation of this relationship at the Exodus appeared almost as a 'magic carpet' experience, wonderful and astonishing in its effects upon the people's life.

New Testament Reading (Epistle)   **1 Peter 2: 1–10**

It is not surprising that when the first Christians reflected upon their coming into being as a new community, they found inspiration in Exodus 19:1–6. What had been true of Israel was now truer still of the Church. Once more God had formed a people for himself. But now it was universal in scope, not confined to a single race; and whereas it had been a political entity, now it transcended all such limitations, being bound together simply and solely by allegiance to God through Christ and dedicated to the spiritual service of God in every aspect of life. To reinforce his message of Christ as the basis of this community—its principle of coherence—the writer draws upon other images from the Old Testament. In particular, the reference to Christians as a priesthood (that is, 'holy' people dedicated to God's service) leads to the thought of them as a temple—a building dedicated to God. This in turn directs his attention to a number of Old Testament passages using the image of the cornerstone, which admirably hits off Christ's function in relation to his people. To judge from the number of times these passages are referred to by different New Testament writers, it seems that they were something of a favourite in the early Church. One of them—about the stone

118

upon which men stumble—carried a note of warning: there is
nothing magical or irreversible about membership of God's people,
whose true characteristic is obedience to his word. But the heart of
the experience remains that God has brought light where there was
darkness, mercy where there was despair—through Christ who
himself made the transition from rejection to triumph.

New Testament Reading (Gospel)   **John 15: 1-5**

In one of its few parable-like passages, the Gospel of John draws
upon another of the Old Testament images long used to signify the
unity and cohesion of the people of God. In Isaiah 5, for example,
Israel is seen as God's vine, planted and cared for by him. Now
Christ himself is the vine, his people branches within the vine. That
is, he is the principle of their life, the one from whom they draw all
nourishment and upon whose resources they depend for life and
meaning. The relationship between them and him is to be one of the
utmost stability and permanence—it is 'abiding'; yet it carries with it
the notions of vitality and hope—the bearing of fruit. If it is not
always easy to see these convictions borne out by our experience of
the Church, it remains true that returning to them for constant
renewal is the only godly way for the Christian community to discover its path.

Third Sunday after Pentecost
The Life of the Baptized

Old Testament Reading   **Deuteronomy 6: 17–end**

Israel has never ceased to focus on the transition which it experienced in the Exodus from Egypt. In every respect it had meant the transformation of its fortunes; in effect, its creation as a people with a life and a future. It was the moment of movement from slavery to freedom, from death to life; and the effect was heightened by the dire destruction which that event had brought upon the Egyptians, their former tyrants. It was this moment, the gracious act of God for their good, which led also to their duty to keep the law which was an essential part of God's endowment. Its keeping was their direct and glad response to his generosity.

New Testament Reading (Epistle)   **Romans 6: 3–11**

For the Christian too, there is the moment of transition. In one sense it took place in principle in the dying and rising of Christ. As in the Exodus (and Christians were quick to point to the parallel), there was movement from death to life, from bondage (for Christ's passion was an act of submission) to freedom. But each believer must himself make the journey and experience the movement. Paul locates it at the moment of baptism. There the Christian's coming to faith finds its visible expression and there he makes his identification with his Lord. The effect is a wholly new direction of life and a new impulse to empower it. The passage is full of Paul's confidence and hope: there is no reason, once the depth and thoroughness of the revolution are realized, why we should not share that confidence and hope. From that base, we are to explore what 'newness of life' means.

New Testament Reading (Gospel)   **John 15: 5–11**

For the Christian, as for the Jew, the new life brings the duty of moral response: Christ has his commandments. In the Gospel of John we learn that loving one another is the content of that moral duty. So it is in effect a matter of our working out in our lives the meaning of a gift we have received. For the source is the love of God which he has shown first to Jesus. From that source comes the power for us to act morally; and moral action is essential if we are to remain in touch with God. Without it we lose our grasp of his love which we have known through Jesus.

The dark side of the matter—that membership of Christ's people may be lost—is not the effect of divine vindictiveness: it is a fact of moral life. To lose hold of loving is to lose hold of God. To retain hold of it is to retain the closest intimacy with God and assurance in his gifts. Human relationships make this easy to see: we know well that when love dies, a relationship turns speedily to dust and ashes, so that the moral force has disappeared and all is soured. Love is the condition of stability, and love has to be given before moral demands carry weight. If love is given, then those demands become the most natural expression and nourisher of joy. And joy should be the characteristic of those to whom so much has been given.

Fourth Sunday after Pentecost
The Freedom of the Sons of God

Old Testament Reading   **Deuteronomy 7: 6–11**

The strength of Judaism is its profound vision of God's redemptive purpose and the responsive duty of loving obedience. Though this vision has frequently involved the whole human race, it has focused on the people of Israel, and found its pattern established in the great events of their history, above all the Exodus. The book of Deuteronomy may be read as a thankful meditation on that event and its significance. Thus, in Judaism history, national life, religion, and morality are closely intertwined—and this has about it a striking human realism. It also has its limitations.

New Testament Reading (Epistle)   **Galatians 3: 23–4: 7**

Paul was acutely aware of those limitations, so much so that what to Judaism was a life of thankful freedom expressed in obedience to the Law was to him one of restrictive tutelage—being 'confined under the Law'. This was partly for reasons connected with the Law itself, partly in the light of Christ. To Paul, the Law seemed negative: it restrained from wrong without empowering for good, and it protected man without enabling him to mature in relation to God. He felt too that focusing on Israel as a people was in effect a distortion and denial of God's redemptive purpose for all mankind. He saw Christ's coming as bringing about the end of all these negative factors. 'Born under the Law', he had burst its bonds and established a new structure for the relationship between God and man. First, it was one of new intimacy and closeness—sonship; second, it brought a spirit of daring and assurance—Christ's spirit gave confidence both to call God 'Father' and to walk the world in freedom; third, it was for all equally, regardless of race, social standing, or sex. Paul believed that this new vision was foreshadowed in the older dispensation, limited though it was, so that Christians can properly be seen as 'Abraham's offspring'; God's purposes for the human race have now 'surfaced' and been fulfilled. Paul forces us to attend to the deepest level of man's relationship with God. That relationship depends wholly on his loving gift of himself to us, and on our side wholly on the openness of faith—trusting commitment, neither making demands nor asserting claims. For us, Paul's argument is couched in terms which are technical and alien—they come from the Jewish theology in which he was reared—but that need not prevent us from seeing the religious and human realities with which he wrestles.

New Testament Reading (Gospel)   **John 15: 12–17**

Here we see Christ expounding and forming in his followers that relationship which Paul described. The terms are similar: we are not servants but friends of Christ. Once more, the emphasis is on intimacy and trust. The trust goes both ways. We are admitted through Christ into all that the Father has to say. That is, religion is not a matter of more and more esoteric and ingenious secrets, but of an accessible way of understanding and acting—which Christ has made known and made possible. It is not without cost: first, the cost of his own self-giving in death, the proof of his love; second, the cost of the good life, lived out with the same quality of love. It is not, however, a lone endeavour, but a community exercise: love, in this Gospel, is presented precisely as love for each other—it is the cement which binds Christians together and embodies in practical terms the commission we have received from God through Christ.

Fifth Sunday after Pentecost
The New Law

Old Testament Reading   **Exodus 20: 1–17**

Whatever their dim origins and parallels in the ancient Near East, there is no doubt that the Ten Commandments were from early times the core of Israel's law. They were the heart of ancient Israel's sense of what was demanded by God's choice of them as his people. Notice that the commandments are given in the setting of the Exodus itself: gift leads to response and duty. They express a comprehensive obligation to God and to man. The former centres first on God's exclusive claims and second on his transcendence. It was one of Israel's profoundest contributions to mankind to stress continually God's 'beyondness': he is not to be summed up, not to be identified with any of the images by which we describe him or any of the enthusiasms and causes with which we associate him. The obligation to others is concerned with the proper regulation of social life among people who worship such a God and owe their existence to him: they are bound to him, so they are also bound to each other and must respect each other's lives, property and well-being. For us, living in conditions vastly different from those in which they were first enjoined, these commandments still carry a sense of fundamental practical obligations to those among whom we dwell. But when Christianity came, the focus altered.

New Testament Reading (Epistle)   **Ephesians 5: 1–10**

In the early Christian communities, small, fervent, and close-knit, morality took on a new flavour: less related to society at large, more concerned with the intimate life of an intensely spiritual group; concentrating less on mere outward action, more on the interior motive it reflects; more interested in the deep, mysterious forces involved in the struggle for moral life. Yet at the heart there is great simplicity: 'be imitators of God'. And love is the basic duty, with Christ as its model. At the same time, there is a lively consciousness of evil, not simply as a series of acts but as a threatening, dangerous power. This sense of the seriousness of 'darkness' and its deep opposition to 'light' is never far from the minds of the early Christian writers. It meant that they saw virtue in colours of great brilliance, by the sheer power of contrast: it was the expression of God-given life.

New Testament Reading (Gospel) **Matthew 19: 16–26**

The young man has the right objective—'eternal life', that is life in true relationship to God, seen at the time of Jesus especially as the product of the new world which, as Jews believed, God would shortly bring into being. But he sees its attainment in terms of some 'good deed' to be performed; indeed he claims that already he has led a life of strenuous obedience to God's commands. Such virtue has one deep and pervasive fault: it is carried out from a base of worldly security, while what is required is self-abandonment to God, a radical revolution in a person's whole scale of values. Morality is not enough!

Possessions are singled out as the obstacle to such self-abandonment because they make one of the strongest ties binding us to our world and leading us to be diplomatic and calculating in our adherence to God's cause. Even so, salvation is in God's sole gift: with him 'all things are possible'.

The modern western Christian, surrounded by possessions on a scale undreamt of in the world of Jesus and even discouraged from voluntary poverty by the provisions of the welfare state, is shamed and bewildered by this stringent admonition. Christians have long sought to soften the blow by making it apply chiefly to our attitudes to wealth: we should maintain a feeling of detachment from our money and our goods. We do better to face the message as it stands, even at the price of bewilderment: then we shall see how radically Jesus confronted men with the overwhelming reality of God, changing everything. How that confrontation is to affect us is then the task before us: but we must seize the sense of newness which Jesus brought.

Sixth Sunday after Pentecost
The New Man

Old Testament Reading   **Exodus 24: 3–11**

The key word is 'covenant'. For Israel, God and his people were
bound together, not only by the laws which mapped out a pattern of
conduct and observance, but also by a shared existence. Com-
prehensively and profoundly, they were knitted to each other, by
God's gracious gift. They looked back to the incident described in
this passage as the solemn ritual establishment of this covenant,
shortly after the Exodus. It was an occasion of the utmost significance. In it, blood, signifying life and vitality, was thrown against
the altar and upon the people, uniting them to God. Then there was
an opening of heaven and 'they beheld God'. Henceforth the life of
God's people was conducted in his presence—caught up into the
higher realm: that was where they really belonged, whatever their
outward circumstances in the life of this world.

New Testament Reading (Epistle)   **Colossians 3: 12–17**

What Israel worked out on the wider scale, the early Church applied
more particularly to individuals and small groups. The first Christian congregations were aware of a quite new vision of personal life.
Within their fellowship, new values came to the fore, new moral
skills were learnt: humility, forgiveness, compassion. Here in these
ways, the target of moral aspiration was distinctive—in comparison
with both Judaism and surrounding pagan society. The qualities
which they brought to the fore were not simply the result of the
Church's social circumstances; they sprang from dependence on
Christ. Everything was to be done 'in his name', in gratitude to God
because of him. His life, death, and resurrection shaped their
priorities. He was both the source and the power behind the new
pattern of life which the Church was now establishing and was soon
to find it so hard to maintain.

New Testament Reading (Gospel)   **Luke 15: 11–end**

The parable falls into two parts. The first tells of the father's welcoming love for the wayward son; the second of the elder son's complaining jealousy. The story is told with such human realism that it is hard to resist reading it as pure drama and embellishing it with further details. But it is a model of the themes on which the Gospel of Luke concentrates: God's boundless patience and readiness to receive the penitent; the meanness of the ungenerous heart; recognition of need as the best basis for return to God. So the drama is partly an allegory—in which the father represents God, the elder son respectable Judaism resentful of Christ's claim to lead people back to God, and the younger son the convert who receives Christ's message. It presents the relationship between God and man in terms of the utmost simplicity—no-one could miss the point, above all concerning the character of God. But some things may be overlooked. Thus, there is no suggestion that the younger son is favoured at the expense of the elder—'you are always with me, and all that is mine is yours'. As Luke shows it to us, Judaism is not rejected so much as called to stop rejecting itself. But the symbolic meaning which the two sons undoubtedly possess overlays the deeper and more permanent sense: that penitence is the road to God's heart and alone opens the door to joy. It is a message which is not so much denied as obscured when we see other hurdles on the path which leads us to him. It is necessary only to 'come to oneself' and to turn to the Father.

Seventh Sunday after Pentecost
The More Excellent Way

God is always calling—'stretching'—his people to higher and better things, because his nature is love.

Old Testament Reading   **Hosea 11: 1–9**

Hosea probably understands the love of God more fully than any other book in the Old Testament. However fickle, unreliable, or two-faced we may be, God is always ready to receive us back. He is like a father who looks after his children. Israel experienced this when they were liberated from slavery in Egypt; the 'up-bringing' continued, but they rejected their father, and went after other gods, of their own making.

Like many a human father, God would have the right to retaliate, to treat them like small children, in their immaturity, and send them back to Egypt, under foreign rule, in order to bring them to their knees. But he does not choose compulsion on stubborn hearts—he chooses the harder and longer way of love. He loves his people too much to punish them severely. The motive behind this divine love is not power, but that Israel should live in their land and fulfil his good purposes for them.

New Testament Reading (Epistle)   **1 Corinthians 12: 27–13: end**

Paul is wrestling with the problems which arise in a community which is full of strong personalities and self-interest. There are many gifts, but the highest and best is the gift of love. For without love, our other gifts are fruitless, and our actions, however spectacular, are worthless. Through love, we learn to respect one another's gifts, and not to regard our own as the most important.

Love is the highest and best, because it can conquer our worst tendencies, those things which divide us from one another. Love has qualities which are more lasting—more enduring than any other gift. Extraordinary gifts, like prophecy, ecstasy, knowledge, are very attractive, but they are bound up with our life as it is now, whereas love is a gift which manifests God's nature. It is, therefore, the mark of the mature Christian. All that we do in this world is fallible, limited, but our loving will prepare us to see God face to face. Love is our strongest link between what we are now and what we shall be then.

New Testament Reading (Gospel)   **Matthew 18: 21–end**

The way of love is the way of forgiveness, and this is very difficult for those who are intent on reckoning up grievances suffered at the hands of others. The Parable of the King and the Debtors illustrates this well, because it highlights the essential difference between natural and divine justice.

The king is caught in the dilemma. He begins by demanding his rights, which no court of law could deny him. The first debtor makes a pressing plea for delay until he can repay him, and this moves the king.

But the first debtor is so determined to repay that he presses a very much smaller debt on one of his fellows, even when his fellow makes exactly the same plea for delay. The second debtor is imprisoned by the first debtor; when this comes to the attention of the king, he retaliates, and imprisons the first debtor too, showing no mercy whatever.

Divine justice contradicts natural justice. Like the king, God is ready to forgive those who acknowledge their faults. This is a more excellent way than to press rights, especially when there is no hope of repayment. But also like the king, God expects us to show the same qualities of mercy and love to those who are in our debt. Their offences to us are infinitesimal compared with ours to God. And our forgiveness must come from the *heart*—we must really mean it.

Eighth Sunday after Pentecost
The Fruit of the Spirit

God transforms the human heart, in order to renew our way of life, and this brings us into conflict with the world.

Old Testament Reading   **Ezekiel 36: 24–28**

God promises to restore Israel, and gather her after her exile, but with the specific purpose in mind of renewing her attitude to life. She is to be cleansed of her sin, and given a new heart, made of flesh, completely human, and not of stone, so thoroughly inhuman. With this heart will come the power of the Spirit, which will enable Israel to obey and fulfil God's purposes, and not to turn away from him. By their behaviour, the people of Israel will show what sort of God they worship. The end in view, therefore, is not to exalt the people politically—that would be to repeat the error made by Israel before. Rather is it to demonstrate God as the Lord of his people, the shepherd of an obedient and productive flock.

New Testament Reading (Epistle)   **Galatians 5: 16–25**

The Spirit must be our guide in all things, conduct included; and this brings to light the conflict between the Spirit and our lower nature, between God's power within us, and our baser instincts. The Law acted as a temporary check, for the Jews, but the Spirit supersedes the Law, coming from God, working in Christ.

The battleground is the human soul, which contends between the urge to satisfy these instincts and the 'pull' towards God's will, the harvest of the Spirit.

Paul gives a catalogue of each harvest. The lower nature engenders sexual perversion, superstition, rivalry, and self-indulgence. The Spirit produces its own self-evident fruit . . . which no Law can produce, because the Law is unspiritual, unconcerned with the higher gifts.

How can this good fruit come? Through nothing less than self-crucifixion, the continuous killing of the lower instincts within us, by letting the Spirit rule the heart and will, and thereby becoming our guide.

New Testament Reading (Gospel) **John 15: 16–end**

The conflict between the world and the believer stems from the fact that Jesus chooses us, and he was himself rejected by the world. If we accept this 'choice', and go with him, then the fruit we will bear will be eternal in its quality—our love of the brethren will bind us so close to Jesus and to one another that we ask the right things in prayer, we discern God's will.

We cannot escape this conflict. People do reject Jesus, fully, or partially, by conviction, or apathy. So we must be prepared to face the same kind of hostility which he faced. Goodness threatens people, especially when they will not allow themselves to know the source of all goodness. Those who have heard the message and reject it have no excuse—they are in a worse position than those who haven't heard it. Those who reject Jesus reject God, because they are rejecting God's plan as shown by and manifested in him.

It is the Spirit who equips us to live with this tension, because he is the power through whom we are able to be true to the message and witness of Jesus. The fruit of the Spirit matches up to the pattern of Christ's life by its fidelity to him.

Ninth Sunday after Pentecost
The Whole Armour of God

Those who proclaim Christ crucified must be prepared to fight for the Man who died on Calvary, and to do so with the same weapons which he used.

Old Testament Reading   **Joshua 1: 1–9**

Joshua was, next to Moses, the most remarkable leader in the Old Testament. Here, we see him confronted by the obvious need—the people must be led into the Promised Land. Moses was dead—how could Israel manage without him? And yet, God never fails his people. A different man, with different gifts, and a younger mind, will step into the breach.

God will never fail! Joshua is told again to be 'strong and resolute', in the face of what seem to be insuperable difficulties along his path. The Law must be cherished, as the fundamental guide to the people's attitudes one to another, for without this guide, God's purpose will be thwarted.

Strong and resolute leadership, and self-discipline among the people are the two qualities which shine out from the story, and which originate from a deep awareness of God's activity in the lives of ordinary people.

New Testament Reading (Epistle)   **Ephesians 6: 10–20**

Paul exhorts the Ephesians in a similar vein. They are to 'stand firm' in their faith, and be aware of their need to protect themselves from the onslaughts which will certainly come in the battle of faith. The battle is against those forces of destruction both in the world at large and in the household of faith. Christians of the wealthy and beautiful city of Ephesus are to stand their ground, not give in; they are to fight, not to lose; they are to survive, not die. How?

Against such heavy odds, their armour and weaponry come from God—truth, integrity, peace, faith, salvation, and, above all, the

Spirit. It is a paradoxical picture of a believer who would stand no chance in a military fray, but who has more than enough in the battlefield of the Spirit. For the Spirit is the ultimate weapon, and also the means of real prayer, so easily forgotten or neglected in times of stress, and yet doubly important. They are to keep praying, not forgetting Paul himself, whose physical helplessness in prison is no brake on his immense spiritual strength. Herein lies the secret of this imagery. Christians are to fight with no worldly weapons, but with the weapons of God.

New Testament Reading (Gospel)   **John 17: 11b–19**

The agony is reaching its peak, as Christ gradually accepts his impending death and the helplessness of his flock, who have failed to understand him, and who will soon forsake him.

We are still in the world, and, for all our lack of understanding and faith, want to remain by him. We stand in need of protection, and highest on the list is the need for *unity*, so that the small, insignificant company of believers stands together, and does not fall apart. Christ is the means to that unity, that solidarity, that common conviction. that holy communion.

Next comes *joy*—a strange gift to pray for in the midst of doom and dissension. But joy from above, true and lasting resignation to the goodness of God, is what Christ possesses, in spite of his agony; such a joy is known to those who share in his sufferings, because they know the will of God.

Finally, Christ makes the strong and sacrificial prayer, that we may be '*consecrated in truth*', that we may be steeped, fulfilled, blessed, offered, in God's truth, because the path to that truth takes us along the road of suffering.

Unity, joy, consecration in truth; these are the three ultimate qualites with which to arm ourselves to fight the battle of God's love.

Tenth Sunday after Pentecost
The Mind of Christ

Christ shows us again and again that the mind of God is a complete reversal of human values and pretensions, and that it is only through this reversal that man can really progress.

Old Testament Reading   **Job 42: 1–6**

Job has prospered and suffered, and he has tried to talk through the problem with the qualified religious and philosophical experts available to him. It may have given him intellectual stimulus, but it has failed to satisfy him spiritually. To believe in a God who is greater than man must involve some degree of 'handing over' to him.

So Job acknowledges that God can do all things and that God knows all things. Job's mistake had been to ignore these truths, and he goes on to chide himself for it. More remarkable, he recognizes that he only knew God second-hand, and that now he sees him 'with [his] own eyes', a grand claim in the Old Testament. Finally, he openly confesses his sin in challenging and playing with God, and he repents 'in dust and ashes', the sign of humility and wretchedness.

Like Job, we question suffering in the world, and like him, we come to a better knowledge of God through enquiry, acceptance, repentance, and faith.

New Testament Reading (Epistle)   **Philippians 2: 1–11**

Paul encourages the Philippians to have the example of Christ so much before them that they think and feel alike, so that their 'common life' is indeed a life which is lived in communion. Keeping and maintaining unity in this fellowship must be of the utmost importance to the Church.

He goes on to describe how Christ lived, in humility, because only those who have humility will strive after unity in Christ; unity requires humility. He slips easily into what many writers think was an early Christian hymn, which depicts Christ before, during, and after his earthly life.

Christ existed in the mind of God before his birth, but did not grasp divine nature, in the way human beings snatch at status or possessions; and so he became man, in humility, as slave to God and man, and lived in that condition; and because of this genuine humility, he was exalted, so that his name becomes, paradoxically, a by-word for respect and subservience, he is made the great 'Lord' by virtue of being the true 'slave'.

Such is the way God turns human standards upside down. No slave has the right to the title of 'Lord'—but this is how God chooses to act, because it is the only way of raising man to a better way of life. 'Start from the bottom' is the pattern of incarnation.

Then comes the sting . . . the Philippians are to model their humility on this difficult, almost unnatural humility of Christ's. So will God work through them.

New Testament Reading (Gospel)   **John 13: 1–5**

As he sits at table for the last time, Christ shows the extent of his obedience, as servant of all. Knowing that betrayal and suffering are at hand, he strips, and begins to wash his disciples' feet. Peter stands in the place of the Church, uncomprehending, protesting that the Master should do this, when it would be more seemly that the disciples should wash their Master's feet. But Christ is the real servant, and those who follow him must be cleansed by him, one by one. If anyone is to have fellowship, communion with him, he must be washed. Peter, like the Church, at last sees the point, and over-enthuses—such washing must be thorough!

The mystery of baptism means a continual purification—a turning of the heart to the Master, and a turning of the heart in service to others. This twofold bending of the self is what Christ requires of us. His mind runs against the grain of human nature, but it leads to the path of God's plan—and our own good—in the end.

Eleventh Sunday after Pentecost
The Serving Community

God requires that his people should be of service to others, so that we may be seen to be the people among whom he dwells.

Old Testament Reading   **Isaiah 42: 1–7**

Isaiah sees a particular vocation in a chosen servant, who may be the personification of the whole of Israel. The Spirit falls on him in such a way that he serves a special purpose, to proclaim justice to all the nations. But man's ways are not God's ways, especially in so tall an order as this one. He is to be no sensational idol of the media, no flamboyant darling of the mob. He will not talk or do—but he will *be*—real justice on earth. Even foreign countries will want him for what he is.

The creator God, who made the whole world, has this design as part of his loving purpose for *all*. He is not a tribal deity, concerned only with a locality, and touched by tribal peculiarities. This great, high, and mighty God calls his servant to be 'a light to all nations', a considerable development in Israel's consciousness. By this wider role of Israel, those who are spiritually blind or held fast may see and touch a true expression of God's nature.

New Testament Reading (Epistle)   **2 Corinthians 4: 1–10**

Paul tells the Corinthians to see their calling as coming from Christ, and therefore they should not give up. The community of faith should be honest and open in proclaiming what it believes, and not throw up its arms just because those who are wedded to the spirit of the age are too blind to believe. Christ is the subject and the object of this proclamation—human agency is secondary. He is the manifestation of God's glory.

The 'human' aspect of the Christian must not be overlooked. He is weak, even though chosen to contain something precious. Therefore, it does not matter what happens to him, what his state of life is, provided that Christ is in him. Indeed, the identification of the treasure with its container is so great that the wounds are shared between ourselves and Christ. That is the way in which Christ shows himself to others in the members of the serving community.

New Testament Reading (Gospel) **John 13: 31–35**

The betrayer leaves, so that only the 'inner circle' is left, to hear Christ's parting words. They are simple and direct, but hard. He must go, in order to glorify God, and fulfil his will. The disciples cannot go where Christ goes, even though they will look for him. The search for Christ, and for the meaning of his life, is to continue . . . But they cannot go with him—instead they must learn to love one another. This is his message of farewell. For in loving one another, they will show that Christ is still with them and in them. This is the only way in which others will recognize the disciples for what they are, and come to believe in him . . . The mission of those who follow Christ is to spread his love abroad, and glorify God in so doing.

Twelfth Sunday after Pentecost
The Witnessing Community

God's declared purpose is to spread the knowledge of his light and love to the whole world that all mankind may enjoy his salvation to the full.

Old Testament Reading   **Isaiah 49: 1–6**

The four Servant Songs increase in intensity from service through suffering to death. By these means Israel will fulfil the purpose of her election, not simply in her own interests but for the Gentiles as well. In the first Song, Isaiah 42:1–4, justice will be established in the earth; in this, the second, light will be given to the nations. Justice and light are attributes of God. Not only is he righteous (just), he acts righteously; not only is he light, he drives the darkness away. And he does this through his active and willing servants. These are those who can say, 'my God has become my strength'.

New Testament Reading (Epistle)   **2 Corinthians 5: 14–6: 2**

The coming of Christ is that point in the ongoing history of Israel when God's righteous action, what he does to put men right, has reached maximum intensity. God's light shines in Christ to the brightest degree possible. For Jesus, the greatest of God's servants, is the man of love. And all who are convinced by him, particularly by his service unto death, come under the control of his love. They become a 'new creation' and, through the quality of their lives, they become also the agents by whom the reconciling love of God reaches others. In this way every day is not only a new day but a 'day of salvation' in which, like the sun passing through the sky and bringing light, warmth, and life, God's servants spread the knowledge of his love to others in Christ. This can be summed up in the joyful message, 'For our sake he made him to be sin who knew no sin, so that in him we might become the righteousness of God'.

New Testament Reading (Gospel) **John 17: 20–end**

In these closing words of Jesus's prayer for his disciples and for the Church of which they are the nucleus, he addresses God three times as 'Father'. As Son of God in that unique relationship which is to be found in all that Jesus said and did, he carries out his Father's will through a perfect obedience, serving unto death. This is how he brings many sons to glory, 'the glory which thou hast given me in thy love for me before the foundation of the world'. To know God's 'name' is to be obliged to declare it to others. That name, as Jesus declared it, is love, the love of a righteous Father towards all his children. But men can only come to believe through the word of those who already know God's name. By entering this divine family all become one in the only sort of unity that will convince the world, that which comes to us in Christ as the gift of God.

Our loving heavenly Father, help us in all we are and say and do to witness faithfully to others that they may come to know your reconciling love in Jesus Christ, your Servant and your Son.

Thirteenth Sunday after Pentecost
The Suffering Community

God's righteous activity in history is made known through the suffering of his people.

Old Testament Reading   **Isaiah 50: 4–9a**

In this, the third Servant Song, suffering is mentioned for the first time. Despite his suffering, God's Servant cries twice, 'The Lord God helps me'. The first time it is because God helps him to endure, the second because God shows him to be in the right. The first of these two convictions strengthens the Servant to hold on until the time comes for the second to be fulfilled in his vindication. Such an attitude to suffering enables one to help others whose sufferings are only a burden to them. But it produces deeper spiritual results since it puts the sufferer in a position to learn that suffering is an element within the character of God himself.

New Testament Reading (Epistle)   **Acts 7: 54–8: 1**

Stephen's death is recorded by Luke in language designed to recall the death of Jesus. Not all are called to martyrdom (witness unto death), but the martyr is granted the vision which is true for all. Jesus's entry into glory and triumph is the true meaning of his death in total obedience; he has discovered the glory which is the knowledge that God is a God who suffers on behalf of his creatures. This acceptance of suffering is what divine righteousness really means. Stephen saw Jesus's glory and it enabled him to die as Jesus had died, praying for his murderers. In this same spirit, the Spirit of Jesus, the Church is called to suffer in the world. This it can do because it is sustained by its fellowship with the God whose nature has been made known in Christ as suffering love. Through the Church's acceptance of suffering for God's sake and in fellowship with him, God gets his work, his righteous work, done. The ferocity of the world's opposition to God's will, its failure to see him at work and its power to inflict suffering and death—none of these things should be overestimated. Saul, who that day was consenting to Stephen's death, was to become the great Apostle to the Gentiles and later to write of 'this slight momentary affliction . . . preparing us for an eternal weight of glory beyond all comparison' (2 Corinthians 4:17). And the persecution which followed Stephen's death was to lead to the spread of the gospel far and wide.

New Testament Reading (Gospel)　　　　　**John 16: 1–11**

In this part of Jesus's final discourses, the Fourth Evangelist interprets the faith which had sustained Jesus through his suffering and death. This is no reading back into Jesus's ministry of what had not been there, but a true drawing out of his teaching, the profundity of which had often eluded the disciples when first they heard it. Jesus is well aware that, following his own suffering, excommunication and death may well be inflicted upon his disciples by their fellow-Jews. On both counts he shrinks back. But beyond both lies, he believes, vindication, not only his own but also the complete and final realization of God's righteous will for the world. The coming of the Counsellor will mark the fact that the rule of darkness and death has been broken, and the presence of divine light and life has been made real through the rule of love. This is the proper context in which alone to estimate the fact of suffering. That is why he says, 'it is to your advantage that I go away'.

Lord Jesus Christ, you entered through suffering into glory and thereby opened up death to be the gateway into life; sustain us and all who follow you to suffer with the God of love till righteousness prevail.

Fourteenth Sunday after Pentecost
The Family

The natural context of human life, the family, is to become the means by which we begin to experience the love of God, our heavenly Father.

Old Testament Reading   **Proverbs 31: 10–31**

Despite the very different circumstances of today, the role of a wife and mother is still of central importance for family life. This passage and its context depict her giving herself in service to her husband, her household, and her family, and placing her skills and resources at the disposal of those in the wider society whose needs her family can help to meet. The stability and maturity of the family stem from her faithfulness and reliability, and constitute the central source from which the family's influence flows.

New Testament Reading (Epistle)   **Ephesians 5: 25–6: 4**

Complementary to the role of the wife is that of the husband. Here this is described as emulating and reproducing Christ's love of the Church. If the Church is the family of Christ, so the family is to be a miniature church, motivated and inspired by that same love. The husband's relationship to his wife is a means by which the love of Christ is mediated to the family; he loves with everything at his disposal, with his whole self. To do this requires that he comes out of the family into which he was born and in which his own self developed and grew up to maturity. This reveals the nature of the love which the family exists to nurture, a love that does not keep itself for itself but gives itself away to others. In this respect it resembles the love of God, giving itself endlessly away and thereby creating what is new and sustaining it. Accordingly at this point the passage refers to the children who are born out of the love of husband and wife. Their attitude to their parents is to reflect the love which brought them into being, by willing obedience and respect. Finally, fathers are not to dominate the family and cause their growing children frustration. Rather they are to demonstrate the gentleness of God, his bestowal upon each individual of a measure of freedom consonant with the stage of development reached, and his respect for personality. This is 'the discipline and instruction of the Lord'.

New Testament Reading (Gospel) **Mark 10: 2–16**

Human families, however, are imperfect societies. Relationships between earthly partners can break down. Nor is there any such thing as the perfect parent except for God himself, whose eternal nature is revealed in Christ as limitless, unchanging love. Jesus knew perfectly well how far short of this divine love the love of husbands and wives, fathers and mothers, falls. Yet he is unwilling to lower standards of which human love is capable. These are nothing less than to respond to and reproduce the quality of divine love. This is the purpose of God in creation, and that purpose is unchanging and unchanged. Human life is the material of which the Kingdom of God is composed, and even little children have their place in this; indeed in some respects they can teach their parents, for the Kingdom of God belongs to the child-like, and only the child-like can enter it, since God is the Father of us all. As Ephesians elsewhere puts it, God is 'the Father from whom every family in heaven and on earth is named'.

Heavenly Father, strengthen our family life that the quality of our relationships with one another in it may worthily reflect your mighty love for us revealed in Jesus Christ, your only Son, our Lord.

Fifteenth Sunday after Pentecost
Those in Authority

There is no authority except from God, since God alone is Lord and therefore himself the source of *all* authority.

Old Testament Reading   **Isaiah 45: 1–7**

God is always at work, and he works through the processes of history. History is the sphere in which he exercises his divine authority. He is the Lord of the ages, the King of kings and the Lord of lords. These insights, however, are not given to all, and many exercise authority on God's behalf without knowing that they do so. Thus though God says, 'I am the Lord and there is no other, beside me there is no God', he also says to Cyrus, 'I gird you, though you do not know me. . . .'. Through his conquest of Babylon, Cyrus of Persia became the agent of Israel's return from Exile, the restoration of her national life, and her rediscovery of the God of the Exodus.

New Testament Reading (Epistle)   **Romans 13: 1–7**

By 'resisting the authorities' Paul does not refer here to the legitimate expression of opposing views but to the refusal to obey the law. In the last resort 'there is no authority except from God, and those that exist have been instituted by God'. Thus the Christian, in exercising his political function by keeping the law, even when he doesn't agree with it, and paying taxes even when he doesn't like them, acknowledges God as the ultimate source of all authority. Of course, kingdoms come and kingdoms go. Law is for ever changing, and no society can govern itself by a system of laws acceptable to all its members. But behind our imperfect human societies Christians believe, even if they cannot always detect, that God is at work exercising his sovereign authority and working his purpose out. The particular period of history of which we are part may be compared favourably or unfavourably with some other; but more important than all particular times is the end to which they move under God's direction, when his kingdom will have fully come, his universal rule be supreme, when 'all things are subjected to him'. Then God will himself be 'everything to everyone' (1 Corinthians 15:24–28).

New Testament Reading (Gospel)   **Matthew 22: 15–22**

While history continues, Christians must continue to acknowledge the authority of law in the societies to which they belong. In the modern world 'Caesar' appears in different guises, whether capitalist, communist, or non-aligned. By rendering to Caesar what is his, Christians however situated acknowledge the temporary character of all earthly kingdoms, and at the same time the working out of that eternal and unchanging purpose which is finally revealed in Christ. Behind the Caesars and also through them, the sovereign Lord exercises his omnipotent authority, building the decisions of sinful men into the stuff of his kingdom. Nothing can prevent him from achieving his purpose, but he has chosen to work it out through human co-operation, where that is offered to him; and despite human foolishness and blindness where it is not. And the nature of his omnipotent authority is love.

O God of love, we acknowledge that you alone are the Lord. Of you and through you and to you are all things. Hasten the time when all mankind will confess you alone as rightful Lord, and the design of your great love is realized; through Jesus Christ we ask it.

Sixteenth Sunday after Pentecost
The Neighbour

What we are in relation to God is to be reflected in what we are in relation to others.

Old Testament Reading   **Leviticus 19: 9–18**

This passage is part of the Holiness Code (Leviticus 17–26) deriving from the basic statement, 'You shall be holy; for I the Lord your God am holy' (Leviticus 19:2). The purpose of God in revealing himself is to bring into being a people whose character matches his own. The touchstone of their relationship with him is their relationship with one another. Hence the emphasis of consideration for the poor and the stranger, and the condemnation of theft, deceit, exploitation, and revenge. Our relationship to others is to show forth our relationship to God.

New Testament Reading (Epistle)   **Romans 12: 9–end**

Any element of threat for failure has now been replaced by grace, the grace given to Paul himself and that given to all believers (*vv.* 3,6). He who repeatedly declared, 'I am the Lord' (Leviticus 19:4, 10, 12, 14, 16, 18, etc.) has now revealed himself as the God of mercy (*v.* 1). This is what calls out from our human side the response which Paul describes as 'your spiritual worship', and it is to show itself in a correspondingly gracious quality of relationship with others. The fundamental difference is that now this is not so much what we do, as what God by his grace does in us. We are to look to God, love like God, leave everything to God, live together in the grace of God. In a word, we are to reproduce in all our relationships the life of Christ who is God's grace personified. Our relationship to others is to show forth God's relationship to us in him.

New Testament Reading (Gospel) **Luke 10: 25–37**

Here the lawyer brings together two Old Testament passages expressing total love for God (Deuteronomy 6:5) and total love for others (Leviticus 19:18) in response to the suggestion of Jesus that Scripture itself tells us where 'eternal life' is to be found. The story of the Good Samaritan which follows illustrates the truth that the possession of eternal life affects the way we behave in relation to others. We become forgetful of ourselves, anxious only to serve, willing to use the resources we have been given to help and heal as opportunity presents itself, to show mercy as we have been shown it. Jesus can be seen either as the Good Samaritan ministering to mankind who lies wounded and dying by the wayside and bringing him healing, hope, health, and wholeness; or as himself the victim, wounded for our transgressions and suffering in all who suffer. In tending to their needs we are tending to his. 'I was hungry and you gave me food, thirsty and you gave me drink, a stranger and you welcomed me, naked and you clothed me, sick and you visited me, in prison and you came to me' (Matthew 25:35f).

Teach us, good Lord, to be to others what you have been to us that in serving them we may serve you as you deserve; for you are the God of all mercy and the giver of eternal life.

Seventeenth Sunday after Pentecost
The Proof of Faith

Life is to be worshipful, and worship the offering of life.

Old Testament Reading   **Jeremiah 7: 1–11**

The voice of the prophet sounds out the word of the Lord to expose
the hypocrisy in worship that is not the offering of life, and life that is
not consistent with worship. What men are in the temple of the Lord
and what they are in their everyday lives require consistency, for the
Lord of the temple is the Lord of life. Not only his house but also his
people are to be called by his name; their behaviour at all times and
in all places must show forth the character of the God whose people
they are called to be. Theft, murder, adultery, falsehood, idolatry
are 'abominations' for this reason. God's people must therefore
amend their lives in accordance with the character of him in whom
they believe.

New Testament Reading (Epistle)   **James 1: 16–end**

Out from the unchanging character of God come 'every good
endowment, every perfect gift'. The word of truth which he has
spoken, implanted in us, issues in deeds of righteousness which
work his work and bear witness to his eternal nature. To visit the
needy, the helpless, the afflicted, and to live out God's life in a
wicked world is described as 'religion that is pure and undefiled
before God and the Father'. True worship is worshipful living, life
that is constantly offered up to God in the service of others. This in
turn builds up a character which bears witness to what God is like,
and reveals what he is always busy doing in the world.

New Testament Reading (Gospel)   **Luke 17: 11–19**

The encounter between ten unnamed outcasts of society in an
unnamed village and Jesus, whom they address as 'Master', becomes
the occasion when they experience the action of God in healing; yet

in only one of the ten does an answering gratitude spring up, causing him to turn back, fall down at Jesus's feet, and praise God; and he was the one from whom Jesus's hearers would least have expected such behaviour. True worship is one long-drawn-out 'Thank you' addressed continually to God in return for his never-ceasing mercy, forgiveness, cleansing, and healing. Once men become, through faith in Christ, recipients of God's limitless grace and love, once they experience its liberating power, they are in a position to live out their lives in a constant expression of gratitude.

Jesus, Master and Lord, turn us back from the selfishness of our wicked ways and make us to know the goodness and love of God that we may never cease to give him thanks who ever cleanses our sins and heals our sicknesses.

Eighteenth Sunday after Pentecost
The Offering of Life

Old Testament Reading   **Deuteronomy 26: 1–11**

Deuteronomy professes to be a review by Moses of God's great acts
in bringing his people through their Exodus wanderings to the point
of entry into the Holy Land. In fact the author is probably writing
many centuries later, in the light of what had actually happened in
between. He has a strong sense of God's providence, and so calls on
his people to respond to God's goodness by obedience and thankfulness. In particular, they must make a practical acknowledgement of
his favours in supplying their needs, by a sort of Harvest Festival
offering. This offering of produce was to be a token and symbol of
the offering of the worshipper's own whole life and work.

'The place the Lord your God shall choose' refers to the Temple in
Jerusalem, which was not established till hundreds of years after
Moses. It became the centre of Jewish worship, and so was regarded
as the right place for making offerings.

Note the wide-ranging sympathy of the writer—he thinks not
only of God's own people, but also of 'the stranger who is among
you' (*v.* 11).

New Testament Reading (Epistle)   **2 Corinthians 8: 1–9**

Paul's Second Letter to Corinth is not easy to follow, as it probably
combines parts of several letters he wrote to the church there. Here
he is encouraging the Corinthians to copy the good example of their
fellow-Christians in Macedonia (Northern Greece), who had contributed very generously to Paul's collection for the poor church in
Jerusalem. Paul set great store by this collection as a token of church
unity and as a recognition of Christians' mutual responsibility.
Christian giving should be sacrificial—they had given out of their
poverty, not their wealth—and also a matter of joy. Compare the
gospel story of the widow's mite.

As always, Paul bases his advice and instructions about Christian duty on Christ's example—the immeasurable sacrifice of God's Son in discarding his heavenly glory and embracing human poverty and suffering for our sake.

New Testament Reading (Gospel) **Matthew 5: 17–26**

The Sermon on the Mount draws together teaching given by our Lord on various subjects and occasions. It has been called 'The new Law of God's new people'. Jesus's contemporaries found it hard to understand his attitude to the Mosaic Law, which controlled their whole lives. Sometimes he caused offence by seeming to overthrow it completely, as with his actions on the Sabbath. But here he claims to fulfil it. This is true radicalism: not destroying, but getting behind the letter of the Law to the principles it enshrined—God's call to his people to 'be holy as I am holy'. No one could have tried harder than the Pharisees to obey the letter of the Law, but, as Paul found, human efforts to be good end in frustration. What is needed is a quite different attitude to God and his will—that of a loving son. That provides a far better motive for obedience, but an even more exacting one: the Christian must outdo the Pharisee! So take a new look at the old commands: don't suppose you are innocent of the Sixth if you haven't actually killed someone. Murder is the supreme example of ill-will; but lesser kinds can be equally bad. *Any* ill-will poisons relationships with our fellow men and with God. So get those relationships straightened out quickly (even if churchgoing has to take a back seat while you do so!).

Nineteenth Sunday after Pentecost
The Life of Faith

Old Testament Reading   **Genesis 28: 10–end**

Bethel, now the hamlet of Beitin, stands on the edge of a stretch of moorland and rock, where the ground falls away sharply to the Jordan valley. This old story was handed down partly to account for the origin of the ancient shrine there. Bethel later became a rival to Solomon's temple, but was subsequently destroyed. Jacob was fleeing from his brother Esau, whom he had cheated out of his father's blessing and birthright. His vision here sustained him during many weary years before he could return.

Bethel means 'house of God'. Jacob knew that he had had a genuine experience of contact with God, and he commemorated it by erecting a pillar-shrine and worshipping there. Most sacred places and buildings have the same aim—to mark out somewhere where God has 'shown his hand', where men have met him, and may meet him again. But there is a danger of trying to 'localize' God, and pin him down to selected spots. The reference to this passage in John's gospel (1:51) shows that, for the Christian, Jesus is the true 'ladder', linking heaven and earth, God and man. The vision was given to Jacob, not just for his own sake, but for all who would come after; the Jewish destiny was to be the channel through which God's blessings would flow out to all mankind.

New Testament Reading (Epistle)   **Hebrews 11: 1, 2, 8–16**

'Faith' in Hebrews means a firm grasp on the great unshakable facts of God and of spiritual reality (whether we can see them or not). In this passage the picture is of a cavalcade of pilgrims journeying through this life and through history towards the still unseen goal of the heavenly life of glory. The heroes and heroines of Old Testament times, in all their struggles and sufferings and achievements, did not succeed in reaching their destination; that had to wait for the fullness of the Christian revelation. This picture of the Christian pilgrimage towards the heavenly city, where the final life of glory awaits God's servants of both B.C. and A.D. times, underlies many hymns, such as 'Jerusalem the golden. . . .', 'Jerusalem, my happy home. . . .' Meanwhile, in the days of our pilgrimage here on earth, we must not get so set in the ways of this world, that we lose sight of our unseen destiny.

New Testament Reading (Gospel)   **Matthew 6: 24–end**

Here, in the Sermon on the Mount, Jesus is urging us not to be so involved in worldly concerns—business success, prosperity, our material needs—that we forget everything else. 'Mammon' means worldly wealth, money, property. It can easily become an idol, which we worship in place of God. Christian standards mustn't be reserved for Sunday only, while we indulge in 'business morality' on weekdays. If we heard the comment: 'He's too good a man ever to be very successful in business', would we regard that as praise, or blame?

God knows our needs far better than we do; so we need not always be worrying about things. *V.* 34 does not mean that we must not make any advance plans for future commitments; that is one of today's proper duties. But fretting about what may or may not happen is unworthy of a trusting disciple.

Twentieth Sunday after Pentecost
Endurance

Old Testament Reading   **Daniel 3: 13–26**

Daniel was almost certainly written at the height of the terrible
persecution of the Jews by Antiochus IV Epiphanes in 168 B.C. But it
is cast in the form of stories about a traditional hero, Daniel, supposed to have lived three or four hundred years earlier, in the days
when the Jews were under Babylonian or Persian rule, and other
tyrants reigned. It was written as a 'Tract for the Times', to encourage Jews of the writer's own day to follow the examples of earlier
heroes of the faith, and to stick to their religion no matter what it
might cost. These earlier heroes are Daniel himself, and his three
companions, the 'Three Holy Children', Shadrach, Meshach, and
Abed-Nego, who are the same as the Ananias, Azarias, and Misael of
the Prayer Book canticle *Benedicite*. In these stories their courage is
vindicated, and they are delivered from the persecuting tyrant.

But note the magnificent resolve and defiance of *vv.* 17, 18. If God
willed to rescue them, he would; but even if he did not save them,
come what may, their duty was still to be faithful to him. Against
such courage and faith, no tyrant can win. Whether God delivers
from torture and death or not, his presence is still with his faithful
servants (*v.* 25)—a reassurance for Christians of today, or of any age
and country, who are persecuted for their beliefs.

New Testament Reading (Epistle)   **Romans 8: 18–25**

Life in this world inevitably entails suffering of one sort or another;
it is the condition of physical existence. Even the natural universe we
live in is clearly far from perfect. In a metaphor from childbirth,
Paul pictures the whole world as struggling and longing for redemption—to enter on a new life. We all hope and long to be set free from
the cramping limitations of this present life. Even Christians are not
immune from this, although, in receiving the Holy Spirit at our
Baptism and Confirmation we have already received the 'first-fruits'

of that new life of Christian rest and glorification with Christ. First-fruits is the equivalent of the down-payment, the first instalment, that guarantees the delivery of the full amount later on. Life is not just 'a vale of tears', but 'a school for eternity'.

New Testament Reading (Gospel)   **Luke 9: 51–55a, 56b–end**

There is a stern side to the character of Jesus as shown in the Gospels. The later stages of his ministry depict him as resolute and determined to let nothing stand in the way of his coming passion and death. That, he knew, was the only way in which he could accomplish God's will. He had counted the cost, and then deliberately discounted it.

The Samaritans occupied an area in the centre of the Holy Land (some of their descendants are still there today). They had a sanctuary on Mount Gerizim, as a rival to the Jerusalem temple. They were always at loggerheads with the Jews, and many Jewish pilgrims to Jerusalem from the north went out of their way to avoid the hostile territory altogether. James and John, the 'Thunder-boys' as Jesus nicknamed them, wanted to copy the fiery-tempered example of the Old Testament prophet Elijah (see 2 Kings, ch. 1), but were quickly rebuked. Violence must not be the Christian response to those who annoy or injure us.

Following Jesus demands of us too determination, commitment, and counting the cost of discipleship. This may involve homelessness (*v.* 58), and the giving up of family commitments (*vv.* 59, 61). How many of those we honour as saints have taken Jesus at his word! What does our vocation involve for us?

Twenty-first Sunday after Pentecost
The Christian Hope

Old Testament Reading   **Habakkuk 2: 1–4**

Little is known of the prophet Habakkuk. Most of the early
prophets had an inner conviction of what God wanted to say to his
people through them, and then uttered the message: 'Thus saith the
Lord . . .'. Later, such messages were written down; and here the
prophet is explicitly told to write down the vision for anyone to read.
'He that runs', that is, can take it in at a glance without pausing to
spell out the words. God's messages were thought almost to have an
existence of their own, so that their potency could not be exhausted
until they had been fulfilled. Sooner or later, the thing prophesied
must come to pass.

 V. 4 contains the famous phrase, 'The just shall live by his faith',
which was to stimulate pages of commentary—among the Dead Sea
Community at Qumran, the Rabbis, and in the New Testament.
There Paul uses it in his argument for faith replacing the Mosaic
Law as the true way of life. Here, faith means rather faithfulness,
'sticking at it'.

New Testament Reading (Epistle)   **Acts 26: 1–8**

Paul had been arrested in Jerusalem, and is now awaiting trial as a
prisoner at Caesarea, the Roman provincial headquarters on the
coast of Palestine. Much of the Roman city remains has recently
been excavated. Agrippa, the last of the Herod family, was on a sort
of state visit to Festus the Governor. He was not an independent
king, but had a position not unlike that of the Indian Rajahs under
the British Empire. The speech given here by Acts does not necessarily reproduce Paul's actual words, though Luke himself may well
have been present. It was a well-recognized literary convention for
an author to represent his characters saying what the author himself
judged appropriate to the occasion. After a complimentary introduction, Paul cites his own impeccable Jewish background, and then

moves on to the central Christian belief—Christ's resurrection. That is the base both for our Christian hope and for the Christian mission to the world.

New Testament Reading (Gospel)   **Luke 18: 1–8**

Jesus's favourite method of teaching was the parable—taking some everyday incident, and using it as a vehicle to convey some deeper truth. The details of the incident used do not matter; like most good teachers, Jesus usually wanted to get across one important lesson at a time. But of course in the telling and retelling of these parables, before they 'came to roost' in their present position in our written gospels, the original context in which Jesus had spoken them was often forgotten, and we cannot always be certain which of several possible lessons he was trying to draw from the story. He often used what is known as *a fortiori* argument (if A is true, how much more must B be true too). So here: if an old woman on her own can eventually get results out of a bad man by constant nagging, how much more can we expect to get results, not from a reluctant and bad man, but from a good and generous God, if we are persistent and do not lose heart.

Twenty-second Sunday after Pentecost
The Two Ways

Old Testament Reading   **Deuteronomy 11: 18–28**

This section repeats what has been said in an earlier chapter, after recapitulating the Ten Commandments, which form part of the covenant relationship between God and his people. Texts from that chapter with other verses were in fact written on slips of parchment and worn by Jews of a later period (the 'phylacteries' of the Gospels) and fastened near doors of houses (the *mezuzah* which a practising Jew has by his door today) as a constant reminder of this relationship.

The writer of Deuteronomy has a rather over-simplified philosophy: if as a nation you obey God, you will prosper, and your boundaries will expand from the Euphrates to the Mediterranean, from Lebanon to the southern desert (borders rarely actually achieved in Jewish history); if you disobey him, you will meet calamity. Life is not quite as straightforward as that; but the message remains important: national morality matters, just as individual morality matters.

New Testament Reading (Epistle)   **1 John 2: 22–end**

Traditionally both the Gospel of John and this Epistle were written by the Apostle in his old age. Whether that is so or not, the author writes in a reminiscent, sometimes almost rambling, style, slowly turning over in his mind the great truths of the gospel he has preached and thought about for so long.

He has had to combat various heresies—false claimants to be the Messiah (as Jesus had warned); here he is concerned to reiterate the basic Christian faith—Jesus was, and is, the Christ. The familiar name or title 'Christ' represents the Greek translation of the original Aramaic 'Messiah'; both mean the same—The Anointed One. If anyone denies this fundamental fact, he is anti-Christ, a liar. The AntiChrist came to be thought of as an almost mythological figure, who would be the champion of evil, and lead the world astray, usurping the place of God. Things would have to get worse before they could get better, but in a final showdown with God AntiChrist would be destroyed.

We are part of Christ by virtue of our anointing (*v.* 27)—the same root word as for Christ the Anointed. If we keep 'in him', we shall not be led astray into heresy or wrongdoing. Possibly Christians were actually anointed at their baptism.

New Testament Reading (Gospel)   **Luke 16: 1–9**

The Parable of the Unjust Steward has caused many difficulties, mainly because people make the mistake of trying to allegorize it by saying: The rich man equals God, and so on. But all Jesus is doing is to take a slice of life—the sort of case a popular newspaper might report—and then use it to convey some teaching or challenge about deeper things. In fact more than one lesson is drawn from the story; perhaps Luke himself was not sure about Jesus's original application of it. The Authorized (King James) Version does not help, by giving us a misleading rendering; *v.* 9 does not mean that we are to 'make friends of mammon', i.e. cultivate worldly wealth; but 'make friends by means of . . .', i.e. use material things to make lasting friends, so that when 'it' (mammon or money, not 'ye') fails and 'is a thing of the past' (*NEB*) you may have 'an eternal home'. Perhaps *v.* 8 should end in a question mark: Did the master commend his sharp-practising bailiff? People are smart enough in business affairs where their own welfare is concerned; are we half as business-like in what we do about our eternal destiny?

Last Sunday after Pentecost
Citizens of Heaven

Old Testament Reading   **Jeremiah 29: 1, 4–14**

When Jerusalem was captured by the Babylonians in 597 B.C., many of the inhabitants, including all the most influential, were forcibly deported to Babylon. Jeremiah stayed with the impoverished and defeated remnants of the population in Judea. Unlike his prophetic predecessor Isaiah, who had a century or more earlier encouraged resistance to the invader, Jeremiah had realized that this time the Jews must lose their freedom, and must learn a hard lesson through defeat, which was interpreted as God's punishment for their national disobedience and sins. Understandably, he was regarded by many as a 'quisling' and traitor, and suffered accordingly. Yet he would not abandon his people in their discouragement, and in this letter to the exiles he tells them to settle contentedly in their new land. Most of them had been feeling either rebellious or full of self-pity—compare Psalm 137: 'By the waters of Babylon . . .'. But God had not abandoned them; they could still know and worship him, though far from home; and in two generations' time ('seventy years'), when they had learned their lesson, he would restore them to their own land again. The prophecy was fulfilled.

New Testament Reading (Epistle)   **Philippians 3: 7–end**

Paul is perhaps thinking that he has not much longer to live; and as he looks back on his life, he can see how he had had to discard his inherited advantages, and his own achievements, counting them 'loss', in order to make progress in 'gaining' Christ. Any merits he has are not his, except insofar as they are Christ's merits in him. Total union of will and purpose with Christ is all that matters, so that sharing in his sufferings he may share in his resurrection too. We can never claim that we have reached perfection in this life. Paul uses here, as elsewhere, the picture of a race-course—no serious competitor gives up half-way; he keeps concentrating on the winning-post. So, don't lower your standards, but keep aiming higher.

New Testament Reading (Gospel)   **John 17: 1–10**

This chapter has been called the High Priestly, or Consecration, Prayer of Christ. John represents our Lord as speaking it a few hours before his arrest and passion. In it, he seems to be standing back from the immediate events, and looking at his whole incarnate life in the light of God's eternal purpose for the world.

The earthly ministry is nearly over; 'the hour', the crucial moment, of his supreme work is upon him, and soon to be accomplished—the work of bringing God's alienated world (or at least those who will respond) back to him, through his own complete dedication and consecration of himself to God's will, even to death.

In the other gospels, Jesus proclaims the Kingdom; John prefers to talk about eternal life. By this he means, not an extension of this life, but a whole new quality or dimension of life. It consists in 'knowing' God the Father and Jesus Christ as his Son—and 'knowing' in the biblical sense implies a closeness and unity far greater than just a mental process. We can enter into this eternal life here and now, even if we cannot know its fullness till after death.

John sees the glorification of Jesus as something that actually includes his cross and passion; God's glory is revealed there just as much as in the joy of Easter and the Ascension.

YEAR TWO

Ninth Sunday before Christmas
The Creation

Christian belief in God the creator does not deduce that because the world of nature is beautiful, it must have had an originator. Belief in creation is belief in purpose—a purpose for man in the world now, set in the context of God's eternity. Man can know of this purpose only when he is enlightened by the Spirit of God, and in worship catches a glimpse of the majesty of the creator.

Old Testament Reading   **Genesis 2: 4b–9, 15–end**

Like all ancient peoples, the Israelites had stories about the beginnings of things, and these stories were meant to explain familiar institutions and facts of daily life. In Genesis, however, the stories have been deeply influenced by what Israel had learned through its history about the nature of God. Some of this learning had been a painful process. In the light of this experience, Genesis 2 states what is God's *ideal* purpose for mankind. First, mankind is dependent upon God for its life (*v.* 7) and is placed in a position of trust and responsibility in the world, to enjoy it to the full, in obedience to the commands of God. Second, mankind is not to be thought of as isolated individuals. Human love and companionship, especially as expressed in family life, are to be an essential part of the enjoyment of the created order. There is a condition to all this, however. If mankind tries to usurp the position of God (*v.* 17), the result will be not merely physical death. It will bring disorder, uncertainty, and alienation into the world, because the unaided power of mankind to sustain and understand the world is quite inadequate. Set in this context, physical death becomes frightening, because the world seems purposeless. In fact, the Bible presupposes throughout that mankind indeed seeks to usurp the place of God, and that only the suffering love of God can reverse the process. It does invite us, however, to glimpse what God ideally intends for his creation, and to work and pray for its realization.

New Testament Reading (Epistle) **Revelation 4**

This vision of the Creator being worshipped by the heavenly hosts is perhaps the most magnificent in the Bible. It draws upon many traditional images in its attempt to express the inexpressible, and perhaps it affords us a glimpse of the eucharistic worship of the early Church, with the elders surrounding the altar. If we ignore the worship of God's Church, we will cut ourselves off from sharing a vision that will give hope and life.

New Testament Reading (Gospel) **John 3: 1–8**

In Genesis 2, God breathed life into man, and enriched that life with human companionship. Both life and companionship need to be renewed by God if we are to know and live out the purpose of creation in a world marred by mankind's belief in its self-sufficiency. To be born anew (or, from above) means both to become by baptism a member of the new people of God whose existence depends upon the death and resurrection of Jesus, and to have one's mind and heart illumined by the truth of Christian teaching. For some, the illumination of the mind and heart is gradual, while for others it is sudden. While the failures of the Church and of its members are perhaps only too obvious, the fact remains that through the Church, God wills to fulfil the purpose of creation.

Eighth Sunday before Christmas
The Fall

The fact of the presence of evil in human thoughts and actions is a major problem for all religions. Christianity and Judaism make this problem more acute by insisting upon the oneness of God, thereby making God responsible at least for allowing the possibility of evil. However, with the help of today's passages it is possible to identify something of the root cause of evil, and God's remedy in Jesus Christ.

Old Testament Reading   **Genesis 3: 1–15**

Israel's neighbours tended to explain evil in terms of struggles between gods, in which man had become involved against his will. Genesis 3 rules out any such approach, and places the responsibility squarely upon man himself. The serpent is not a divine or angelic creature, but a created 'beast of the field'. But because in the chapter the serpent also symbolizes that evil which seems to be outside of man, and to which man responds, later Jewish and Christian interpretation saw the serpent as an agent or a disguise of the devil. The important thing is that we do not minimize man's responsibility in the story for breaking God's commandment because of desire for what had been forbidden. At the same time, evil seems to be more than the sum of individual evil human wills, as we can readily appreciate when we remember the extermination of millions of human beings before and during the second World War. This is why the Christian view of salvation involves more than individuals merely resolving to use their freewill aright, and why Genesis 3 sees the disobedience of Adam and Eve as somehow affecting the created order.

New Testament Reading (Epistle)   **Romans 7: 7–13**

It is significant that Paul selected the most inward of the Ten Commandments: 'Thou shalt not covet'. This is a law which can hardly be enforced legally, and yet it is a sign of a human disposition from which much other evil derives. Adam and Eve had coveted what truly was reserved for God alone. In speaking about sin, Paul almost personifies it, seeing it as a force which has used the occasion of his coveting to make him a captive. Redemption must defeat sin in this external sense.

New Testament Reading (Gospel)   **John 3: 13–21**

Numbers 21:4–9 records that when the Israelites complained that God was treating them badly during the wilderness wanderings, they were afflicted by deadly poisonous serpents. God ordered Moses to make an image of a serpent, and to put it on a pole, so that those Israelites who looked at it in faith would be healed. Whatever may be the historical reality behind the story, its symbolism is profound. It teaches that disaster comes if man's selfish desires lead him to reject God, the source of life and hope. Healing and renewal also come only from God, who requires that man turns in faith to what outwardly appears to be a representation of that which is causing his affliction.

Using this symbolism, today's Gospel reminds us that outwardly, the crucified Son of man presents the results of man's alienation from God, and the evil that man works in the world. Because of his obedience to God, the Son of man suffers grievous bodily pain as his fellow men use their ultimate weapon—their power to deprive another of his life. Worse than the bodily pain is the disloyalty of his followers and the apparent desertion by God himself. But paradoxically, at the moment of his humiliation, the Son of man is robbing evil of its power to have the last word. His obedience is the counterpart to Adam's disobedience. In him, God is reconciling the world to himself, and is inviting mankind to look in faith at the Crucified One, in order to find pardon and hope.

Seventh Sunday before Christmas
The Election of God's People: Abraham

The redemption of the world through our Lord was something achieved once and for all, at a decisive point in history. However, it was also the culmination of a process begun with God's choosing of Abraham, the father of the Hebrew nation. Yet the redemption and its rejection were anticipated in the history of Israel, as successive generations judged themselves by their response or indifference to divine grace.

Old Testament Reading   **Genesis 22: 1–18**

Chapters 12 to 21 of Genesis record how God's promise to Abraham both that he would become the father of a great nation, and that through the nation all mankind would receive blessing, was realized in its first essential by the birth of a natural son to Sarah and Abraham. Chapter 22 is a shock—in it, God tells Abraham to sacrifice the son whose very life is necessary if the divine promise is to be fully realized. Abraham's obedience, spread out over a three-day journey, and costing so much in terms of the prospective loss of his only son, contrasts with the ease and pleasure of the disobedience of Adam. Such is the cost in human and divine terms of overcoming the effects of evil, and it is no accident that similarities have long been seen between the 'sacrifice' of Isaac and God's gift of his son for the world's redemption. In Genesis 22 the divine plan is rescued at the last minute. On the cross, the divine plan appears to have had no rescue, except that the eye of faith sees there the victory of God.

New Testament Reading (Epistle)   **James 2: 14–24 (25, 26)**

Faith is not simply an attitude of mind. It is the conviction of heart and mind together that the hidden purpose of life has been declared in Jesus Christ. It is not merely the assent of the mind to certain propositions about the divinity of Jesus or the Persons of the Holy Trinity. It is a readiness to live a particular sort of life and to champion particular values, because these are believed to be based upon the reality of God. The faith of Abraham issued in action, surrounded though it was with doubt and foreboding. It was based upon the deep conviction that God is trustworthy, and that his purposes will be ultimately vindicated.

New Testament Reading (Gospel)   **Luke 20: 9–17**

The story of the Hebrew people that begins with the faith and obedience of Abraham is by no means a success story. It is rather a narrative of a struggle between a small band of God's servants, and a people that wanted a god to assist their own particular interests. No wonder the prophetic calls for social justice, for honesty in the courts, and for sincere worship of God led sometimes to the rejection or death of God's servants. It seems amazing that God should have persisted with such a stubborn people, but happily, God's patience and his redeeming love are stronger than human ungratefulness. This hope is strengthened when we consider how people such as Abraham have responded positively to God. Our Lord told this parable in order to remind the people of his day how their own history set out their purpose in God's plans, and how they had often rejected it. This same parable, and the same history, serve a like purpose for the Church, God's people of the New Covenant.

Sixth Sunday before Christmas
The Promise of Redemption: Moses

The Exodus from Egypt was for the people of the Old Covenant what the Resurrection is for the people of the New Covenant. Both events were preceded by God's choice of servants: of Abraham, Isaac, and Jacob before the Exodus, and of the disciples before the Resurrection. But without the Exodus there would be no Israel, and without the Resurrection there would be no Church.

Old Testament Reading   **Exodus 6: 2–8**

The origin of the name Jehovah (or, as it was more likely pronounced, Yahweh) is unknown. Its origin is less important than two other factors, first, that its meaning is explained in Exodus 3:14; second, that it was first made known to the Israelites at the time of the Exodus, and is thus closely bound up with the manifestation of God's grace and power at the time Israel was delivered from slavery. Although Exodus 3:14 has been the centre of intense scholarly discussion, it seems to be clear that the biblical writers connected the name Yahweh with the first person of the verb 'to be'—I am. This means that the name is not to be linked with any object in the natural order; nor is it the sort of name that enables God to be pictured or otherwise visually described. God is the one who is, and his being is dependent on nothing other than himself.

The one who is, however, is not remote from the world. In Exodus 34:6–7, God's name is expounded in terms of compassion and forgiveness, and in today's passage these qualities are related to the specific situation of Israel in slavery in Egypt. For Israel, God will not be a postulate of reason achieved by reflection upon the nature of being. He will become known to his people when his compassion is joined to his power over being, to give freedom and hope to his people, in fulfilment of his promises to their forefathers.

New Testament Reading (Epistle)　　　　　　　**Hebrews 11: 17–31**

According to Hebrews 11:1, faith gives true existence to what is
hoped for, it is the test of the reality of the unseen. Because of faith,
things that are hoped for become a possibility *now*. This is amply
illustrated from the life of Moses. The thing hoped for in his case was
deliverance from slavery for his people, and possession of their own
land. To see the final possession of the land was to be denied him,
and the achievement of the Exodus was beset with difficulties, not
least those caused by lack of conviction on the part of the Israelites
themselves. However, Moses was able to have such a sure grasp of
the certainty that God would fulfil his purpose, that faith sustained
him at every point in the enterprise. From the standpoint of the
writer of Hebrews, things looked clearer than they must have done
to Moses himself. It is to the faith of such great men of God that the
people of God owe their very existence. In turn, they are challenged
to consider the quality of their own hope in God's purpose, and their
translation of it into reality now, through faith.

New Testament Reading (Gospel)　　　　　　　**Mark 13: 5–13**

The discourse about the last things in Mark 13 contains allusions to
many popular Jewish beliefs of the time. Themes such as famine,
earthquake, war, and family division form part of Jewish belief in
the woes and 'birth-pains' that would precede the final establishment of God's kingdom. A distinctively Christian note is to be found
in *v*. 10. If the passage is considered in the light of Hebrews 11, the
key words are the conclusion of *v*. 13—'he that endures to the end,
the same shall be saved'. Just as the faith of Moses gave substance in
his lifetime to the future for which he hoped, so Christian faith in the
final establishment of God's purposes must endure to the end, in the
face of all trials and difficulties that may ensue. This is far more
important than trying to calculate when the end might be.

Fifth Sunday before Christmas
The Remnant of Israel

The story of the Old Testament contains much about the unfaithfulness of Israel in the face of God's grace and mercy. Indeed, there always remains true to God a tiny minority which escapes divine punishment and holds fast to hope in the future outworking of God's purposes; but God must look beyond this remnant for the fulfilment of his plans for the world.

Old Testament Reading   **Isaiah 10: 20–23**

This passage is probably an early commentary on the teachings of the prophet, stemming from one of Isaiah's later disciples. It deliberately introduces a note of pessimism into the book. 'A remnant shall return' was the name given by Isaiah to one of his children as a sign of hope for the deliverance of Israel from her enemies in the reign of Ahaz (7:3). In 10:21–3, the promise has become a threat. The statement about Israel being as the sand of the sea is a reference to God's promise to Abraham (Genesis 22:17), but here the promise has been reversed. Only a tiny number will escape the destruction that God will bring upon the earth (v. 23), a destruction in accordance with justice (v. 22). At this time, there will be no automatic immunity for Israel, and the only hope for the people who survive will be to place their trust once more in God (v. 20). Such gloomy pessimism is not surprising in view of the continued apostasies and disloyalty of the chosen people. Such pessimism can be the final word, however, only if we think that the indifference and selfishness of mankind are finally able to frustrate the purposes of God.

New Testament Reading (Epistle)   **Romans 9: 19–28**

As a 'Hebrew of the Hebrews' (Philippians 3:5) Paul was much exercised to understand why the chosen people had rejected Christ, and why non-Jews had become the heirs of the promises made to Abraham. Without ever accepting that God had rejected his ancient people for ever (Romans 11:25–32), Paul understands the story of Israel's disobedience as designed to teach the wrath of God, his longsuffering and his grace (*vv*. 22–3), so that those who have been chosen under the New Covenant might understand the divine purposes. In quoting Isaiah 10:22–3 in verse 27, Paul gives the passage a different sense from what it means in Isaiah. For Paul, the remnant referred to is that group of Jews who have accepted Christ, and, together with non-Jews, entered the Church. Paul's experience of Christ places the pessimism of Isaiah 10:21–23 in a wider context of divine purpose.

New Testament Reading (Gospel) **Mark 13: 14–23**

It is impossible to know whether verse 14 contains a prediction by our Lord that the temple would be destroyed, or whether it was written after the destruction of the temple in A.D. 70. In either case, the verse is based upon Daniel 9:27 and its parallels, and expresses the Jewish horror of foreigners entering the temple and then desecrating it. The passage also contains other allusions to traditional Jewish images of the travail of the last days. At this time, the elect (or remnant) will be delivered (*v*. 20), even although it may sometimes find it hard to discern what is the truth (*v*. 22).

If the passage was written before A.D. 70, then the writer confused a decisive act of God with the final consummation of his kingdom. Yet there is always something of the final purpose in a decisive act of God. In A.D. 70, the destruction of the temple was a decisive part of the separation between Judaism and Christianity, on the basis of which the gospel has taken on its universal character.

First Sunday in Advent
The Advent Hope

Old Testament Reading   **Isaiah 51: 4–11**

The whole book of Isaiah is permeated with great hopes centred upon Jerusalem. But in the sixth century B.C. when Isaiah 51 was first written, the community being addressed was in exile far from Jerusalem. In these depressing circumstances, the Lord raised a prophet full of words of hope. Just as in the past God had worked great marvels in Creation and Exodus (the two themes are inextricably interwoven in *vv.* 9–10), so the people should look forward to an equally great deliverance in the future—a joyful and triumphant return to Jerusalem. All through this reading the prophet exhorts and encourages the people to prepare themselves for God's victory (or deliverance, or salvation—all three words bring out different aspects of the meaning).

Already in the New Testament there is evidence that the Christian church used 'Jerusalem' as a symbol of hope (e.g. Revelation 21). So, too, many Christian hymns have similar expressions about a 'heavenly Jerusalem'. We rightly look to a glorious life beyond death, but we must not abandon our hopes in the here-and-now. The Christian hope is concerned also with this world, and the individual Christian has to be God's transforming agent here.

New Testament Reading (Epistle)   **Romans 13: 8–end**

At first glance the two parts of this reading might seem quite unrelated to each other. In *vv.* 8–10 the summary of the Ten Commandments is concerned with ethics, how we are to live here and now. From *v.* 11 the emphasis changes to concern for the future. But the division is in our minds, not Paul's. Behaviour now and concern for the future—ethics and eschatology as they are sometimes called—were for him and must be for us all part of the one demand. Our hope for the future must dictate the way we live now;

the way we live now will demonstrate what kind of a world we really believe we inhabit.

New Testament Reading (Gospel)   **Matthew 25: 31–end**

Few Gospel parables are more liable to misinterpretation than this. Too often it is used simply as a kind of sanction for good neighbourliness, as if to be concerned for the various outcasts of society is the only important thing. In fact, the parable enshrines the same duality of behaviour now and concern for the future as the Epistle. The parable is one of judgement, reflecting the belief that judgement was imminent, that the world would shortly come to an end. It is this emphasis on judgement which lies behind the choice of this reading for Advent Sunday.

Christians today for the most part do not share the belief of those in New Testament times who expected the imminent return of Jesus to bring the present world-order to an end. Today the theme of judgement which underlay that belief must be expressed in different terms. Nevertheless, belief in judgement is a fundamental part of any Christian world-view, and all our actions must be taken in that light. The ideas of hope and of judgement are symbols expressing our belief as to the kind of world we live in: one in which there is ultimate meaning, one in which demands are made upon us. The Advent hope asks us: What kind of a world do you think you are living in?

Second Sunday in Advent
The Word of God in the Old Testament

Old Testament Reading   **Isaiah 64: 1–7**

The prophet is characteristically God's messenger, bringing his words to the people. In these verses, by contrast, the words are addressed *to* God, praying to him for help. In other words, this is really a passage like one of the psalms of lament in the Book of Psalms. These verses are only part of this 'psalm', which should be read in its entirety (Isaiah 63:7–64:12) to grasp the full force of the original. Whether the prophet himself composed this passage or incorporated an existing prayer into his words, we see him here acting as the people's representative before God, just as at other times he brought God's message to the people.

As in other psalms of lament, the theme here is the plea—almost the demand—that God should act. The Israelites knew of God's decisive saving acts at different times in their history; and when they found themselves in fresh trouble it was natural to ask for new manifestations of his power. Such a plea contains a right instinct, but it can be dangerous, for, as the prophet elsewhere points out, it is the people's own sin which is responsible for their humiliation and God's apparent lack of response.

Most important of all, however, is the testimony which these verses give to the nature of the God whom they worshipped. He might appear unpredictable, his ways hidden from human understanding, yet he was essentially just in his judgement against sin and in his welcome for those who showed any sign of turning from their evil ways.

New Testament Reading (Epistle)   **Romans 15: 4–13**

Most of us are probably ambivalent in our attitude to the Old Testament, seeing it sometimes as God's word for us, sometimes as an outdated series of precepts which can no longer be relevant. Paul's solution to this dilemma was that in itself 'the Law' had been superseded, but interpreted in the light of Christ it was still the vehicle of divine truth.

These verses enshrine this latter attitude. First, the continuing applicability of the Old Testament scriptures is stressed (*v.* 4), with the same implication as we saw in the Old Testament passage—that God's acts revealed in Scripture provided a basis for encouragement and hope. Then Paul cites a number of passages which show how the Christian may interpret those Old Testament writings in his own situation. We may feel that the quandary is not entirely removed, but an important pointer for its resolution is provided.

New Testament Reading (Gospel)   **Luke 4: 14–21**

The same principle which we saw in the Epistle, of interpreting the Old Testament scriptures in the light of Christ, is here applied by Luke to Jesus's own teaching. Quoting verses from the same section of the book of Isaiah as our own Old Testament reading was drawn from, a principle of interpretation is suggested. The lament that the prophet had uttered on the people's behalf, that God seemed inactive and indifferent to his people's misfortune, is here resoundingly answered. God has indeed acted; it is in Jesus that the answer to the people's anguish can be found. 'Good news', 'release', 'sight', 'liberty'—these powerful symbols retain their force, and the Scripture announcing their availability is fulfilled in Jesus.

Third Sunday in Advent
The Forerunner

Old Testament Reading   **Malachi 3: 1–5**

The idea of the 'day of the Lord' is a common Old Testament theme. It may have originated in a popular belief that God would intervene decisively in war against Israel's enemies, but the prophets transformed this into a warning that God's anger would be directed against his own people for their failure to recognize and carry out their obligations. The complex of ideas surrounding the 'day' gradually developed, and so here in Malachi we find, alongside the basic condemnation of all those who break the covenant (*v.* 5), an elaboration aimed against those who were in a particularly responsible position—the Levites, with their special cultic duties (*v.* 3).

A further refinement is the idea of a kind of final warning associated with the sending of a messenger. It seems as if this figure was associated with a threat of judgement, like those of the earlier prophets, warning of the consequences of the people's wrong actions. Malachi probably had no particular individual in mind, but a kind of footnote to the book (4:5) suggested that the expected messenger would be a returning Elijah, and early Christian tradition associated this messenger with both Jesus himself and with John the Baptist. For us, it may be wiser to concentrate on the stern message rather than engage in speculation about the identity of the messenger.

New Testament Reading (Epistle)   **Philippians 4: 4–9**

Paul still looked forward to a 'day of the Lord'; 'the Lord is at hand' (*v.* 5). But where the prophet had stressed the foreboding aspect, Paul is serenely confident of the outcome for those who are 'in Christ'. They should 'rejoice' and 'have no anxiety', for he knows the power of his own and their prayer. The passage lays much stress on the peace of God, and perhaps reflects the fact that Paul's relations with the Christians at Philippi seem to have caused him less anxiety than those with other churches. This passage well illustrates his serene confidence, and transforms the idea of 'the day'.

New Testament Reading (Gospel)   **Matthew 11: 2–15**

A different Christian tradition is enshrined here. The day of the Lord is not pictured as a future event; instead, the coming of Jesus had fulfilled that expectation. Verses 2–6 seem to identify Jesus with the coming messenger, but the remainder of the passage goes further and—often in enigmatic words—identifies John with the forerunner and Jesus with the one who is 'least in the kingdom of heaven'. Verse 14 seems to suggest that not everyone will accept the identification of John with Elijah—John 1:21 represents quite a different view—and *v.* 12 poses interpretive problems that have never been satisfactorily resolved. Some English translations have understood the 'violence' as a bad thing, referring to the outrages of evil men; others as a good thing, referring to the triumphant and inevitable progress of the kingdom. (Compare the text and footnotes of this verse in *Revised Standard Version*, *New English Bible*, or the *Good News Bible*.) But despite these difficulties of detail the basic message is clear: John prepared the way, and with Jesus the power of the day of the Lord has already broken in.

The tension between these three readings with their combination of the backward and the forward look is always present in the Christian world-view, and especially during Advent. We look back to Jesus, his birth and life, his death and resurrection, but we must also be looking forward. The message of the forerunner, be he Malachi's messenger or John the Baptist, is a word both of warning and of encouragement.

Fourth Sunday in Advent
The Annunciation

Old Testament Reading   **Zechariah 2: 10–end**

When we read in the opening verse of this section the direct address to the 'daughter of Zion', with the promise, 'I come and I will dwell in the midst of you', it would be easy to suppose that here in some way Mary is being prefigured, with the promise that Jesus will miraculously be implanted in her womb. To interpret this verse in such a way, however, does violence to the sense of the passage as a whole. That makes it clear that not an individual but the whole community, not an inhabitant of Jerusalem but the city as a whole, is being addressed.

This may seem to lessen the predictive element of the prophecy, but it has an important corresponding advantage. It enables us to see that the Annunciation is not a once-for-all event in the past, but an important theme with a continuing message. Three points in particular emerge from these verses which Christian communities of this and every age will need to make their own: God dwells among his people who are his own possession (*vv.* 10 and 12); this will be an example that can lead others to join the faithful community (*v.* 11); and the only proper response to these marvellous deeds is one of the deepest awe (*v.* 13).

New Testament Reading (Epistle)   **Revelation 21: 1–7**

Once again the theme of Jerusalem is found as a symbol for the whole community. Here it is a new Jerusalem, part of a new heaven and a new earth, a visible sign of the promise that all things will be made new (*v.* 5). Yet the expressions 'Alpha and Omega' (the first and last letters of the Greek alphabet), 'the beginning and the end', should not be understood merely temporally or historically; they express the completeness of God's control, manifested in Jesus and offered as free grace to all who will commit themselves to him.

The newness of which the passage speaks so vividly should not therefore be regarded simply as a future event. We have already been made new, incorporated into Christ in our baptism and committed to him in our lives. The approach of Christmas gives us an opportunity to reflect that the status of 'son of God', an expression most characteristically and appropriately applied to Jesus, is one that is offered to all of us. Our reading ends with the promise once made to the Davidic king (2 Samuel 7:14) now being applied to every Christian.

New Testament Reading (Gospel)   **Matthew 1: 18–23**

These familiar verses read at first sight like a simple story expressed in Matthew's characteristic way with an appropriate Old Testament reference, a prelude to his account of the birth of Jesus. Sometimes, or with part of ourselves, we shall love and treasure them as part of the familiar Christmas ritual; at other times, or with other parts of ourselves, we shall be embarrassed by their apparent unreality. Angels and dreams and girls having babies without sexual intercourse—all this seems light-years away from the world we live in.

Christians will differ as to how much of this story they accept as literal historical fact. But Matthew is not simply naive. The heart of this reading is *v.* 21: Jesus as saving his people from sin. The opening verses of the gospel are the family-tree, preserved not out of genealogical interest, but as showing Jesus to be the heir to the Old Testament hopes which had so regularly been thwarted. Just as the new Jerusalem theme in the other readings meant that there was hope once more for a despairing people, so the birth of Jesus brought new hope of deliverance to a people from whom hope had almost disappeared.

Christmas Eve

Old Testament Reading   **Isaiah 62: 1–5**

In the first verse God announces his plan through the prophet: that it is his intention to bring deliverance to his people from all their miseries. For Christians that deliverance is to be found in the mission and message of Jesus, who has brought that salvation of which the prophet speaks.

The remaining verses are the prophet's reflection on the meaning of this great promise. It will be a cause for marvelling all over the world, it will bring joy to those formerly desolate and forsaken, there will be all the signs of rejoicing. Here too it is natural and proper for the Christian to see that the birth of Jesus was the event above all others which brought this transforming power into the world. On Christmas Eve, the Christian can look forward, like the prophet, in the confident assurance of God's power at work.

But it is noteworthy that the prophet is addressing Zion, or Jerusalem, pictured as representing a community, the whole people of God. The marvellous acts of God were to be reflected in the nature of his people, pictured in vivid metaphors as 'a crown of beauty', 'a royal diadem'. The transformation that we believe to have taken place through Jesus is one that is demanded in the life of the whole community of believers.

New Testament Reading (Epistle)   **Acts 13: 16–26**

The prophet had spoken of God's transforming plan in the language of vivid metaphor. Now we find a different way of setting out the acts of God. Paul in these words to his fellow Jews gives an outline of the history of his people showing how all the promises made to David are now fulfilled in his descendant Jesus. Not only that, but the words of Jesus's great contemporary, John the Baptist, also pointed to Jesus as the one promised by God.

The reference to John brings out another point which made Paul's speech a stumbling-block to its original hearers and can still have the same effect today. John's preaching was 'a baptism of repentance' (*v.* 24). Only those who had acknowledged their unworthiness and were open to receive God's forgiveness would be able to recognize and welcome Jesus.

New Testament Reading (Gospel)   **Luke 1: 67–79**

The gospel reading will be most familiar to many as the canticle *Benedictus*, used at Morning Prayer. It is, in effect, a Psalm, closely similar in style to the hymns in the Psalter, and especially to the doxologies at the end of some of the Old Testament Psalms (e.g. Ps. 72: 18–19).

Two basic themes run through this hymn. The first is that God is faithful to his promises of old, an idea vividly expressed in *vv.* 72–73. The covenant and the promise made long ago have not been forgotten; God has remained loyal, and so must his people (*v.* 75). The second is that these promises are now on the point of being fulfilled. God *has* visited and redeemed his people; he *has* brought salvation. The hope for a new son of David is now achieved, and in the closing verses the child John (in thanksgiving for whose birth the hymn is sung) is pictured in markedly less stern terms than elsewhere in the gospels. Here he is the one who draws people to Jesus, and, though there are darker shadows ahead, it is appropriate at Christmas to stress this note of hope:

> To give light to those who sit in darkness
> and the shadow of death,
> to guide our feet into the way of peace.

Christmas Day

Old Testament Reading   **Isaiah 9: 2, 6, 7**

The prophet is so certain of the future that he speaks of it as having already happened. What is certain for him is Yahweh's eternal covenant with David that Yahweh's own king should sit on David's throne. In the light of this the prophet speaks of him in the language reserved in Israel for the ideal king—the Son of God and godlike, wise, powerful, exercising fatherly care and bringing harmony and well-being (peace). For Christians the ideal became actual in Jesus, the Christ, the King.

New Testament Reading (Epistle)   **Titus 2: 11–14, 3: 3–7**

Two statements of the coming of God in Jesus as 'epiphany' (appearing)—a word commonly used of the godlike Roman emperor. In the first epiphany God's goodness and philanthropy (love of mankind) was at work in the gift to men of his salvation, in a second birth as God's children, and in the renewal of their life by the Spirit. The gifts of salvation and renewal both discipline us now to a godly life in this world, and also direct our minds to the second epiphany in glory, when God in Christ finishes and consummates what he has begun in us.

New Testament Reading (Gospel)   **Luke 2: 1–14**

All unwittingly the emperor in Rome, the lord of the world, brings it about that a humble pair from Nazareth come to Bethlehem, the city of king David, because the man was of Davidic stock. There in the humblest circumstances a child is born. To the lowliest (shepherds were little thought of at the time) the birth is revealed from God as that of the highest—the birth of the one who is to be Christ, Israel's true Davidic king, and Lord, the true bearer of God's authority among men. Through it there passes praise from earth to God and peace (true well-being) from heaven to men.

Alternative Readings

Old Testament Reading   **Isaiah 62: 10–12**

The city of Jerusalem stands for God's people, for it is there that the God of Israel is worshipped as a present God. His presence is known through his deeds, in which he will deliver his people from what oppresses them and will restore them, so that they may belong to him and live with him. Then the people will stream into the city to worship him.

New Testament Reading (Epistle)   **1 John 4: 7–14**

God is invisible. Who he is, is spelt out to us in what he does. His supreme deed is to give us his Son. This spells love. So God not merely loves, but is himself love. There is no other God to be known. But to know him is to share in his life, to have his abiding presence, to reproduce his character, and so to love. Love communicates, gives, and transmits itself. To love one another is to live the life of God, to have the life of God living in us.

New Testament Reading (Gospel)   **Luke 2: 8–20**

The birth of Jesus, like his life and preaching, is 'gospel'. That is, God's own good news, and so the cause of the greatest possible joy. It is so because it is the birth of the one who in his life and preaching, his death and resurrection, is to be the messiah or king of Israel whom God has led his people to expect, and is to be the Lord, who will rule over men and in men in God's own way. Because it is God's good news, only God can convey it to men, and this he does to his humble ones by means of heavenly visions.

Alternative Readings

Old Testament Reading   **Micah 5: 2–4**

In the purpose of God greatness and littleness are found side by side. The littleness is of men. Bethlehem is insignificant as a place. The greatness is of God, who will bring out of Bethlehem the ideal ruler of Israel, of which David of old was a type. He will rule with the qualities of a shepherd like David; under his rule all will return home, and there will be no limit to his sway. So the prophet discerns in his own way the rule of God in Christ.

New Testament Reading (Epistle)   **Hebrews 1: 1–5 (6–12)**

The first four verses are in the Greek a single sentence. It is the most carefully written, and the most closely packed, sentence in the New Testament, setting forth what the divine Sonship of the man Jesus had come to mean for Christians. It is a word of God to men, single and final as compared with the many and fragmentary words of God in the prophets. It stretches from beginning to end, since as God's Son he is the world's creator, preserves it in its course, and has its ultimate destiny in his hands. As Son he reproduces as directly as may be on earth the nature and character of God himself. His work on earth completed, he shares the divine throne itself. With this not even those closest to God can compare. (To underline this last the author contrasts Jesus the Son with the angels by applying to him statements from the Old Testament which there were originally applied to God.)

New Testament Reading (Gospel)   **John 1: 1–14**

A hymn of the divine Sonship of the man Jesus, providing the key to the gospel story of his life which is to follow. He is the Word—God's self-utterance—and has been so always. To hear him is to hear God. He has shared in the creation of the world, and the world is his world. In him is the way to live in it and the way to understand it, and nothing in the world can master that. Heralded by the Baptist he came as man to his own possession, the world, and to his special people Israel. Entering into the life of the world, he so lives it as the Son of the Father as to make the splendour and life of God visible. But more, in those who take him to themselves he is able to reproduce his own sonship, to give them a new life and the true life from God.

Sunday after Christmas Day
The Presentation of Christ

Old Testament Reading   **1 Samuel 1: 20–end**

Samuel is the last of the judges or saviours of Israel from her enemies and the first of her prophets, the one who is to be Yahweh's agent in giving Israel a king—first Saul, then David. His conception is the gift of God in response to urgent prayer of the barren Hannah in the sanctuary at Shiloh, where the ark of the Lord was kept. She not only performs the regular sacrifice in relation to a first-born son, but goes further and offers the boy himself to Yahweh in the form of his being from childhood the personal attendant of the priest of the sanctuary. (Her thanksgiving which follows is the model for Mary's *Magnificat*).

New Testament Reading (Epistle)   **Romans 12: 1–8**

The point in this epistle where Paul passes from expounding the gospel of the grace of God in Christ for all men, to expounding its consequences ('therefore') for living. These consequences are summed up as 'offering' and 'sacrifice', which are here given a deeply spiritual and personal meaning. Christians—not individually but together—are to offer to God, not the blood of a dead animal, but their own selves (the body for Paul means the self). This sacrifice is alive because they possess God's Spirit. It is their rational worship, because it is what they are made for and alone makes sense of life. It involves a radical change of thinking from what is natural in the world, with its self-regard, to what is centred on God and his will. It begins to be learnt and exercised in the corporate life of the body of Christ, where the spiritual capacities of each are not for himself but for the whole.

New Testament Reading (Gospel) **Luke 2: 22–40**

The first event in the life of the babe Jesus after his naming and circumcision. The story begins as the purification of Mary after childbirth required by Jewish law by means of a sacrifice in the Temple—in her case the sacrifice of the poor who could not afford a lamb. It continues, however, as a story (modelled on that of Hannah and Samuel) of the presentation of the babe to the Lord—though it is not clear what this means. There he and his future destiny as Israel's messiah and redeemer are recognized by two representatives of the pious in Israel, a man and a woman. This recognition is divinely inspired, in the case of Simeon by the Spirit, in the case of Anna by the gift of prophecy. It is a mark of Luke's account of the births of John and Jesus that they were accompanied by a rebirth in Israel of prophecy and by the presence of the Spirit. Simeon's recognition is more precise, seeing the coming salvation as involving the Gentiles as well as Israel, and a unique participation in it of Mary the mother.

Second Sunday after Christmas
Christ the Light of the World

Old Testament Reading   **Isaiah 60: 1–6**

Jerusalem and the Temple have been restored by Yahweh from destruction. He has done this by his light and glory, that is, his effective power and presence. Jerusalem is to reflect this, and so to become the centre of the world. She is to attract the nations out of their darkness, and they will come there to praise Yahweh for his acts, bringing with them their wealth to beautify her. With them will also come the Jews who have been exiled amongst them.

New Testament Reading (Epistle)   **Revelation 21: 22–22: 5**

The heavenly Jerusalem—the polity of God and the ultimate dwelling place of men. It is established by God himself through Christ, the Lamb, who is completely associated with him. It does not contain a Temple, being itself all Temple; nor does it contain light, being constituted by the Light himself. The presence of God is ubiquitous and permanent; the worship of him is personal and immediate. The city's scope is universal and all-embracing. It includes all nations and their secular life, once that has been cleansed of its hostility to God. The sacred and the secular are there one.

New Testament Reading (Gospel)   **Matthew 2: 1–12, 19–23**

Two stories from the five which Matthew has of the birth of Jesus.

The first story attests, by a combination of celestial sign and Scripture, the birth as that of the expected Jewish messiah in its most national form of 'the Son of David'. Magi were representatives of the astronomical-astrological wisdom of the East. They are directed by this wisdom to Jerusalem in search of Israel's messiah. Expressed in secular, political form as 'the king of the Jews', this arouses the hostility not only of Herod, the cruel and hated Edomite king of Judea, but also of the Jerusalem he rules. They are further directed by scrutiny of Scripture to Bethlehem; and, guided by the star to the exact spot, do homage with their wealth.

The second story, also by a combination of supernatural guidance and Scripture, accounts for a paradox. Returning as refugees from Egypt the holy family is divinely guided out of the reach of Herod's successor in Judea. Hence it comes about that Israel's messiah does not perform his work in the land of Israel in Judea, with its centre at the holy city (which is to reject him), but in the outlying and semi-heathen region of Galilee, and from residence in Nazareth—a town not found in the Old Testament and not mentioned in literature before the gospels. It remains a mystery how and where Matthew finds 'in the prophets' that the messiah was to be a Nazarene.

The Epiphany

Old Testament Reading   **Isaiah 49: 1–6**

Israel (speaking as an individual) announces to the peoples her status
and vocation. It is God who has brought her secretly into being as the
servant of his purpose, and to make him known as God. He has given
her his word as a prophet, and supplied her with his strength to fulfil
her calling. This calling has been to bring about the true Israel, all
that God's people has it in them to be, and this is still her calling,
despite any failure. But now this service is to be extended. As the
servant of the God of the world, she is given a mission to mankind to
be saved—brought into a living relation with the God of Israel—and
to be brought the light of God's truth.

New Testament Reading (Epistle)   **Ephesians 3: 1–12**

Paul, the servant of God and his steward, peculiarly entrusted with
dispensing the good news of God's free gift and empowered by God,
speaks from prison to the Gentile world concerning the 'mystery' of
Christ. The mystery means the eternal plan which the Creator has
for mankind and for the universe. Its full scope and depth have
previously remained hidden, and even now are not fully plumbed.
Yet they have been unveiled in what the Spirit has taught to the
missionaries of the gospel and to Christian prophets, and especially
to Paul himself. The mystery is, first, universal. It embraces mankind in the common sharing of salvation by believing Gentile and
believing Israel, and their union in Christ in a single body. But it also
embraces the universe. Through the existence of this one body in the
world the multi-faceted truth of God is made known to whatever
spiritual and heavenly powers there may be.

New Testament Reading (Gospel) **Matthew 2: 1–12:** see above, p. 190

First Sunday after Epiphany
Revelation: The Baptism of Jesus

Christmas is a Jewish event; the manger birth, the visit of the local shepherds. Here is Jesus, 'the glory of his people Israel'. Epiphany, the coming of the Wise Men, is a world event. Here is Jesus, 'A light to lighten the Gentiles'.

The Greek word *epiphaino* means 'to show forth'. The word 'Revelation' in the title of each of these six Sundays means exactly the same, but is taken from a Latin instead of a Greek word. These are weeks of 'the showing forth' of Christ. Thus, traditionally, they have always had a missionary flavour: 'Christ for the world we sing'.

Old Testament Reading   Isaiah 42: 1–7

This is the first of the four Servant Songs in the Book of Isaiah. Through suffering humbly and lovingly borne, the Servant will establish God's righteousness in the earth. Christians have always seen in these poems a character sketch of Jesus. 'I will put my spirit upon him' (*v.* 1) reminds us straightaway of Jesus's Baptism, which is our theme today. 'A light to the nations' (*v.* 6) reminds us of the Epiphany world theme of Epiphany season. Verse 7 reminds us of the first sermon with which Jesus began his ministry (Luke 4:18).

New Testament Reading (Epistle)   Ephesians 2: 1–10

This passage is almost a summary of the Gospel as Paul preached it, namely, that we are saved entirely by God's grace, received through faith. The phrase is repeated twice in the reading.

Paul's other great theme is the union of the believer with Christ. The Christian has died with Christ to sin, and has been raised with him to a new and endless life, a life which looks towards God. Baptism is the image Paul uses to convey this teaching. 'We were buried, therefore, with him by baptism into death, so that as Christ was raised from the dead by the glory of the Father, we too might walk in newness of life' (Romans 6:4).

So, in this reading, we who were dead in our trespasses and sins have been made alive. We who once followed the spirit at work in the sons of disobedience have received the Holy Spirit who descended on Jesus at his Baptism, and who unites us to Christ.

New Testament Reading (Gospel) **John 1: 29–34**

The Fourth Gospel tells the story of Jesus's Baptism in its own way, different from the first three. John the Baptist has a smaller part. He is used to give the distinctive witness of this Gospel to who Jesus is. 'Behold the Lamb of God who takes away the sin of the world.' That is who Jesus is: the true Paschal Lamb, the Lamb of our deliverance who releases us from the Egypt of our sins (see Exodus, ch. 12.)

There are two different readings of *v.* 34 in the ancient manuscripts. Most read 'I have borne witness that this is the Son of God'. But some of the very oldest read '. . . have borne witness that this is God's chosen one'. The translators of the *New English Bible* thought this was the better reading. If it is, it takes us straight back to today's First Reading: 'Behold my servant . . . my chosen in whom my soul delights'. Jesus is both the true Paschal Lamb, and also the true Servant of the Lord, the Suffering Servant, as we call him.

Jesus, Lamb of God: have mercy on us.
Jesus, bearer of our sins: have mercy on us.
Jesus, redeemer of the world: give us your peace.

Second Sunday after Epiphany
Revelation: The First Disciples

The three readings all make the same point, namely that the initiative lies with God. Samuel did not realise that God was calling him. Paul was stopped dead in his tracks and turned face about on the Damascus road. Nathaniel—'Can anything good come out of Nazareth!'—had to be convinced almost against his will. We talk of our search for God, and difficulty in finding him. The truth is God's difficulty in getting through to us. 'You did not choose me, but I chose you', says Jesus.

Old Testament Reading   **1 Samuel 3: 1–10**

Samuel was a child of promise, born to a mother who had for long years been barren. She had promised in her pleading with God that if she bore a son, she would 'give him to the Lord'. So, from childhood, Samuel remained in the temple serving the old priest Eli.

Spiritually, things were at a low ebb in Israel. 'The word of God was rare, there was no frequent vision.' But God was not absent. The child Samuel whose spiritual life began with the call we read about in this reading was chosen by God to be his prophet, and the great king-maker in Israel. He anointed Saul the first king, and when he fell from grace, anointed in his place David the greatest of all Israel's kings and the forefather of the Messiah.

New Testament Reading (Epistle)   **Galatians 1: 11–end**

When Paul wrote this letter, both he and his gospel were under attack. His enemies said that he was not a true apostle at all. Here Paul lays down his credentials. He had been called directly by the Risen Christ and sent to the Gentiles. It is interesting that immediately after his call, he withdrew into solitude to meditate on what had happened, just as Jesus withdrew to the desert immediately after his baptism. This is the true pattern of spirituality. Every great spiritual experience needs to be followed by a time for reflection.

We need not worry that Paul's account of his movements here cannot be fully reconciled with Luke's references in Acts. Both men had better and bigger things to do than keep accurate records of their movements over the years.

New Testament Reading (Gospel)   **John 1: 35–end**

Straight after the story of Jesus's baptism, John gives us his account of the call of the first disciples. We might note the humility of John, who willingly allows two of his disciples to leave him and follow Jesus. We may also note that whenever we meet Andrew in this Gospel, he is bringing somebody to Jesus (1:41; 6:9; 12:22). We may note too the way that the Jacob theme runs through the call of Nathaniel. 'Behold an Israelite in whom is no guile', says Jesus. Israel ('ruling with God') was the new name God gave to Jacob (Genesis 32:28). 'Guile' or 'supplanter' was the meaning of his old name, Jacob. The final verse of our reading also refers back to the story of Jacob at Bethel (Genesis 28:10–22).

In the Bible, names indicate character, and to be given a new name means to receive a new nature or character. In this reading Jesus also gives Simon a new name—Cephas (Aramaic) or Peter (Greek), which means a rock.

Lord, open my eyes that I may see what you want me to see: open my ears that I may hear what you are saying to me: open my heart that I may respond to you: open my lips that I may praise you and bear witness to you before others. Amen.

Third Sunday after Epiphany
Revelation: Signs of Glory

Today's readings teach us to think of material things as signs of a greater spiritual reality. The Manna (Exodus 16:1–21) came at the extremity of the Israelites' need, when they were famished with hunger as they journeyed through the wilderness to the Promised Land. It was a sign of God's care for them.

In the same way, Paul receives the material gift which the Philippians sent him as a sign of their concern for him, and of the bond of love which united them and him, even when they were separated.

Whether the feeding of the five thousand was literally a miracle or not, the richness of the story certainly lies in its hidden depths. The whole of chapter 6 in John's Gospel is full of echoes of the Manna in the wilderness. It was Passover time (v. 4), the time of deliverance when Israel had set out from Egypt. There are four extended references in the chapter to the Manna in the wilderness (vv. 31–34; 41–42; 48–51; 53–59). The feeding of the five thousand is a sacramental sign of Messiahship. Jesus is the new Moses who delivers us from the Egypt of our sins into the freedom of the sons of God.

All this leads us straight away to think of the bread and wine of our Communion as the sign of God's care for us; the Manna in the wilderness given to sustain us on our journey to the Promised Land.

Old Testament Reading   **Deuteronomy 8: 1–6**

The sufferings of the journey through the wilderness are seen as God's testing and refining of his People (cf. 1 Peter 1:6–7), so that they may learn to be humble and to look beyond material things to God their giver. Our appointed passage is a prelude to the warning not to be lifted up and forget God when prosperity comes (vv. 11–14). The Bible teaches that the material world is good, but the danger is that we are tempted to seek our satisfaction in it, and not in God; and also that material prosperity tempts us to develop a proud self-sufficiency (cf. Luke 12:16–21).

New Testament Reading (Epistle)   **Philippians 4: 10–20**

This is a perfect commentary on the Old Testament Reading. Paul does not seek his satisfaction in material things. 'I have learned, in whatever state I am, to be content . . . I have learned the secret of facing plenty and hunger, abundance and want.' The secret he has learned is that our sufficiency is not in material things, but in God. 'I can do all things in him who strengthens me.'

New Testament Reading (Gospel)   **John 6: 1–14**

This is the only miracle recorded in all four Gospels. There are suggestions that its real meaning lies deep below the surface. In none of the accounts is it directly said that Jesus multiplied the loaves and fishes. In Mark's account the language reminds us time and again of the Last Supper and of the Breaking of Bread in the early Church (cf. Mark 6:41 and 14:22). In Luke, it looks forward to the Messianic Feast which will be consummated 'when he comes' (cf. 1 Corinthians 11:26). In this Gospel it is knit into a chapter full of references to the Manna in the wilderness and God's deliverance of his People from slavery.

> *Guide me, O thou great Redeemer,*
> *Pilgrim through this barren land;*
> *I am weak, but thou art mighty;*
> *Hold me with thy powerful hand:*
> *Bread of heaven,*
> *Feed me now and evermore.*

199

Fourth Sunday after Epiphany
Revelation: The New Temple

The key to today's theme is Jesus's sentence in the Gospel, 'The hour is coming and now is, when the true worshippers will worship the Father in spirit and truth . . . God is Spirit and those who worship him must worship in spirit and truth'.

The Epistle makes the same point in its last verse, 'Let us be grateful for receiving a kingdom that cannot be shaken, and thus let us offer to God acceptable worship, with reverence and awe'.

Jeremiah teaches the same lesson in the Old Testament Reading. It is no use trusting in earthly temples. An earthly temple, with even the best rituals and services, can never bring us close to God if we are far from him in spirit.

Old Testament Reading   **Jeremiah 7: 1–11**

The fatal mistake of the Jews in Jeremiah's time was to think that no power on earth could harm them because they were God's chosen people. The symbol of this was the Temple in Jerusalem. God was bound to protect them because he could not possibly let his own Temple be destroyed.

This is false, says Jeremiah. God is not tied to his Temple, or to his Chosen People. As he rejected the earlier shrine at Shiloh for the evil of its worshippers, so he will reject them and the Temple in Jerusalem, unless they repent of their evil ways (Jeremiah 7:8–12). Within a few years Jeremiah was proved right. Nebuchadnezzar razed the Temple to the ground and carried the Jews off into exile in Babylon.

New Testament Reading (Epistle)   **Hebrews 12: 18–end**

The philosopher Plato taught that the real things are spiritual and eternal. Earthly things are only copies or shadows of the eternal realities. The writer of this Epistle thinks in a rather similar way of the Old Covenant under Moses and the New Covenant in Christ.

The covenant on Mount Sinai came with awe and splendour, but Jesus brings us to Mount Zion, the heavenly reality, of which the earthly mountain is but a shadow. If those who refused to respond to God's call through Moses did not reach the Promised Land, how much more important is it that we should not refuse to hear God's call in Christ, which comes from Heaven itself.

New Testament Reading (Gospel) **John 4: 19–26**

When the Jews returned from their exile in Babylon, they debarred the Samaritans from the Temple which they re-built in Jerusalem. The Samaritans set up a rival sanctuary on Mount Gerizim which was also a holy mountain, associated with Joshua and the blessing of the people of Israel. This sanctuary had been destroyed a hundred years before Jesus was born, but the Jews and Samaritans still wrangled about which was the true shrine.

Jesus and the woman could see Mount Gerizim from where they were sitting. Perhaps she brought the subject up as a talking point to fend off this uncomfortable stranger. Jesus does not argue with her as she expected, but lifts the issue to a higher plane.

Almighty God, we come to you through Jesus Christ, that living Stone, rejected by men yet chosen and precious in your sight: grant that we, like living stones, may be built into a spiritual temple, to worship you in spirit and truth; through the same Christ our Lord.

Fifth Sunday after Epiphany
Revelation: The Wisdom of God

The Wisdom of the Greeks was speculative philosophy, such as we find in Plato and Aristotle. But this kind of philosophy was totally foreign to the Hebrew mind. The Jews never speculated about the existence or Being of God. God was the point from which all their thinking started, and God was the source of all wisdom. 'Whence comes wisdom? And where is the place of understanding? . . . God understands the way to it, and he knows its place' (Job 28:20f). The last verse of this same chapter sums up the Hebrew attitude: 'And he said to man, "Behold, the fear of the Lord, that is wisdom; and to depart from evil is understanding"' (Job 28:28). Thus, Hebrew wisdom is rooted in a right attitude to God, and is moral and practical rather than speculative.

In some places, Wisdom is treated almost as a person who was with God at Creation. 'The Lord created me at the beginning of his work . . . before he made the earth with its fields . . . When he established the heavens I was there' (Proverbs 8:22f). The prologue to the Fourth Gospel could be said to be the crown of Hebrew Wisdom literature. The Wisdom (Word) which was with God in Creation has become flesh in Jesus.

The readings today present us with a challenge to choose God's way, the way of Wisdom, and to live for him.

Old Testament Reading   **Proverbs 2: 1–9**

The best commentary on this reading might well be found in John: 'If any man's will is to do his will, he shall know whether the teaching is from God' (John 7:17). The wisdom of God is revealed to those who will 'seek it like silver and search for it as for hidden treasures' (*v.* 4).

or   **Ecclesiasticus 42: 15–end**

One of the outstanding things about the Book of Ecclesiasticus is the poetic beauty of its language. This passage is a beautiful hymn of praise of the wisdom of God. No thought escapes him. He is from everlasting to everlasting. He knows all that may be known.

New Testament Reading (Epistle)   **1 Corinthians 3: 18–end**

Paul contrasts the false wisdom of an age which is in rebellion against God, with true wisdom which begins with obedience to God. 'The fear of the Lord is the beginning of wisdom' (Proverbs 9:10).

New Testament Reading (Gospel)   **Matthew 12: 38–42**

The question of the unforgivable sin, or the sin against the Holy Spirit, has worried many people. The sin against the Holy Spirit is to call good evil. The Pharisees saw Jesus heal a man who was both dumb and blind, and said, 'This is the work of the devil'.

The reason why such a person cannot be forgiven is that while he is in that state, he cannot repent and ask for forgiveness. If he cannot recognize the good when he sees it, he cannot desire it, and if he cannot recognize evil as being evil, he cannot turn away from it. The whole reading is a challenge to see the wisdom of God in Jesus and to turn to him.

O Wisdom which camest out of the mouth of the Most High, and reachest from one end to another, mightily and sweetly ordering all things: come, and teach us the way of prudence.

YEAR TWO

Sixth Sunday after Epiphany
Revelation: Parables

In the Bible, 'parable' can mean anything from a proverb or pithy saying, 'Physician heal thyself', through a similitude such as 'The Kingdom of heaven is like leaven which a woman took and hid in three measures of meal, till it was all leavened', to the full blown story such as The Prodigal Son.

The heart of the matter is the likeness between the natural and the spiritual world. The simple definition 'an earthly story with a heavenly meaning' is not far wrong. Jesus is the master of parables. Apart from him, fully developed parables are few. Jesus's parables are without compare: simple and beautiful stories on the natural level, they yet carry depth after depth of spiritual meaning.

Old Testament Reading   **2 Samuel 12: 1–10**

David committed adultery with Bathsheba while her husband Uriah was away at the war. Hoping to cover it, David summoned Uriah home. But he refused to sleep with his wife whilst his comrades were suffering danger and hardship. The ploy having failed, David arranged Uriah's death, and then married Bathsheba.

Nathan's parable illustrates one quality of parables which Jesus used to perfection. The parable demands an opinion on its own natural level. The listener gives it, 'The man who has done this deserves to die', without realizing that he has lowered his guard and left himself defenceless. Before he is aware of it, the sword thrust has gone home: 'Thou art the man!'. Compare Jesus's parables of The Two Debtors (Luke 7:41f) and The Wicked Husbandmen (Matthew 21:33f).

New Testament Reading (Epistle)   **Romans 1: 18–25**

This reading teaches us something about the theological basis underlying teaching by parables. Because God is the author of the kingdom of nature and of grace, the natural world can be a window through which we can see into the nature and the mind of God. The love of an earthly father for his son, and his joy in forgiving him, can show us something of the nature and the mind of God. The whole world can be a parable. 'Ever since the creation of the world his invisible nature . . . has been clearly perceived in the things that have been made.' But,—and here Paul is talking about the Gentiles—instead of seeing through the world to God, men have worshipped images resembling mortal man or birds or animals or reptiles.

New Testament Reading (Gospel)   **Matthew 13: 24-30**

This parable appears only in Matthew. Bearded darnel is a poisonous weed which is closely related botanically to bearded wheat and closely resembles it, especially in the early stages of growth.

'Reapers' (*v.* 30) are employed extra to the usual servants at harvest time. The weeds are bound in bundles to be dried and used for fuel. Palestine lacks forests, and fuel is scarce.

A parable usually makes one main point. We are not to press every detail of it. The main point here seems to be patience with the very mixed situation of good and evil in the Christian community. We are not to try to purge the Church down to a 'pure' sect. We cannot see into the heart as God can. True and false believers are as confusingly alike as wheat and darnel. Further, evil and good are so intertwined and intermingled now that we cannot root out the one without damaging the other. Therefore, we are to judge nothing before the time until the Lord comes who will bring to light the things now hidden . . . (1 Corinthians 4:5f).

'Earth's crammed with heaven and every common bush aflame with God . . .' Lord, give me eyes to see and a heart to understand.

Ninth Sunday before Easter
Christ the Teacher

We are all familiar with the role of the teacher as imparter of information and guide of character. Jesus shows himself to be one of the best kind of teachers—those who encourage their pupils to think things out for themselves and learn through their own perception and responses. He also underlines the importance of receptiveness in the pupil if the teaching is to be effective.

Old Testament Reading   **Proverbs 3: 1–8**

In the Old Testament teaching was always related to life in a practical way, and never reduced to the mere acquisition of facts for their own sake. This accounts for the strong emphasis on moral qualities such as loyalty, and spiritual qualities such as humble dependence on God's guidance. Qualities such as these lead indirectly to success in human relationships and in the conduct of life generally. Of particular importance is the injunction not to be wise in one's own eyes; such an attitude immediately undermines the humble receptiveness which is essential if God's guidance is to be discerned.

New Testament Reading (Epistle)   **1 Corinthians 2: 1–10**

In the cosmopolitan university city of Corinth Paul was at pains not to present the Christian message as a product of human wisdom, in other words as just one more philosophy of life. He could never forget that God vastly exceeds the scope of human comprehension, and presented himself as a witness to God's mysterious and eternal purpose which was even now coming to fulfilment in Christ. In particular the crucifixion, at first sight incomprehensible to human intelligence, was the focal point of God's activity. But Paul does not despise wisdom as such, only the proud and independent wisdom of men; to those who have accepted the Gospel in humility and faith, he speaks the wisdom of God as revealed through the Spirit.

New Testament Reading (Gospel) **Luke 8: 4–15**

This is one of Jesus's parables which seems most clearly to have allegorical meaning. It is not so much a parable of the Sower as of the different kinds of soil on which the seed is sown. Just as, for one reason or another, the farmer's seed does not always produce a crop, so God's message can fail to find a response in men's minds and hearts for different reasons. In the first instance the parable seems to be addressed to the deceptive appearances of Jesus's popular following: not all the crowds who come eagerly to hear his teaching will in fact assimilate it and respond with a 'fruitful' life. On some it makes only a momentary impression; others lack the staying power when discipleship begins to make costly demands; yet others are preoccupied with the affairs of everyday life. But there are always some who respond, and these are characterized as those who come to the teaching with an honest and good heart, and put it into practice with patient perseverance. To those who do not respond in this way the teaching remains obscure; yet for those who are prepared to think out the implications, the message is clear, and to such it is given to know the secrets of God's kingdom.

Lord Jesus, help us to come to you as our Teacher in a spirit of humble receptiveness. Guide us by your Spirit as we ponder your teaching, and show us how to apply it in our lives, so that we may be wise in God's eyes, and help us to remove the obstacles in our hearts and minds which prevent us from bringing forth fruit with patience, for the glory of your holy name.

Eighth Sunday before Easter
Christ the Healer

In recent years we have come to recognize that physical health cannot be isolated from mental and spiritual health, and that there is an important relationship also between health and harmony in personal relationships. Jesus is portrayed in the Gospels not only as the healer of physical disease, but also as the healer of human personalities, and the one who brings reconciliation between God and man, and between man and his fellow man. Healing is thus seen as the restoration of wholeness, which is God's will for every man.

Old Testament Reading   **2 Kings 5: 1–14**

In the ancient world the disease called leprosy, which is not identical with modern leprosy, was particularly harmful because of the isolation it entailed for its victims. The Israelite king's question shows that the healing of disease was regarded as a divine power, comparable to the conferring of life itself. Elisha prescribed the treatment which Naaman must undergo if he wished to receive divine healing, and Naaman's first instinct was to despise the suggested procedure. But he was humble and wise enough to heed his servants' advice and thus put himself in the way of receiving divine healing. We too must never despise the appointed means of grace, lest we forfeit God's grace itself.

New Testament Reading (Epistle)   **2 Corinthians 12: 1–10**

Paul is presenting his credentials as an apostle in comparison with some false apostles who keep parading their spiritual experience and authority. In the course of his statement he tells of his experience over a sharp physical pain, which he regards as of Satanic origin, and which was proving a hindrance in his apostolic ministry. Three times, he tells us, he prayed for this to be removed. But God's answer to his prayer was even better than the healing he desired. The pain made him continually conscious of his own weakness and dependence on God's strength, and thus he became more receptive than ever to God's power at work within him. This teaches us that healing can take different forms, and does not always result in the removal of physical pain or disease.

New Testament Reading (Gospel)   **Mark 7: 24–end**

Mark recounts two of Jesus's healing miracles, both typical but showing some special features. Both healings are performed in answer to prayer offered by others on behalf of the patient. The Syro-Phoenician woman's faith is severely tested and found to possess the qualities of humility and perseverance as well as confidence. Her daughter's illness is treated as a case of demon-possession and, whatever precisely we make of this, this healing illustrates Jesus's ministry as a victory of the Kingdom of God over the powers of evil that threaten to spoil men's lives (see Matthew 12:28). In the case of the deaf-mute, as in that of Jairus's daughter, Mark has preserved the Aramaic word addressed to the patient by Jesus—a word which is at once a command in form, and a word of release in its effect. We are reminded of Jesus's insistence on another occasion (John 5:6) that a patient should genuinely want to be healed as part of the receptiveness of true faith, without which healings are impossible (Mark 6:5, 6).

> *Thy touch has still its ancient power;*
> *No word from thee can fruitless fall.*

O Son of Man, sharer of our weakness and healer of our infirmity, help us to come to you with a simple, humble, and persevering faith, and to put ourselves into your hands without reserve, that we may experience your healing power in our lives, and be reconciled to God and to one another in the fellowship of your Church, to the glory of your holy Name.

Seventh Sunday before Easter
Christ the Friend of Sinners

Numerous passages in the Old Testament bear witness to the struggle within Israel to maintain racial and religious purity. Unfortunately this was often considered more important than Israel's function as a witness of God to the Gentile world, and by Jesus's time the narrow puritan emphasis was dominant. While a good Pharisee refrained from the contamination of contact with sinners, and remained aloof in his self-conscious devotion to God, Jesus shocked public opinion by befriending sinners and redeeming them by what has been called his 'transforming friendship'.

Old Testament Reading   **Numbers 15: 32–36**

This passage illustrates the sense in which Paul found that the Law, though in itself good, had the practical effect of bringing men under condemnation. The Sabbath, which according to Jesus's teaching was a merciful provision of rest from daily toil, is already seen here as an obligation, the penalty for whose infringement is exclusion from the people of God and death.

New Testament Reading (Epistle)   **Colossians 1: 18–23**

The Christian Gospel brings a completely different message: in place of condemnation, exclusion, and death, Christ came to bring about reconciliation. This passage hints at the mystery of redemption—its cosmic scope, its achievement by Christ's sacrifice of himself on the Cross, its relation to his victory over death, its working out in his mystical body the Church, and its effect in the dedicated and consistent lives of Christian people.

New Testament Reading (Gospel)   **John 8: 2–11**

This passage, which occurs in several different places in John or even Luke in the Gospel manuscripts, seems to have circulated at first independently. It illustrates the dilemma in which the Jewish authorities more than once tried to trap Jesus. If he refused to endorse the penalty prescribed in Scripture, he would be laying himself open to the charge of setting himself above what was generally recognized to be God's Law, and thus implicitly challenging the authority of God himself. If he endorsed the penalty, he would be acting inconsistently with his general practice of befriending sinners. In fact he did neither, but brought a new factor into the situation by raising the question of the innocence of the accusers. If they themselves had broken God's Law they were hardly in a position to pass judgement on a fellow-sinner. Jesus's writing on the ground may reflect the practice of a judge recording his verdict before announcing it, or it may simply have been a device to lessen the embarrassment of all concerned. When all the accusers had disqualified themselves, Jesus, the only sinless one, declined himself to execute the sentence of the Law. But his forgiveness was no mere condoning of the woman's sin: in the same breath he charged her not to sin again.

To think over

I am often inclined to think of forgiveness merely in terms of being 'let off' a penalty and restored to favour with God, and content that Christ should have made this possible for me by his sacrifice of himself. I must learn that his friendship is not only a rescuing but a transforming one, and that as a forgiven sinner I must change my attitude to sin. Do I long earnestly enough for inner cleansing and victory over temptation, as well as for forgiveness for the sins I have already committed? Do I bring forth fruits worthy of repentance? If not, Lent affords an opportunity to deepen this side of my life.

O God, have mercy on me, sinner that I am.

Ash Wednesday

A number of alternative passages are appointed for this day, and brief notes are given on the three Old Testament Lessons together and the Epistles and Gospels separately.

Old Testament Readings   **Isaiah 58: 1–8** *or* **Joel 2: 12–17** *or* **Amos 5: 6–15**

The three lessons from the prophets share a common concern that the people should not rest content with the outward observance of religious rites such as fasting. Fasting is intended to be an expression of repentance, but genuine repentance always makes a difference to daily life. The Hebrew word for 'repent' means literally 'turn back'. The Joel passage thus points out that the repentance required by God is a broken heart and a changed life; it also shows that repentance itself is inspired by the revelation of God as gracious and compassionate, merciful and always ready to forgive. The other two prophetic passages are primarily concerned with the practical outworking of repentance in social justice. It does not require much imagination to relate this teaching to the needs of the hungry millions of our modern world, and to see how our Lenten self-denial can be a direct means of helping the under-privileged.

New Testament Reading (Epistle)   **1 Corinthians 9: 24–end**

In this passage Paul draws an analogy between the Christian life and an athlete training to compete in the sports. The difference is that the prize is not restricted to the winner! But the same kind of self-discipline and self-control are required, and find both their purpose and their inspiration in the goal of our call in Christ (see Philippians 3:13–14).

or   **James 4: 1–10**

This passage is worth reading and pondering again and again. It has much to teach us about social relationships, ambition, frustration, worldliness, and the problem of unanswered prayer. It diagnoses the root of our trouble in undisciplined and selfish desire, and a failure to turn to God in humble dependence and submission to his will. This teaching is not only fundamental practical Christianity, but acutely relevant to the pressures and tensions of modern life.

New Testament Reading (Gospel) **Matthew 6: 16–21**

This passage from the Sermon on the Mount follows Jesus's teaching about almsgiving and prayer. He makes the same point about fasting—that if it is undertaken to enhance one's reputation for sanctity it is useless. Jesus goes on to speak about our scale of values: fasting in the widest sense (self-denial in all that concerns temporal possessions and enjoyments) will strengthen our love for God and the things of God.

or **Luke 18: 9–14**

This well-known parable contrasts the attitude of the man who is complacent about the quality of his religious and social life with that of the one who recognizes the depth of his sin and failure and casts himself entirely on the mercy of God. If we are tempted to complacency, we need only to recall our Lord's summary of the Law, with its demand for love of God with our whole being and love of our neighbour as ourself, to realize the hopeless extent of our failure to live as God requires. True self-knowledge will make it impossible to exalt ourselves. We can never hope even to make adequate amends, let alone to be acquitted at God's judgement-bar on our own deserts. But by virtue of the Cross our appeal to God's mercy will never be in vain, provided we come as penitent sinners, dependent solely on his grace. This is the secret of humility, and the way to receive God's forgiveness.

First Sunday in Lent
The King and the Kingdom: Temptation

It is easy to forget that the word 'Christ' is not really a name but a title. It means 'anointed' and is a translation of the Hebrew word 'Messiah', the title of the divinely chosen King of Israel, the arrival of whose victorious rule was awaited eagerly by the Jews. To confess Jesus as the longed-for Messiah, however, is to serve one whose Kingship is 'not of this world' (John 18:36). The readings for the first five Sundays in Lent form an extended comment on the nature of Jesus's Kingship. Today, we are reminded that he must be enthroned first of all in our hearts. Only if he is, will we be able to resist, and indeed to benefit from, temptation when it comes.

Old Testament Reading   **Genesis 4: 1–10**

In this passage, sin is pictured as a demon lying in wait for Cain, who can easily be overcome because of his pride. Being a farmer, Cain is naturally suspicious of the shepherd Abel. When Abel's offering alone is accepted, Cain is crestfallen. The Epistle to the Hebrews (11:4) says that the difference between the two brothers' sacrifices was that Abel's alone was offered in faith. Cain offered his in the wrong spirit, as though it were God's duty to accept it. Cain's injured pride shows itself in his anger and jealousy, and, fuelled by these uncontrolled feelings, leads to Abel's violent death and Cain's attempt to lie to God.

New Testament Reading (Epistle)   **Hebrews 4: 12–end**

Temptation is an inner experience, a battle involving 'the thoughts and intentions of the heart', and this is why resisting it can often be so difficult. We can take comfort, however, from the fact that we have in Jesus a merciful high priest who not only understands our weakness, but understands it better even than we do ourselves. We know the power of temptation only in part, because we have frequently yielded to it. God's Son alone can know its full force, because he alone never yielded.

New Testament Reading (Gospel) **Luke 4: 1–13**

Temptation is a process of testing as well as enticement to sin. In particular, temptation always tests the reality of our relationship with God, and faithful perseverance under temptation always strengthens that relationship. The devil first tempted Jesus through his hunger. This temptation was extremely subtle, because in yielding Jesus would also have allowed doubt to creep into his relationship with God. He was then invited to accomplish God's purposes, using the devil's means, and finally his trust in God's promises was sorely tried. Jesus rebuffed the tempter with texts from Scripture, each of which refers to Israel's past failure to resist similar temptations. The point is that, where Israel yielded, God's new people will be enabled to resist, for at the heart of their life are Jesus and his cross. It is therefore significant that the closing words of this passage point forward to the cross, where the tempter was finally defeated.

Direct and rule our hearts, Lord Jesus, so that we may stand firm against temptation and grow more like you day by day.

Second Sunday in Lent
The King and the Kingdom: Conflict

The final book of the New Testament looks forward to the time when 'the kingdom of this world' will have become 'the kingdom of our Lord and of his Christ' (Revelation 11:15). God's people are called to fight continually against the evil which at present disfigures the world and must be eradicated before God's Kingdom is revealed in its fullness.

Old Testament Reading   **Genesis 7: 17–end**

The story of Noah is very closely related to other ancient tales of a world-wide flood. One of the most important differences between the biblical version and the others is that the biblical story-tellers alone interpret the flood as God's act of judgement on sinful man. The flood story gives us a symbolic picture of the inevitable consequence of rejecting God's rule. At the same time, because he is righteous, God is not only judge but also saviour, and so he preserves the family of Noah and, with them, representatives of all animal life. Noah, the one righteous man, is chosen (as his Hebrew name suggests) to be the instrument of God's plan to give mankind *rest* from their troubles.

New Testament Reading (Epistle)   **1 John 3: 1–10**

This passage attacks a distortion of Christian truth. Some people were claiming that the Christian is involved in no battle against evil, because sin can be forgiven and it is God's business to forgive. But the truth is that our hope of being like Christ rests on the fact that we are God's children already. God's children are called to become daily more like the sinless Christ, which they cannot do without opposition from the world. It is not simply a matter of the world not giving us recognition. We can expect to be hated for our discipleship.

New Testament Reading (Gospel)   **Matthew 12: 22–32**

At first sight, this passage seems to speak of three different conflicts. The first is between Jesus and the powers of evil, whom he overcomes in healing the demoniac. Secondly, there is the dispute between the Pharisees and the other bystanders: could this man who drives out evil spirits be the Messiah, or is he demonically inspired? The third conflict is between Jesus and the Pharisees: if he casts out evil spirits by the power of the prince of demons, then the same must be true of their exorcists too. If, on the other hand, his power over the evil spirits comes from God, then they must recognize it as a sign that God's kingdom has come and commit themselves wholeheartedly to the cause of that kingdom. All three conflicts in the story are intimately connected. Behind the disputes, and manifesting itself in them, is Christ's victorious battle against the powers of evil. To try to remain neutral when challenged by Christ to fight at his side is in fact to join the opposing army.

Lord Jesus, give us the strength to fight manfully under your banner against sin, the world and the devil, and to continue your faithful soldiers and servants to our life's end.

217

Third Sunday in Lent
The King and the Kingdom: Suffering

A particularly distinctive mark of Jesus's kingdom is that its citizens are called not merely to endure, but actually to rejoice under suffering (Romans 5:3). Such rejoicing would be impossible, had our king himself not suffered. In suffering, we are free to tread Christ's own path to glory, and to grow in faith, hope, and love.

Old Testament Reading **Genesis 12: 1-9**

Because the world is sunk in sin, Abram's response to God's call is bound to involve him in suffering. But the call itself is not to suffering. God's plan is for salvation. He calls Abram in order to bless him and, through him, all mankind. The suffering Abram experiences most acutely as he responds to God's call is the feeling of uncertainty. Having left Haran with faith in God's promises, he soon finds himself wondering whether this God who leads him into a promised land occupied by Canaanites can really be trusted. The question becomes more pressing when he moves on through Palestine only to find himself on the edge of the desert. Driven to Egypt by a famine, Abram can no longer bear the uncertainty, which is why he pretends that Sarai is his sister. His subsequent experiences in Egypt show him that God has been in control of the situation all along, and that he *can* be trusted, despite all appearances to the contrary. Thus it is through the suffering of uncertainty that Abram's faith and hope in God are deepened.

New Testament Reading (Epistle) **1 Peter 2: 19-end**

More than half the people in the great cities of the Roman Empire were slaves. Some slaves suffered horribly under vicious masters, and it is to them that this passage is addressed. They must not lose heart. Their Lord also suffered unjustly on the cross and, as Christians, they are called to follow his example of patient faith. To do this is certainly not easy, but neither is it impossible, because every

Christian is always united with Christ. Our individual pains and sorrows and anxieties are not really so many little crosses. The Christian knows only one cross—the cross of Jesus. He honours us, like Simon of Cyrene, by letting us share it with him when we suffer.

New Testament Reading (Gospel)   **Matthew 16: 13–end**

The disciples were horrified by what Jesus said after Peter, their spokesman, had confessed him to be the Messiah. Jewish belief was that the Messiah's God-given destiny was the exact opposite of what Jesus now foretold for himself. It is therefore little wonder that Peter should have objected so vehemently to Jesus's words. In the light of subsequent events, however, they came to realize that Jesus's death was the greatest of all possible victories. Only a crucified Messiah could make known the full extent of God's love for sinful mankind and throw wide the gates of his kingdom. Likewise, since God's kingdom is the kingdom of love, our only way into it is the way of the cross. The cross alone can transform our sorrows into joy and our self-centredness into love of God and man.

Lord Jesus, mark all our sufferings with the sign of your cross. Strengthen our faith, deepen our hope and purify our love, that we may know the joy of your kingdom ourselves and share it with others.

Fourth Sunday in Lent
The King and the Kingdom: Transfiguration

God's kingdom means 'righteousness and peace and joy in the Holy Spirit' (Romans 14:17). It is present wherever the Gospel message is proclaimed, heard and acted upon. At the same time, it also lies ahead of us in God's future, when he will be all in all. The central role of Jesus in the ushering in of God's kingdom is strongly emphasized in the story of the Transfiguration.

Old Testament Reading   **Exodus 3: 1–6**

On the mountain of God, Moses is made deeply aware of God's holiness: he stands barefoot on the holy ground, hiding his face in godly fear. At the same time, he learns that God's holiness, his inmost being, is full of love for mankind. The holy God once guided and cared for Abraham, Isaac, and Jacob, and now he intends to carry his plan of salvation one stage further by rescuing their descendants from slavery in Egypt. God's holiness is his love, his mercy, and his faithfulness to his promises.

New Testament Reading (Epistle)   **2 Peter 1: 16–19**

In moments of sorrow, anxiety, or disillusionment, it is all too easy to doubt the power of God to help us. And if we doubt this, it obviously makes no sense to believe that he is merciful and faithful. We come to think of life as a grey, shapeless succession of events, haphazard and completely outside God's control. This passage points us out of the darkness of such doubts to the clear light of the transfigured Christ. God is not powerless, for he sent his beloved Son to mankind and revealed his glory on the holy mountain. Nor does God act haphazardly: he sent his Son in accordance with his saving plan, revealed in the scriptures, and that plan is now moving on to its fulfilment. The kingdom for which we pray has come and will come in Christ.

New Testament Reading (Gospel)   **Matthew 17: 1–13**

As often in the Bible, the overshadowing cloud symbolizes God's presence. The words from the cloud, which are full of Old Testament allusions, explain the true nature of Jesus's glory. He is the beloved (or only) Son whom God will give up in love for mankind, just as Abraham was once prepared to offer Isaac. Being God's Son, Jesus is also the Messiah, come to begin his reign on earth. And he is the humble servant in whose obedient love his Father delights. The presence of Moses and Elijah in the vision indicates that God's saving plan, which began with Israel, has reached its climax with the coming of Jesus. It would be quite wrong for Jesus and the three disciples to remain indefinitely on the mountain as Peter suggests. The holiness of divine love, mercy and faithfulness revealed in Jesus demands that they move on towards Jerusalem, the cross and the tomb. Because of a prophecy of Malachi (4:5, 6), the Jews believed that Elijah would return to earth before God's kingdom arrived. In claiming that John the Baptist has already fulfilled Elijah's role as forerunner, Jesus is really pointing to himself as the one through whom and in whom the kingdom comes.

Father, we rejoice that in Jesus your kingdom has already come. Keep us faithful and attentive to him, and hasten the time when all your creatures shall confess him as Saviour and Lord.

Fifth Sunday in Lent
The King and the Kingdom: The Victory of the Cross

An unknown pagan artist in the Roman Empire once drew a picture of a man hanging on a cross, with the head of an ass. How could the victim of such an ignominious death ever be called victorious? How could this tortured wreck of a man have power to save? Each of today's readings has something important to say about these questions.

Old Testament Reading   **Jeremiah 31: 31–34**

During Jeremiah's youth, king Josiah of Judah carried out a religious reform based on the law of Moses. In the years that followed, Jeremiah came to realize that Josiah's reform was a failure, because it was more concerned with correct external observance than with man's heart and its yearnings. So it was that Jeremiah spoke in God's name of a time when the relationship between God and his people would be renewed, and each individual would have deep personal communion with God. Jesus referred to this prophecy of Jeremiah at the Last Supper when he said that the new covenant would be sealed by his blood. The new relationship with God is now open for all who would enter it. God has spoken his word of welcome to each one of us. He spoke it through the death of his Son.

New Testament Reading (Epistle)   **Hebrews 9: 11–14**

Men may hear God's welcome uttered from the cross but still hang back because of a guilty conscience. But the truth is that we need not fear. On the cross, Christ has set us free for ever from sin and its effects. As each year the high priest used to enter the inner sanctuary of the temple bearing sacrificial blood to free Israel from ceremonial pollution, so now Jesus, by virtue of his self-oblation, has entered God's heavenly presence once and for all on our behalf, and so freed us from the inner pollution of sin.

New Testament Reading (Gospel)   **Mark 10: 32–45**

Although the sons of Zebedee were disciples, their attitude in asking Jesus to enthrone them beside himself in his glory was essentially the same as that of the pagan artist and, indeed, of the world at large. Jesus's way to glory is not man's way but God's. His glory is the glory of sheer love, and love means self-sacrifice and humble service. These things are his cup and his baptism. A crucified Messiah is a catastrophic and grotesque failure by worldly standards. And yet those whose gaze is directed by love will always see in that broken figure the source of the world's true joy, for the victory of the cross is the victory of perfect love.

Jesus, Lamb of God: have mercy on us.
Jesus, bearer of our sins: have mercy on us.
Jesus, redeemer of the world: give us your peace.

Palm Sunday
The Victory of the Cross

Old Testament Reading   **Isaiah 50: 4–9a**

The Servant of God speaks, in this third 'servant song', as a faithful pupil of the LORD. His knowledge is obtained daily in the LORD's schoolroom, and is used to support those in need (*v.* 4). And then the picture changes to a courtroom: the prophet is on trial, but he can challenge his adversaries because God will have him cleared by being a decisive witness. (The courtroom picture is frequent in the Old Testament, particularly in the prophecy of Isaiah 40–55.)

But the prophetic experience remains predominant; 'the LORD has spoken, who can but prophesy?' asked Amos. And the vocation of the prophet involves accepting the consequences of obedience; the word of God may not be popular; its proclaimer may be subjected to maltreatment, rejection and insult (*v.* 6—plucking out the beard was a common humiliation in ancient times).

To all of this he submits patiently, and his faith remains. The humility of the true servant of God is shown in the true wise man or the true prophet. And we can begin to see why this and other so-called 'servant passages' in Isaiah 40–55 were found so apt for helping to portray our Lord's passion.

New Testament Reading (Epistle)   **Philippians 2: 5–11**

'Let your manner of life be worthy of the gospel of Christ' (1:27). That is the apostle's appeal; and in chapter 2 he goes on to urge his hearers to Christian humility on the basis of the humility of Christ. In what is possibly an early Christian hymn, our Lord is shown as laying aside his primal heavenly glory and becoming man—taking the form of a slave (*v.* 7). In voluntary obedience he accepted a shameful death (*v.* 8), one reserved for rebels and outcasts.

Because of his obedience and humility ('therefore', *v.* 9) Jesus has been raised to the place of honour in heaven, 'sitting at the right hand of the Father', as we say in the Creed. The phrase 'given a name' (*v.* 9) evokes a practice known from the Old Testament: one makes another his servant by giving him a name, thereby creating a relationship of protection and loyalty (e.g. Genesis 32:28, 35:10).

Obedience to God, says the apostle, calls forth what our Lord has shown. If the Lord himself can lay aside the trappings of majesty and be obedient in this imperfect world, so must we and so can we by participating in the mind of Christ (*v.* 5). And the heavenly glory to which Jesus was raised is the consummation of our Christian hope.

New Testament Reading (Gospel)   **Mark 14: 32–15: 41**

The suffering and death of our Lord do not need commentary. Yet the events narrated are understood by the evangelist, and by us, in the light of the belief that in them lies the redemption of the world. The themes of faithfulness and humility found in the life of a prophet are brought to completion in the setting-at-nought of God, which is the ultimate significance of the Passion; and then by our participation in the death and resurrection of Christ through baptism (Romans 6:4) we are called to be sharers in and imitators of the humility Christ has fully shown.

Open our hearts, O Lord, to share anew in the commemoration of your Son's passion; that we may go with him in humility and faith and so come to know the joy of his resurrection.

Alternative Readings
The Triumphal Entry

Old Testament Reading   **Zechariah 9: 9–12**

This passage is of a type occasionally found in the Old Testament, in which normal patterns are reversed. The king was normally thought of as a mighty warrior, riding a war horse or an armoured chariot; but here the prophecy shows him riding on the lowliest animal. 'Triumphant and victorious' (*v.* 9, *RSV*) is literally 'righteous and saved'—emphasizing that it is God who has vindicated his cause, and that the idealized king is his faithful servant.

The extent of the King's dominion is that contained in the old promises (e.g. Psalm 72:8, Genesis 15:18), and possibly exceeds the area of Solomon's rule. But again, we must notice the way the nationalist claims are reversed in this oracle of peace and blessing. Our ways of thought must be ruled by what God shows us of himself.

New Testament Reading (Epistle)   **1 Corinthians 1: 18–25**

The theme of reversal is continued in this passage. The methods of knowledge we might expect to apply cannot work; for at the heart of the mystery of our redemption there is a crucified saviour, not obviously glorious. This is both scandalous (= a stumbling block) and hardly acceptable in a respectable philosophy (= foolishness). The categories our systems prescribe are burst open. The depths of God's nature are revealed to us in the ultimate paradox, that in a broken man on a gibbet should be incarnate the source of all life. And as a consequence, since the categories become irrelevant before the cross, the cross opens up the way of life to everyone (*v.* 24), whatever his past history. It would be a mistake, however, to use this passage as an invitation to theological incoherence: for God is Lord of the world of thought.

New Testament Reading (Gospel)   **Matthew 21: 1–13**

By presenting Jesus's triumphant entry into Jerusalem as one of the key episodes in his life which fulfil Old Testament prophecy, the gospel writer is showing how the life and death of Jesus achieve God's will for his people. Notice the presentation of Jesus as King (*vv.* 5, 9 – son of David; *v.* 8 cf. 2 Kings 9.13), even to the extent of misusing 'Hosanna' as a greeting instead of a prayer.

It is helpful to compare this passage with Mark 11:1–10. We note how a demonstration by the disciples has become in Matthew a reception by a great crowd, and Mark's use of Psalm 118:25f has been applied to the person of Jesus. Any idea that the King of Glory is to be understood politically (compare 'the coming kingdom of our father David' in Mark 11:10) is omitted—the kingdom of heaven for Matthew is foreshadowed in the Church.

By these variations and the use of Old Testament prophecy, Matthew is showing in his way that Jesus was the special person sent by God to Israel, his lowliness and rejection notwithstanding.

Lord, you hid your glory for our sakes, so that we should respond to you in love. Help us always to follow your way of humility so that we may worthily share in your resurrection.

Monday in Holy Week

Old Testament Reading   Isaiah 42: 1–7

The Lord speaks of his servant (*vv.* 1–4) as one who will establish
justice in the earth, but who will do it in quietness and confidence,
without aggression. He is called by God ('chosen', *v.* 1) and has the
gift of his life-giving power ('spirit'). Since 'to put my Spirit upon
him' also means to set the servant apart as his designated one (cf even
the alien Cyrus in 45:1), the servant is shown as one who is empowered to achieve what God wills. He is God's agent; God does not act
apart from his creation, but achieves his will in it and through it.

The question 'Who is the servant?' is much debated, but his role is
clear: he is to rescue all in oppression—he is to be a saviour, he is to
show all peoples (the nations, *v.* 6) the saving power of God. And
God who created all things intends such a redemption—in the
thought of this prophet creation and redemption are of a piece. For
redemption brings newness of life, as does creation.

Is the servant in this passage an individual prophet, or is it a figure
for Israel as a prophetic people? We may not be able to answer the
question, but it is not difficult to see that such a figure is apt as a
model for helping us understand God's saving work in Christ, as a
faithful servant and the one in whom the vocation of Israel comes to
fulfilment.

New Testament Reading (Epistle)   Hebrews 2: 9–18

In the thought of Hebrews, Christ is the son and heir of the household (cf 1.1f), who shares in God's nature. Yet he came to earth to
speak to us for God and to heal the breach which sin had established
between man and God. This breach is symbolized by the curtain of
the temple, and only the obedient Son can pioneer the way through
for others to follow (10:20, cf Mark 15:38) by suffering for all
(*vv.* 9f).

All of us come from God (*v.* 11) since all things exist for him and by
him (*v.* 10). So we too are sons, who have to be sanctified; and Jesus,

the Son and heir, acknowledges us as brothers and makes God's call to us known. (The use of quotations from Psalm 22:22 and Isaiah 8:17–18 is typical of the method of the time.)

Not only does Jesus acknowledge us as brothers, he becomes our brother by sharing in our nature (*v.* 14), and destroys death which causes human bondage (*v.* 15) by means of death itself. As an Easter hymn puts it: 'Christ has risen from the dead, by death trampling upon death, and has bestowed life upon those in the tombs'.

The redemptive work of God is proclaimed and achieved by the one who fulfils his vocation. The different models (prophetic servanthood and sonship) need not disturb us; they and others are mere pointers for our own understanding and acceptance of God's redeeming outreach to us.

New Testament Reading (Gospel)   **Luke 22: 1–38**

Note the irony of a dispute about precedence, occurring at the Lord's last meal with his disciples. The humility of Christ is again emphasized (*v.* 27); so is his acceptance of suffering (*vv.* 15, 22, 28).

Verses 35–8 reflect the needs which will be experienced by the disciples when they come to spread the gospel: equipment which might once have been a hindrance is now necessary in the face of hostility. But not with swords—force has no place in the work of Christ and his gospel—and so the Lord dismisses the apostles' further lack of understanding (cf. Deuteronomy 3:26 for the idiom).

Lord, you came among us and called us back to your Father and our Father. Help us to know that when we suffer and are put to the test, you are with us in the darkest valley, for you tasted death for us all.

Tuesday in Holy Week

Old Testament Reading   **Isaiah 49: 1–6**

There is no doubt whom the servant represents in this passage! The prophet describes his call in terms reminiscent of Jeremiah's (1:5)—he has a destiny prepared by God and God gives him the tools (*v.* 2). Even the address 'Israel' in *v.* 3 can be seen as the prophet's adoption of this name for himself to indicate his fulfilment of the call of God's whole people to be a faithful spokesman, and to be faithful even when all seems hopeless (*v.* 4).

The message of the prophet is that the judgement of Israel has already occurred in full measure and that a new age is to dawn. Such an expectation was not fulfilled, and that is why Christians came to feel it appropriate to apply these prophecies as a way of understanding God's work in Christ. We should do the prophet's preaching violence, however, were we to regard it as a direct foretelling of the life and death of Jesus. The continuity is always to be found in God's nature as revealed to us.

The culmination of the prophet's understanding of his work comes in *vv.* 5f: he is not just to restore the ancient people, but to transcend the boundaries of nationality by extending the realm of God's victorious reign world-wide. This dimension of the prophet's insight picks up the interweaving of creation and redemption, for if the one is of universal extent so is the other.

New Testament Reading (Epistle)   **Hebrews 8: 1–6**

In this passage we have a further sample of the argument of the letter to the Hebrews—indeed a summary of the argument so far (*v.* 1). The Jewish high priest is appointed to offer gifts and sacrifices on earth (*v.* 3); but Jesus, who is seated at the right hand of God (*v.* 1), makes an offering of himself in the perfect heavenly tent (*v.* 2), because, since he comes from the tribe of Judah, he cannot be a priest in the line of Levi (7:14), offering sacrifices on earth.

Not an argument we might construct today, perhaps? But the

mystery of man's redemption, which is the common thread of all our worship and meditation this week, is multiform. Underlying the argument in Hebrews is the conviction that the old covenant had been shown to be insufficient, inadequate to bring man into the fellowship of heaven, but that God had now broken through the barrier of sin in the perfect self-offering of Christ (7:27f).

The sacrifice of Christ can be legitimately understood in a number of ways in Christian doctrine; in Hebrews it is presented in terms of true as opposed to incomplete priesthood.

New Testament Reading (Gospel) **Luke 22: 39–end**

Notice the obedience of our Lord (especially in *v.* 42). It is a mark of Luke's presentation of the gospel story that Jesus *must* go up to Jerusalem and suffer there.

The council want an easy answer (*v.* 67); but they cannot have it because they do not ask in faith. To know that Jesus is God's appointed servant is sterile unless it is quickened by our response of love.

Lord, as we go nearer with you to Calvary, we ask you to draw us all into the obedience of love. You gave yourself for us; prepare us to offer ourselves in whatever way you may require, in union with your perfect sacrifice.

Wednesday in Holy Week

Old Testament Reading   **Isaiah 50: 4–9a**
See Palm Sunday (p. 224).

New Testament Reading (Epistle)   **1 Peter 2: 19–end**

The redemption wrought in Christ also gives us an example to follow. Throughout the story of Christ's passion as told in the gospels, we find exemplified the qualities of the innocent sufferer (cf *vv.* 22f). For the Christian the 'imitation of Christ' is the model on which he will wish to form his character.

Now there are many who say that Jesus was a great teacher of ethical truths. But that is superficial; for not only was he a teacher who lived out what he taught, but much more important, instead of merely pointing sadly to the ills of the world, he claimed it for God, and announced and showed God's love for it.

For we must not forget to relate all this to the docrine of the incarnation. It is God who in Christ reconciles the world to himself; it is God who in Christ is reviled and put to the test but endures patiently. 'By his wounds we have been healed' (*v.* 24)—Christians who are maltreated can unite themselves with the sufferings of their teacher and their God. For God's condescension in becoming man means that of his own free grace he has submitted himself for our sake to the limitations of our human condition and to the effects of sin and disorientation in our imperfect world (*v.* 24).

New Testament Reading (Gospel)   **Luke 23: 1–49**

We follow our Lord from his hearing before Pilate to his crucifixion and death. We can see how the theme of the innocent sufferer, now so familiar to us from this week's Isaiah passages and today from 1 Peter, is brought out in Luke's narrative. See *vv.* 14 and 16; the prayer for his executioners in *v.* 34 and the confession of one of the thieves in *v.* 41.

Luke, possibly more than any of the other evangelists, stresses that Jesus was the righteous teacher of spiritual truths who suffered undeservedly. He stresses too the disciple's call to the imitation of his Lord's obedience, suffering and death (12:8–12, 21:12–19). Hence the centurion's confession in Luke's form (*v.* 47; compare Mark 15:39 and Matthew 27:54): 'Truly this man was innocent'.

Teach us, good Lord, to serve you as you deserve; to give and not to count the cost; to fight and not to heed the wounds; to toil and not to seek for rest; to labour and not to ask for any reward, save that of knowing that we are doing your will.

Maundy Thursday

Old Testament Reading   **Exodus 12: 1–14**

This passage sets out the Jewish understanding of the reason for
keeping the Passover. It 'consolidates and re-enacts' earlier legisla-
tion. All the regulations are designed to remind the people of the
Lord's mighty act of deliverance, by reproducing in the observance
some of the conditions of the original escape (or exodus) related in
the traditions, especially the food and clothing (*v.* 11) appropriate
for a hasty journey.

In the Jewish Passover law it is taught that 'in every generation a
man must so regard himself as if he came forth himself out of Egypt'.
The liturgy in part recounts the story of Israel's deliverance by
means of the father instructing his young son in its significance (cf
Exodus 13:8). And the Jewish rule goes on: 'Therefore are we bound
to give thanks, to praise, to glorify, to honour, to exalt, to extol, and
to bless him who wrought all these wonders for our fathers and for
us. He brought us from bondage to freedom, from sorrow to glad-
ness, from mourning to a festival day . . .'.

Thus we see that the memorial (*v.* 14) enacted in the celebration is
no mere remembrance of a dead past; the deliverance was achieved
once and for all, but the people redeemed by God share anew in that
deliverance as they celebrate it in each generation.

New Testament Reading (Epistle)   **1 Corinthians 11: 23–29**

We cannot fail to notice how during Holy Week the Church enacts
the memorial of the suffering and cross of its Lord, to culminate in
resurrection on Easter Day. 'In every generation', we may say, 'a
Christian must so regard himself as if he himself suffered, died, and
rose' (cf Romans 6:4). So today we celebrate the last meal of Jesus
with his disciples.

The tradition which Paul received presents this institution of the
Eucharist in a manner somewhat reminiscent of that of the Passover.
Thus 'Do this for my memorial' means to renew our sharing in the
saving work of Christ (*v.* 26). This we do at every eucharist, but

today especially we are in the upper room; yet instead of looking back with sadness to the final meal, we share in its transcended significance. We look back in order to look forward; 'I am with you always'; the last meal becomes the first of the new meals because the Lord of the Church is risen and the new life he brings is given to us.

We thank God therefore for our creation and redemption in Christ, for the gift of the Holy Spirit, and for calling us to his service as his people. In celebrating God's mighty acts of loving-kindness we offer the fruits of the earth as symbols of our joy in God's bounty, making our 'sacrifice of praise and thanksgiving' in union with Christ's eternal sacrifice of love. 'His manhood pleads where now he is, on heaven's eternal throne.'

We share in Christ's body, which symbolizes his life—so we belong to him and no other; we share the cup which is the new covenant sealed with his blood, so we are bound in fellowship with God through Christ (cf Exodus 24:8). In the eucharist we proclaim God's saving work in Christ, we receive anew his power into our lives, and we look for his coming in glory.

New Testament Reading (Gospel)   **John 13: 1–15**

John associates the last supper with a different memorial: the example the master gives of humble love is one a disciple must follow. The foot-washing is an enacted parable of the love Jesus has for his own (*v.* 1).

The incarnate Word stoops and shows what the love he has with the Father is to mean among his disciples (cf 17: 26). And note that Judas Iscariot is there (*v.* 2), his plans already made. The love of God is consummated on the cross, where man destroys God; the master is abased by the servant; love is expressed in its ultimate self-giving. The Christian can and must give himself too, first being washed by Christ (*v.* 8); such service is also Christ's memorial, a showing forth of his love. For it is God's love which redeems us.

Father, you have shown us your love in Christ and given us the wonderful sacrament of his body and blood as a continuing sign of your goodness and his presence among us. Help us by your power to follow his example and to give ourselves in service to one another and to you.

Good Friday
Christ Reigns from the Cross

The Gospel chosen for today warns us against turning this liturgy into a great lamentation or mourning rite. Indeed, in all of the readings the feeling of victory gained, of something achieved for us is very much to the fore.

Old Testament Reading   **Isaiah 52: 13–53: end**

This is the last of the so-called 'Servant Songs' in Deutero-Isaiah. It appears where the great prophet of Israel's exile has called upon Israel to seize the moment of redemption and come forth from Babylon. Whatever our discussions as to the identity of this Servant figure, in that setting we are dealing with the collective Israel, a suffering Israel. There is much terrible detail about the ugly aspect of the Servant's appearance; about his suffering and rejection; about the violence of his persecution to death. Through it all his innocence and his bearing in suffering are appealed to. So strong is this note of suffering that we have to remind ourselves that the poet opens and closes by singing of the final exaltation and vindication of the Servant. Mystery it may be, but somehow it was the Lord's will to bruise him, somehow he carried the griefs and sorrows of others—it was for our iniquities that he was wounded.

New Testament Reading (Epistle)   **Hebrews 10: 1–25**

The language is that of sacrifice and blood, and that in reference to man's sin: since we are all sinners, in reference to our sin. The author of Hebrews looks at the Old Testament ritual law and particularly at the Day of Atonement. He is concerned to stress its inadequacy, its ineffectiveness—it is only a shadow of what is to come. The passage, however, rings out a note of confidence, of assurance, of hope. What is to come is Jesus Christ. His death is understood as sacrifice, a single sacrifice, one offering, but an offering which sanctifies, perfects, brings about forgiveness of sin. This is because of his obedience, expressed in the words of Psalm 40: 'I have come to do thy will, O God'. We are then exhorted, we who are perfected in this new covenant, to hold fast, to exercise love and good works. God is faithful.

or   **Hebrews 4: 14–end; 5: 7–9**

As in the passage in Hebrews 10, we are encouraged to hold fast. We may be weak but the source of our confidence is Jesus, the Son of God. We have access to grace through him. He was made perfect through obedience and became the source of salvation for us.

New Testament Reading (Gospel)   **John 18: 1–19: 37**

Today in our meditation upon this account of Jesus, we stop before the account of his Resurrection. Yet even here John presents Jesus, not as a victim, but as an agent. He is in control. Note the incidents in the garden, Pilate's questioning about the kingship of Jesus, and the final 'It is finished'. The meaning of this last sign in John is glorification, victory—so much, if not all, of John's Gospel points forward to this sign. In the cross we have not a disaster awaiting its reversal—John's Jesus reigns from his cross. Today, we give thanks for our promised share in that victory.

Easter Eve
Time for Reflection

Liturgically, we are halted at Christ's death. The readings are selected to help reflection upon the significance of death: Christ's death, our death. Yet they turn our attention to life.

Old Testament Reading   **Job 14: 1–14**

The author of Job cannot turn our attention to life. Here he offers us no hope, no future. Job is speaking out of the disaster which have befallen him, his feeling of estrangement from God. We might regard his characterization of man as pessimistic, or merely as a realistic view of life: man is of few days and full of troubles. If Job's difficulties could be explained in terms of God's judgement (as his friends suggest), Job is here asking why God should bother with such a poor specimen as man is. His plea is really: leave me alone. The two images (the tree cut down and the dried up lake) emphasize that death is final. In a piece of wishful thinking he imagines that God might hide him in Sheol (the abode of the dead according to Hebrew thought) till God's wrath has passed. Job reminds himself that there is no return from Sheol.

New Testament Reading (Epistle)   **1 Peter 3: 17–end**

The author is aware of the difficulties of life. In the context of offering, Christ's suffering is an example. Peter says that Christ died. The purpose of that death was to bring us to God. He was put to death in the flesh (his human condition) but made alive in the spirit (the power of God). Here we do not stop at death as Job does—Jesus is alive, in heaven, at God's right hand. That is our future, too. Tradition has made much of the preaching of Jesus to the spirits in prison. Perhaps we should see it simply as the proclamation of his victory over death. What is important is the comparison that follows (even if the image is a little strained). In Noah's time eight persons were saved (hardly 'through' water), so we are saved through the water of baptism which constitutes an appeal to God through Christ's Resurrection.

New Testament Reading (Gospel)   **Matthew 27: 57–end**

Whatever Matthew's reasons were for including this discussion between the Jewish authorities and Pilate, it turns our attention away from the attendant circumstances of death—tomb, shroud, and burial—to the thought of life. The authorities are afraid of a deception because Jesus had foretold, 'After three days I will rise again'. We who read the story today are aware of the denouement which we will read on Easter Day, and indeed the Gospel, the story of Jesus, is told and has to be read in the light of the affirmation of new life in Jesus.

or   **John 2: 18–22**

John brings forward to early in his story the incident of the cleansing of the temple. The audience of Jesus misses the symbolism which John explains here, the pointing forward to the Resurrection of Jesus.

Easter Day
'The end is where we start from'

We may apply these words of T. S. Eliot to our Easter triduum. We have reflected upon death, the end, the death of Christ. Today we affirm in faith our beginning, life and all it offers, and we give thanks.

Old Testament Reading   **Isaiah 12**

The enthusiastic tone of the hymn-like praise, which rounds off this first collection of oracles in the book of Isaiah, sets the tone for our Easter Day. God is my salvation, my strength, my song. Our thoughts are turned from sin and death to the trust and comfort which God offers us today. The image of the well from which we draw with joy suggests life, richness, fullness. If we are allowed to mix metaphors, we approach that well, the table of the Lord, proclaiming his deeds on our behalf.

New Testament Reading (Epistle)   **Revelation 1: 10–18**

The Book of Revelation is a proclamation of Christ's continuing presence with his Church, of his power and lordship in history. John is commissioned to write to the seven churches this message which is summed up in his vision. The figure which he sees in the midst of the churches (these symbolized by the seven lampstands) is Christ as the fulfilment of the figure like the Son of Man in Daniel, chapter 7 (see p. 254). Here this figure is definitely placed in a divine realm by the majestic description. John reacts properly to the hyperbole in the description by falling down in fear, but the figure offers him comfort and support: 'Fear not'. The visionary figure characterizes himself with thought-provoking titles. What strikes us today, perhaps, is the attribution of life and of the power (symbolized by the keys) over death and Hades. He who has that power is the Lord present with his Church.

240

New Testament Reading (Gospel) **Matthew 28: 1–10**

Matthew's account of the first Easter Day is remarkably brief. Through the eyes of the women we can be present at the tomb. At first Jesus does not appear on the stage. By means of the device of the earthquake and the legendary element of the angel descending to roll back the stone, we are introduced to what is the new beginning for us: 'He is not here, for he has risen as he said'. The surprising nature of the assertion merits indeed an earthquake and an angel. Only after the women are commissioned to carry the news to his disciples do they, in fact, meet their risen Lord. We give thanks for his presence with us especially in this liturgical celebration.

Alternative Readings

We pin our faith in the Resurrection. The victory over sin and death, wrought by God for us, is there. There it begins, there is the type of the risen life in which we share by our baptism. We reaffirm our faith.

Old Testament Reading **Exodus 14: 15–22**

There are many images used here: the crossing of the sea, the pillar of cloud, the pillar of fire, the image of battle. All convey Israel's faith that the Lord is with her, guiding and protecting and fighting for her against her enemies. We know how these images, used in connection with the traditions about Israel in the wilderness and the traditions of her exodus from Egypt, are celebrated again and again in her liturgy, as she rejoices in what God has done for her. What Israel has experienced in the Exodus is a type of all human experience. In the change and insecurity of life, we all need security and assurance. Often we turn to these images used by Israel as we reflect on God's presence with us in life.

New Testament Reading (Epistle) **1 Corinthians 15: 12–20**

In Corinth, it seems, there was question as to the possibility of there being any resurrection for man after death. We might feel that Paul reverses the argument in a curious fashion—'If so, then Christ did not rise from the dead'. He is, however, intent in presenting the Christian proclamation: God raised Christ from the dead. If he did not, says Paul, we are in a pitiable state, still in our sins and with hope only for this life. With the image of the first fruits Paul extends our hope beyond this life. Christ is the first fruit; we share his resurrection.

New Testament Reading (Gospel) **John 20: 1–10**

John's account of Easter Day appears colourless. In one sense for John's gospel there is no place for resurrection. The cross is already exaltation and ascension. However, he does give us from the tradition three resurrection appearances in this chapter. This first one presents the tomb (empty) as a sign of resurrection. Throughout John's gospel sight is a symbol of faith. We have for example the curing of the blind man in chapter 9. Here, in John's language, the beloved disciple sees and believes. The Lord is risen. Later, John is to call blessed those who do not see and yet believe.

Alternative Readings

The scene may be the empty tomb, but the interest is the proclamation: 'He has risen, he is not here'. This is presented as a wonderful new thing.

Old Testament Reading **Isaiah 43: 16–21**

This great prophet of Israel's exile reflects upon the preaching of Isaiah of Jerusalem, upon Israel's great religious traditions. In response to the questioning and doubt occasioned by the disaster of the exile, he reaffirms and proclaims his faith in Yahweh, the God of Israel. He turns to creation to experience the power of that God, a power shown on Israel's behalf as narrated in the story of the Exodus. Yet he tells Israel to forget the former things, her old traditions. Now a new thing is imminent, and the prophet proclaims a glorious new exodus in which Israel is led in procession back to her land. This glorious future is to be worked out in Israel's history.

New Testament Reading (Epistle) **Colossians 3: 1–11**

Past, present, and future. On the basis of what God had done in the past, Isaiah looked forward to restoration, renewal. The writers of the Christian community looked back. Christ has died and is risen. In him something new has happened. We worship Christ seated at God's right hand, a symbol of his victory and power. We proclaim our faith that we are there too, already present in his victory. Therefore, put away, in contrast to those things that are above, the earthly things. These are listed as sin, greed, envy, the things which bring about God's wrath. These are the former things we are to forget. They are our old nature, but we now have a new nature. We who have been created in God's image are continually being renewed in that image in Christ.

New Testament Reading (Gospel) **Mark 16: 1–8**

According to some manuscripts it is possible that Mark's gospel originally ended here with the seeming abruptness of *v.* 8. The tradition of the empty tomb is presented. The burial of Jesus emphasized the reality of his death. This addition of the empty tomb is a proclamation of the divine miracle and power in the face of death and human incapacity. The reaction of those who first experienced it is fear. Thus does Mark emphasize the suddenness, the abruptness, and the marvel of what has happened. Only later in the other gospels do we have appearances of the risen Lord. Here there is merely a foretelling of a leading into Galilee. What this means is much disputed, but perhaps it symbolizes the preparation for the mission of the community of the resurrected Lord.

Monday to Saturday in Easter Week

See pages 86–97.

243

First Sunday after Easter
The Bread of Life

Old Testament Reading   **Exodus 16: 2–15**

In this passage God provides food in the desert for his hungry people. Despite their complaints he acts graciously towards them, so that eventually his worship is established among them and his promises to them can be fulfilled. All that he does is intended to help the people to grasp his purpose for their lives. He gives them manna, he tests their obedience, he makes special arrangements for the seventh day of the week, he instructs their leaders. The reason for all this care is that Israel should recognize how much the nation owes to God, that God is their only source of hope. 'You shall know that I the Lord am your God' (*NEB*). In Psalm 78 the manna and the quails are sent as a punishment upon Israel for testing God. Here in Exodus 16 it is God who tests the people. They ask what the flake-like substance is that is spread over the ground (the Hebrew in *v*. 15 *'man-hu'* is an unusual form of the question 'What is that?', hinting already at the answer 'Manna!'), and Moses replies that it is bread from heaven. For all their disobedience God remains willing and able to bring them to their promised land.

New Testament Reading (Epistle)   **1 Corinthians 15: 53–end**

To be 'in Christ' is not to have arrived. According to Paul, there will have to be many changes in us, if we are to share God's final victory. In the end, if we are to be fit for the final days of God's conquest, we shall need to be thoroughly transformed. In harmony with the traditions of his own day Paul depicts this victory as including the end of death (see Revelation 21:4). For such a new kingdom we shall need to be changed. But in the meantime also there is still much to be done. Daily, Christians must share Christ's death to the tyranny of sin ('sting' in *vv*. 55–56 implies that sin is death's instrument of torture or mastery), so that with him they can enjoy victory over the law of sin and death. The result of this sharing in the life of Christ should be a distinctive style of living, confident, purposeful, and fearless, whatever the cost may be.

New Testament Reading (Gospel) **John 6: 32–40**

The Lord's Prayer includes the petition to the Father for the bread we need. The same request is made in John 6:32–40 by those who are listening to Jesus: 'Sir, give us this bread now and always' (*v.* 34). Jesus's reply 'I am the Bread of Life' summarizes his own obedient commitment to the Father's way of meeting our need, a commitment in his life and his death to the Father's will. Through his obedient offering of himself he is like 'the bread from heaven', sustaining all who receive him. All who receive him receive eternal life in the here and now and a share in God's kingdom hereafter. The elements at the Eucharist are symbols of this sustaining power. They also express, as this lesson indicates, Christ's welcome to us, meeting our need before we make it known: 'and the man who comes to me I will never turn away' (*v.* 37). Those who are hungry and those who are thirsty will find satisfaction there, now and always.

Second Sunday after Easter
The Good Shepherd

Old Testament Reading   **Ezekiel 34: 7–16**

What did 'shepherd' mean in the world of the Bible? It could mean hired labourers minding sheep in the hill-country. But it could carry far wider associations too, some of which are lost today. 'Shepherd' could refer to rulers exercising authority over their subjects. It could be used of men. It could be used of God. According to Ezekiel, God himself is the standard by which all shepherds, all those in authority, are to be judged. As 'Shepherd of Israel' God recalls men to the ideal of wise oversight and unselfish protection of the weak which condemns all misuse of authority. It is this self-interest and misuse of authority that Ezekiel has noted among his nation's leaders. He finds that this has led to disaster, the fall of Jerusalem, and the dispersion of the people. In times of irresponsible leadership Israel had often returned to the ideal ruler and shepherd, and drawn from God the inspiration and strength to begin again. This is what Ezekiel does, blending together the picture of the rustic shepherd who cares for his sheep with the picture of the ruler who will judge those under him. So, for Ezekiel, God is seen as about to draw together once again his dispersed flock in a new restoration (the *NEB* translation of *v.* 12).

New Testament Reading (Epistle)   **1 Peter 5: 1–11**

The church has often had to face testing times. 1 Peter belongs to an era like that, and testifies to the reliability of God's care whatever may happen. Part of that care should be God's provision of a generous and devoted leadership. The latter will of course be judged by the standards of Christ, the Head Shepherd. His ideal was that of girding on humility, like a slave dressed for menial service, as when he tied a towel round himself to wash his disciples' feet. Such an ideal is however not only for church leaders to follow. The whole church, alert and self-possessed, should follow it also, seeking to express the ideal of service as part of a wider understanding of the whole of life under God's hand. God provides the measure of all our possibilities and responsibilities. To serve others is part of the recognition that God provides the context of our life and work, and we must be humble enough to recognize it. If we do so, we have found a firm foundation for our lives, whatever tests may come our way.

New Testament Reading (Gospel)   **John 10: 7–16**

Jesus calls himself 'The Good Shepherd'. Are we then to picture to ourselves a good shepherd, and then attempt to fit Christ into that pattern? The Gospel of John suggests a different approach. Begin with Jesus Christ, and see how radically you must adapt your picture of a shepherd's work. That is the way the Gospel of John usually proceeds. Jesus gives his life for his sheep. His relationship with his flock reflects his own close relationship with the Father. In both these respects Jesus sets a new standard as shepherd of his flock. It is true that a rural shepherd might well have to risk his life at some time in the course of caring for his sheep. But Jesus's obedient sacrifice is central to his whole mission. He gave his life for his own. This of course enables us to see how Christ's relationship with his flock reflects his own relationship with his Father. For the self-giving love which is at the heart of the Father-Son relationship determines the character of the life of Christ's flock. This has surprising results. It means that many are drawn into Christ's flock whom we might not have expected to see there. The writer of the Gospel may have had in mind the entry of Gentiles into the primitive church. It also means that there is 'one shepherd, one flock'. The relationship of Father and Son is reflected in the unity of purpose that should characterize the flock of Christ.

Third Sunday after Easter
The Resurrection and the Life

Old Testament Reading   **1 Kings 17: 17–24**

God has power over life and death. That affirmation is central to the Old Testament: 'when thou takest away their breath, they fail, but when thou breathest into them, they recover' (Psalm 104:29, 30). A 'man of God' therefore may be expected to possess that power also. In addition to providing food or rain, in addition to seeing into the past or the future, a 'man of God' may be expected to give life or take it away. I Kings 17:17–24 records such a story. The woman of Zarephath finds her dead son given back to her alive, and confesses that Elijah truly speaks the word of God. We do not need to concern ourselves here with suggestions as to how Elijah achieved this, nor with the kind of person Elijah must have been for such a story to have been told about him. Here we may simply concentrate on the interpretation given by the widow, that God's power to make alive had been displayed in her home. There is an obvious parallel between this story of Elijah and the record in the gospels of the raising of Jairus's daughter and of the raising of the widow of Nain's son. In the case of Elijah and the case of Jesus, God is proclaimed as at work, the God who is Lord of life and death.

New Testament Reading (Epistle)   **Colossians 3: 1–11**

Christ is our life. That could serve as a summary of this passage, which considers two ways in which our daily lives are affected by Christ, our life. First, there is what Christ has done for us. He has demonstrated God's power over life and death and through that power has delivered us from all the powers that could have enslaved our lives. Second, there is what we must do for Christ. We must reflect the effectiveness of Christ's power in our lives by the kind of decisions we make. Our old habits, life-style, inclinations must give way to those which are appropriate to life in Christ. They must suit the mutual responsibilities of a mankind restored to its true unity by

Christ. All this does not, however, mean that we can expect what is apparent to *us* to be apparent to all our contemporaries. Nor ought we to expect that all the mysteries of God's providence should be disclosed to us. Much of Christian life remains 'hidden'. What we can say is that Christ is our life. He is our life now, our new life in a new humanity. He will be our life, full of promise for the future that we shall share with him.

New Testament Reading (Gospel)   **John 11: 17–27**

The Gospel of John includes many individual personalities who are helped by conversations with Jesus to a new understanding of his life and work. This is true for Martha. She first addresses Jesus as a kind of 'man of God' who can bring her brother back into the land of the living: 'Even now I know that whatever you ask of God, God will grant you' (*v.* 22). In the discussion that follows Martha is led to a very different conclusion. She begins to see that, when Jesus raises Lazarus, this is not a demonstration of his or of God's power primarily. It is to help her to recognize that God, in his Son, is offering men eternal life. By 'eternal life' is meant a life free from fear of God's future judgement, a life away from the darkness in which people stumble around, and a life that cannot be annulled by death because it is drawn from unbroken fellowship with God. So Martha, as distinct from Thomas, who sees the visit to Bethany only in terms of the danger it brings, is able to respond to Jesus with faith. In that way, she, and everyone who follows her example, is able to see not only the raising of Lazarus, but more importantly Christ's own death and resurrection as part of God's act of redemption on behalf of mankind, opening up for mankind a new quality of existence and of fellowship with God.

Fourth Sunday after Easter
The Way, the Truth, and the Life

Old Testament Reading   **Proverbs 4: 10–19**

We like our responsibilities presented in a clear and precise way.
The teacher of wisdom in the book of Proverbs is admirable in this
respect. He presents with clarity and precision the two ways, the way
of life, which commends itself by being well-marked and free of
obstacles, and the way of destruction, which lures travellers into
danger and leaves them, like men addicted, living by and for violence. In other words Proverbs is concerned with the consequences of
the choices we make. Men reap what they sow. The Old Testament
as a whole varies between approval of this principle, and a recognition that this is not always how things turn out. Sometimes, for
example, those who choose the way of destruction appear to enjoy a
remarkable easy and trouble-free existence, whereas those who
choose the way of life find nothing seems to go right for them. The
New Testament also speaks of two ways. Matthew 7:13–14 affirms
the usefulness of straightforward alternatives as a guide to living.
But there are New Testament passages which recognize how
dangerous it would be to assume that illness and misfortune are the
result of sin, and that if you speak of the inevitable consequences of
certain choices and actions, you may leave too little room for forgiveness and hope.

New Testament Reading (Epistle)   **2 Corinthians 4: 13–5: 5**

In contrast with the Old Testament teacher of wisdom, Paul presents the way of life as being far from easy and certainly not free of
obstacles. He even suggests that the way of life can often feel like a
kind of death. The demands of Christian living make severe
demands on our physical resources, and we feel ourselves being
worn down in the process. However the Psalmist discovered how to
live confidently and thankfully because of God's ability to help those
in distress, and Paul has experienced the same. 'Scripture says, "I

believed, and therefore I spoke out", and we too, in the same spirit
of faith, believe and therefore speak out' (*v.* 13). Above all, in the
very middle of our work, God builds up our inner resources, and
through the gift of the Spirit gives a guarantee of a life that survives
the terrors of death. We should like to be able to avoid the latter, but
they are part of a life in which God in Jesus Christ has shown his
power to deliver.

New Testament Reading (Gospel)   **John 14: 1–11**

Thomas' uncertainty about the way of Jesus provides an opportunity
for Christ to declare himself to be the Way, the Truth, and the Life.

I am the Way, says Jesus. No one comes to the Father except
through him. The Son alone could blaze the route to the Father's
side, but now the route is open and his disciples may follow. It is,
however, the way of the Cross, and the way of obedience to the
Father. If this is so for the Son, it is true also for his disciples.

I am the Truth, says Jesus. The one who has seen the Son at work
knows the truth about the Father, for in the Son's activities the
Father is uniquely known. To be open to Christ, to be decisive in
following his ways and a home for the Spirit's work is to discover
Truth.

I am the Life, that is, the life which only God can give. This life
means a break with man's self-seeking past and a new beginning,
with God's self-giving love known in Jesus opening up the chance of
unlimited, unending life. The dialogue with Philip suggests that this
kind of claim can only be accepted because of faith in the special
relationship between the Father and the Son, perhaps on the basis of
what we have seen Jesus doing.

Fifth Sunday after Easter
Going to the Father

Old Testament Reading   **Deuteronomy 34**

This chapter brings the story of Israel's desert wanderings to a hopeful conclusion. The prophetic vigour of Moses is commemorated; through him God has led his people out of captivity; the allocation of the Promised Land to the tribes is complete; and their possession of the land is already secure. God has chosen and empowered a successor to give leadership in the same spirit as Moses. It is true that there is some poignancy in the description of Moses's exclusion from the Promised Land, but he leaves them with his people's future secure. He is not remembered as a dead leader. There is no tomb to give evidence of his death. He is commemorated in his full powers, as the one through whom God achieved his purposes for his people. It is a moment to which Israel could look back, and from which Israel could draw inspiration, particularly during the period of exile from the Promised Land. The parallel between Moses's departure and Jesus's departure to the Father is poetic, and only the associations of restoration and renewal link the two.

New Testament Reading (Epistle)   **Romans 8: 28–end**

The Christian has nothing to fear from God or men. This is part of the real change effected by Christ's victory in our human situation. Nothing is left outside of Christ's range of influence, for what God has achieved in Jesus is of cosmic significance. Romans 8:28–39 brings the first main section of that letter to a conclusion with the claim that no power of any kind can separate us from him, when once his rule has been established over our lives. The mystery remains of how and why we have responded to Christ's rule, while others do not, and it is wisest not to be more definitive than Paul is on that subject. Here Paul speaks of God's choice of us; elsewhere he speaks of our choice of Christ. What is beyond doubt is the difference which such commitment to Christ's power makes. Once a man or woman shares Christ's victory, then the fears which might have held us slaves, fears about our past, about our present, or our future, are overcome by a greater reality, the reality of God's love operative in Jesus Christ. For Paul this seems to include freedom from fear of the criticisms of contemporaries, who might disapprove of his methods and Christian life-style. It includes also freedom from fear of God's judgement. For God's act of salvation in establishing Christ as Lord of all is an all-sufficient security and safeguard.

New Testament Reading (Gospel) **John 16: 12–24**

When a child is born, a safe birth makes the worry and the pain a thing of the past. In the same way the departure of Jesus to the Father, a traumatic moment for the disciples, presents itself as a moment of great joy and opportunity. Christ's life and teaching take on a new perspective through the interpretation offered by the Spirit; a new relationship between the disciples and their heavenly Father begins; and their vision of God's work gains new horizons. The sorrow and uncertainty associated with Christ's departure turns into jubilation at his continuing life, and as free access to God is opened up by his work. The good news of what Christ has done must be presented in new situations, and the Spirit will make this possible. To the glory of the Word at creation, and the glory of the Son in his incarnation, is now added the glory given by the Spirit: 'He will glorify me, for everything that he makes known to you, he will draw from what is mine' (*v.* 14).

Ascension Day

The meaning of Ascension Day for Christians does not depend chiefly upon the particular means by which the visible presence of the risen Lord was withdrawn from the disciples. Indeed, three of the four Gospels do not contain any account of such an event. So we may let these readings concentrate our attention on some of the great Christian beliefs which the Ascension illustrates or symbolizes, rather than on the details of the story in Acts.

Old Testament Reading   **Daniel 7: 9–14**

Supreme authority

This is the climax of a vision of the movement of human history which began at *v*. 1. A succession of empires precedes the coming of the everlasting kingdom of 'one like a son of man'. After the judgement scene (*vv.* 9–10) some of the worldly empires (symbolized by animal figures) are allowed to survive for a time, though the worst of them is completely destroyed (*v.* 11). But all other kinds of dominion are subordinated to the rule of the human figure who represents the 'saints of the Most High' (*v.* 22). This vision, probably recorded in the second century B.C. to hearten the Jewish people in a time of bitter persecution, was the source of later speculations about a supernatural Son of Man. The Christian Church sees in it a prophetic declaration that Jesus, as Son of Man, is entrusted with supreme authority. But just as the Ancient of Days sits in judgement along with other assessors (*v.* 9), so the 'one like a son of man' is not an isolated figure, but exercises his supreme authority as representative of the saints of the Most High (*vv.* 18, 25; cf. Matthew 19:28).

New Testament Reading (Epistle)   **Acts 1: 1–11**

Power from on high

The words of the risen Jesus and of the two men in white direct attention away from what is in the future and in the heavens, to what is present and on earth. The removal of Jesus's visible presence should not turn men's eyes to a home 'above the bright blue sky'. They should not even trouble themselves with speculations about the future of their own nation. One thing alone was necessary: the assurance that the same power which had been so evident in the ministry of Jesus would now be available, to the ends of the earth, in the work to which he was sending them.

New Testament Reading (Gospel)   **Matthew 28: 16–end**

Universal presence

Matthew does not explicitly describe this as the last appearance of Jesus to the disciples, and the story only hints at the possibility of an ascension by saying that the meeting had been arranged on a mountain top. But the essential meaning of this passage corresponds to the meaning of today's Epistle. The disciples, reduced to eleven by the defection of Judas Iscariot, are given a task and the ability to do it. The promise, in Acts, of power from on high is suited to the setting of that ascension story; it is replaced here, just as appropriately, by the promise of Jesus's own perpetual presence. The disciples' task is here stated more specifically as baptism and instruction. Probably the form of words has been influenced by the experience of the early church. Its doctrine is reflected in the threefold baptismal formula, and the tendency of its moral instruction is shown in the description of Jesus's teaching as the source of commandments to be obeyed. No doubt the work of the Church needs to be organized, and any organization brings the dangers associated with formulas and rigid rules. But these dangers can be overcome by realizing the everyday presence of Jesus, who has withdrawn from sight in order to be present universally by his Spirit.

Sunday after Ascension Day

Old Testament Reading   **2 Kings 2: 1–15**

The same spirit

We know nothing about the birth of Elijah. Like Jesus in Mark's
Gospel, he comes on the scene in mature manhood. But we have this
story of his life's end, and it is one of the most striking among the
many stories told about him. It says that he did not die, but was
taken up to God's presence. Centuries later it came to be believed
that he would return as the herald of the great Day of the Lord
(Malachi 4:5). But the relevance of this story in today's readings is
that it deals with the continuation of his work. Elisha inherits his
mantle, and with it receives the gifts of his spirit. A man's work and
witness may easily be forgotten and fruitless, unless he is succeeded
by others who continue his work in the power of the same spirit.

New Testament Reading (Epistle)   **Ephesians 4: 1–13**

Diversity in unity

The unspoken assumption of the writer is that Christ, having
ascended above the heavens, has been followed (like Elijah) by those
who witness to the power of his spirit. But as Christ is incomparably
greater than Elijah, so the continuation of his work requires much
more than a single successor. His spirit activates the great company
of his disciples, each one receiving a measure of his gifts (*v.* 7). Of
course, there are all kinds of ways in which Christ's disciples may
share in his work. Here the writer concentrates on ministries within
the Christian community (*v.* 11). It is beyond the scope of his
argument to describe the Christian's ministry to the world at large.
His theme is the creation of a loving community in which every
member, having different gifts, helps to realize the God-given unity
of the whole by devoting those gifts to its service. This is what it
means to 'build up the body of Christ' (*v.* 12). Its unity is truly the
work of the Spirit; but the Spirit's work is only effective when the

members of the church spare no effort (*v.* 3 *NEB*) to live at peace with each other.

New Testament Reading (Gospel)   **Luke 24: 45–end**

God's unchanging purpose

In these concluding verses of Luke's Gospel we have a kind of overlap with the beginning of the Acts of the Apostles. Verses 48–53 say more briefly what we have already read in the Epistle for Ascension Day. The interest, therefore, falls upon *vv.* 44–47, which claim that the death and resurrection of Jesus and the universal preaching of a gospel of forgiveness are 'written in' the Old Testament. There are different ways in which Christians explain this claim. Some would argue that there are particular texts which foretell the events in question. Others would say that the New Testament story fulfils the deepest aspirations of Old Testament religion, and that this is true whether or not the 'proof texts' can be shown to make detailed predictions. What matters most, and what the Christian Church has never doubted, is that God's purpose for mankind is unchanging, and therefore the same in Old and New Testament. The supreme revelation in Jesus Christ cannot contradict any other genuine revelation. Rather it is the full truth which completes all partial truths. Most importantly, it shows in a unique way how innocent suffering can reveal a loving God.

Pentecost

Old Testament Reading   **Genesis 11: 1–9**

Language is one of man's most precious possessions. It enables us to
share thoughts and experiences with our fellow men. But we know
all too well that words can divide as well as unite. Misunderstanding
is almost as easy as understanding. The ancient legend of the Tower
of Babel was told to explain why different peoples had different
languages. But it can be read as a kind of parable. It seems to say that
man's pride and ambition make it impossible for him to understand
his fellows; or that technological achievement itself depends on a
proper humility.

or   **Exodus 19: 16–25**

This passage is shot through with a feeling of awe, or holy dread.
God's presence on the mountain top is represented by frightening
phenomena (*v.* 16). Only Moses and Aaron are allowed to enter the
sacred zone marked out by God's command (*v.* 23). It all sounds
very odd to us, if we have allowed our picture of God to get too much
like an amiable grandfather. But suppose there is in God a 'deep and
dazzling darkness'. Then might we not expect him to reveal himself
at times through unexpected acts of power—through wind and
flame and pentecostal speech?

New Testament Reading (Epistle)   **Acts 2: 1–11 (*or* 1–21)**

The second part of this reading (*vv.* 12–21) must be borne in mind,
even if it is not read aloud in the service. For it is there to explain the
meaning of the strange events which are described in the previous
verses. As with many descriptions of vivid spiritual experiences
(Paul's conversion on the Damascus road, for example) it is impossible to be sure whether the events described were objective, observ-
able events, or whether the description is a vivid way of presenting
the inward experience of the group of disciples. There is room for a
difference of opinion, too, about the exact nature of the gift of

tongues. Some readers believe that the disciples miraculously spoke foreign languages; others believe that to speak 'in tongues' is to speak no actual language, but to communicate through unstructured sounds the spiritual excitement, and even the gist of the message, which the speaker himself understands. Again, other people may seem to be hearing their own languages. What matters chiefly, however, is that the strange events are interpreted by Peter as the fulfilment of a prophecy. The promised day has come, and God has made his Spirit freely available to every man. Now it is not only Moses and Aaron who may approach God's presence. Now languages are no longer a barrier, as at Babel. Communications are open, as they never have been before, between God and man, and between man and man. And it has all been made possible by Jesus of Nazareth.

New Testament Reading (Gospel)   **John 14: 15–26**

The meaning of the passage lies in the linking of key words and ideas: love—commandments—Spirit—indwelling—life. The love of the disciples is shown in their obedience to his commandments. Their obedience ensures the presence of the Spirit as counsellor and guide. This presence is not just nearness; it is actual indwelling, which is unobservable by the world. And the indwelling of the Spirit is life itself, the life of the Master in the lives of the disciples.

or   **John 20: 19–23**

In John's Gospel the glorification of Jesus is connected with his triumphant death (cf. 17:1) rather than with his ascension. So we find the gift of the Spirit following that glorification (cf. 7:39) even before the appearances of the risen Jesus have ceased. By the gift of the Spirit the disciples are so intimately associated with Jesus that they can continue his ministry of forgiveness and judgement.

Trinity Sunday

Old Testament Reading   **Isaiah 6: 1–8**

This striking passage needs little comment: its meaning is conveyed in such memorable images. It declares the majesty of God, before whom even the most devoted of men must feel unclean. Yet as God's majesty is, so is his mercy. And that mercy not only cleanses man's sin, but actually honours man with a share in his own work in the world.

New Testament Reading (Epistle)   **Ephesians 1: 3–14**

By contrast this reading is remarkably difficult to understand. It has evidently been chosen for Trinity Sunday because its movement of thought is from the Father (*v.* 3) to Jesus Christ, and so to the Holy Spirit (*vv.* 13–14). In fact little is said about Father and Spirit. It is the Father whose purpose is fulfilled in the Son (*vv.* 9, 11). It is the Spirit who seals the work of the Son and assures the believer of the ultimate triumph of God's purpose (*vv.* 13–14). But the significance of the Son is more fully described. Notice that the *NEB* contains the phrase 'in Christ' five times. The key to understanding the passage is the idea of incorporation (*v.* 13); that is, the involvement of the believer by faith in all that Christ has done for him. The same general idea is presented in different words in two other places: first as the bestowal of spiritual blessings (*v.* 3) which are Christ's by right and ours only in as far as we are 'in' him; and secondly as the sharing of a heritage (*vv.* 11, 13) which is already ours 'in Christ', yet is still waiting for us to enjoy fully when God's purpose is finally achieved. But the general idea is also developed in detail. The believer shares step by step in the achievement of Christ. As Christ dedicated himself, was accepted by God, secured man's release and forgiveness, and established the true basis for mankind's unity; so by incorporation in him the believer, too, is dedicated by God (*v.* 4), is accepted as a son (*v.* 5), is released from sin and forgiven (*v.* 7), and shares in the unity of creation (*v.* 10). All this is not an afterthought or improvisation of God. It has been his plan since before the creation of the world. (*v.* 4). The writer is not here expounding Trinitarian orthodoxy. Rather he seems almost carried away with excitement as he struggles to express his conviction that the plan of the Father, triumphantly carried out by the Son, will achieve its full realization through the work of the Spirit.

New Testament Reading (Gospel)   **John 14: 8–17**

Again we find Father, Son, and Spirit mentioned together in the development of thought in this passage. Philip has asked to be shown the Father. Jesus replies that the Father can be seen in him, because his own actions and words belong equally to the Father, who is their real source. He and the Father live in each other. But this is not the only kind of indwelling mentioned. The Spirit abides in the disciples and enables them to continue the work of Jesus (*v.* 12). The thought of the passage is complicated by the insertion of another idea, in *vv.* 13–14. These refer to prayer by the spirit-filled disciples to the Father in the name of the Son. But although this is almost an aside to the main argument, we can take it as a reminder that the doctrine of the Holy Trinity matches the experience of the Church at prayer. God in the heart moves us to offer our prayers, shaped by all we know of God incarnate, to God in the heavens. The pattern of Christian belief corresponds to the pattern of Christian worship.

Second Sunday after Pentecost
The Church's Unity and Fellowship

Old Testament Reading   **2 Samuel 7: 4–16**

The prophet Nathan, through a vision, learns that king David may not build a temple for God, but the king is promised that his royal house will continue, and will be blessed by God.

There is a play upon words here. 'House' can mean both 'a house for God' (temple) and also 'a royal house' (lineage). Similarly, for us, 'church' can mean 'parish church' (building) or the Christian community (people). By far the more important reality in Christian belief is *the holy community*. Buildings, though necessary, are comparatively unimportant. The early Church for a long period of time met in various homes suitable for their purpose (Acts 2: 46).

'We are the temple of the living God' (2 Corinthians 6:16, cp. 1 Corinthians 3:17).

New Testament Reading (Epistle)   **Acts 2: 37–end**

Luke, writing about A.D. 80–90, gives us this vivid picture of the life of the earliest Christian community in Jerusalem. The Church's unity and fellowship has five characteristic marks:

1. *Baptism.* 'Those who received Peter's word were baptized.' Baptism is one of the marks of Church membership.
2. *The apostles' teaching.* The apostles had first preached the Gospel and now were teaching both publicly in the temple, and within the Christian fellowship. Holding fast to the Gospel is another sign of Church membership.
3. *The fellowship.* By their baptism and faith in Christ, Christians enter into 'the fellowship', that is, the unity and harmony of those who are united to Jesus Christ and to one another. They are, together, owned by the Holy Spirit. 'Fellowship' means sharing.
4. *The breaking of the bread.* It appears that, at first, the Eucharist was celebrated in the context of a joyful common meal, shared in people's houses. It was in 'the breaking of the bread' that the risen Lord was known to his people (Luke 24:35).

5. *Prayers*. The earliest Christians in Jerusalem continued to share in the Jewish prayers at the appointed hours of day (Acts 3:1) but also met for specifically Christian prayer.

Throughout the passage, we receive a strong sense of *corporate life* ('together', *v.* 44) extending to a sharing of resources. How does your own church fellowship compare with that described in Acts?

New Testament Reading (Gospel)　　　　　　**Luke 14: 15–24**

We have seen that 'the breaking of the bread' is one of the distinguishing marks of the Church's unity and fellowship, and that, at first the eucharist was part of a joyful common meal. In the Gospel for today, the joyful cry goes out: 'All is now ready' (*v.* 17; cp. 2 Corinthians 6:2). What is our response to our Lord's invitation?

'Ye know how grievous and unkind a thing it is, when a man hath prepared a rich feast, decked his table with all kinds of provision, so that there lacketh nothing but the guests to sit down; and yet they who are called (without any cause) most unthankfully refuse to come. Which of you in such a case would not be moved? Who would not think a great injury and wrong done unto him? Wherefore, most dearly beloved in Christ, take ye good heed, lest ye, withdrawing yourselves from this Holy Supper, provoke God's indignation against you. It is an easy matter for a man to say, I will not communicate, because I am otherwise hindered with worldly business. But such excuses are not so easily accepted and allowed before God. If any man say, I am a grievous sinner, and therefore am afraid to come; wherefore then do ye not repent and amend? When God calleth you, are ye not ashamed to say ye will not come? When ye should return to God, will ye excuse yourselves, and say ye are not ready? Consider earnestly with yourselves how little such feigned excuses will avail before God. They that refused the feast in the Gospel, because they had bought a farm, or would try their yokes of oxen, or because they were married, were not so excused, but counted unworthy of the heavenly feast'.

(Exhortation in the Order of Holy Communion, Book of Common Prayer)

Third Sunday after Pentecost
The Church's Confidence in Christ

Old Testament Reading   **Deuteronomy 8: 11–end**

This chapter promises that the people of Israel will find themselves in a land of plenty, their welfare state. The question now arises: 'In her new affluence, will Israel still recognize that she lives by everything that comes from God, or will her prosperity lead her to pride, to forgetfulness of God, and worse?' (G. Henton Davies).

We find ourselves in the same kind of situation, and the question is: *in what do we put our full trust and confidence?*

There are, as Davies has pointed out, three possibilities:
1. *Idolatry*—the danger that we shall abandon the one true God, and put other things in the place of God—wealth, success, sex, the State.
2. *Self-deification.* 'If a man does not worship the true God, and reaches the stage when he is too cultured or educated to worship idols and other gods, he then is inclined to promote himself to the divine vacancy.' '*My* power and the power of *my* hand have gotten me this wealth' (*v.* 17).
3. *Confidence in God.* This is the attitude of the man who knows that, still today in what is one of the world's richer countries, we depend upon God for our knowledge, our achievements, our possessions—for everything.

New Testament Reading (Epistle)   **Acts 4: 8–12**

According to Luke, Jesus had already prepared his followers for persecution, and had given them in advance the assurance that his Holy Spirit would be with them: 'When they bring you before the synagogues and the rulers and the authorities, do not be anxious how or what you are to answer or what you are to say; for the Holy Spirit will teach you in that very hour what you ought to say' (Luke 12:11f). Peter now finds himself in just the situation, and his speech to the Sanhedrin (solemn assembly of Israel's leaders) is marked by *boldness*. The word which is used here means freedom in speaking, openness, plainness, and it occurs no less than three times in this chapter. 'They saw the boldness of Peter and John' (*v.* 13); 'Grant to thy servants to speak thy word with all boldness' (*v.*29); and 'They were all filled with the Holy Spirit and spoke the word of God with boldness' (*v.* 31).

'In the early 1920s, Bukharin was sent from Moscow to Kiev to address a vast anti-God rally. For one hour he brought to bear all the artillery of argument, abuse, and ridicule upon the Christian faith till it seemed as if the whole ancient structure of belief was in ruins. At the end there was a silence. Questions were invited. A man rose and asked leave to speak—a priest of the Orthodox Church. He stood beside Bukharin, faced the people and gave them the ancient, liturgical Easter greeting: "Christ is risen". Instantly, the whole vast assembly rose to its feet, and the reply came back like the crash of breakers against the cliff: "He is risen indeed!" There was no reply; there could not be. When all argument is ended, there remains a fact, the total fact of Jesus Christ. . . . That fact is the authority for the Christian mission. If we are asked for our credentials, we can only answer: "In the name of Jesus" ' (Lesslie Newbigin: *A Faith for this One World?*, p. 59f).

New Testament Reading (Gospel)   **Luke 8: 41–end**

Confidence in Jesus Christ is typified in today's Gospel by the ruler of the synagogue, Jairus, who begs Jesus to come to his house because his twelve-year-old daughter is dying. When he arrives, the mourners laugh at Jesus, for they *know* she is dead. Nevertheless, Jairus puts his confidence in Christ and the girl is restored.

We are reminded of the story earlier in Luke's gospel of the centurion whose expression of unworthiness *and* confidence could well be on our lips as we approach the Lord's Table: 'Lord, I am not worthy that you should come under my roof; but speak the word only, and your servant will be healed'.

Fourth Sunday after Pentecost
The Church's Mission to the Individual

Old Testament Reading   **Isaiah 63: 7–14**

'Evangelism (proclaiming the Gospel) is centred in news which must
be reported in words, about a Person, *an event, a series of events*'
(D. Webster). So today's Old Testament reading is concerned with
the 'steadfast love' of the Lord, demonstrated in his dealings with the
people of Israel, and above all in the great events of the exodus from
Egypt, the crossing of the sea, and his leading them to the land of
promise despite their wilful rebellion. Similarly, the focus in the
apostles' preaching, recorded in the New Testament, is the death
and resurrection of Jesus.

We notice too the connection in this passage between *prayer* and
proclamation. The whole passage is part of a long prayer of intercession by the prophet and his disciples. It consists of a *remembrance*
of the mighty works of God. 'You who put the Lord in remembrance,
take no rest and give him no rest' (Isaiah 62:6). Similarly, in the New
Testament, the Lord's death is proclaimed not only by public
preaching but also in the Church's worship (1 Corinthians 11:26).
We are to offer up spiritual sacrifices in our worship, but also to
show forth the wonderful deeds of God in our mission (1 Peter
2:5, 9).

New Testament Reading (Epistle)   **Acts 8: 26–38**

There are three things to notice here:

1. *The mission is God's.* The meeting between Philip and the eunuch
   from 'Ethiopia' (the modern Sudan) was, humanly speaking,
   improbable. One would hardly expect to meet anyone on a desert
   road, especially 'at noon' (*RSV* margin). But Philip was divinely
   guided. 'The angel of the Lord' means that God was at work. *He*
   always initiates the mission. Its objective and means are to be
   governed by his own character of holy love. It is to God's mission
   that the Church is committed.

2. *Evangelism—an essential part of mission.* Mission is a wide term which must include things like social action. But there is no substitute for evangelism, by which we mean the *proclaiming of the good news* of what God has done, is doing, and will do in Christ, proclaiming it to those who have not heard it, or have not responded to it. Here we find Philip preaching Jesus to the eunuch and bringing him to faith and baptism.

3. *Sensitivity to the needs of the individual.* We observe how Philip was sensitive to the difficulties of this man, and was able to open his mind to the good news of Jesus. Philip starts from where the god-fearing eunuch has got to (reading the scriptures but without understanding them) and from the questions that he is asking (*v.* 34). For effective evangelism there must be a clear grasp of the essential message, a sensitive understanding of the other person, and a message conveyed in relevant terms.'To introduce a person to God we need to know both.'

New Testament Reading (Gospel)   **Luke 15: 1–10**

'If he has lost one of them.' The Gospel for today consists of two of the three parables of the Lost (the sheep, the coin, and the Son), in Luke 15. The parable of the lost sheep is about a fairly rich man; the parable of the lost coin is about a poor woman. But the point is the same in both: 'God rejoices over one sinner who repents'. That is how Jesus himself behaved—receiving individual sinners and sharing table-fellowship with them. And that, says Jesus, is what God is like—a God who rejoices to forgive. He wants the lost to be found because they are his; their wanderings have grieved him and he rejoices at their return home. It has been pointed out that neither a sheep nor a coin can in fact repent! Perhaps we are meant to understand that a man's repentance itself is a gift of God, which follows upon his being found. 'Repentance is joy that God is so gracious' (J. Jeremias).

Fifth Sunday after Pentecost
The Church's Mission to all men

Old Testament Reading   **Ruth 1: 8–17, and 22**

P. G. Wodehouse made one of his characters say: 'a parable is one of
those stories in the Bible which sound at first like a pleasant yarn but
keeps something up its sleeve which pops up and knocks you flat!'
That is supremely true of the parables of Jesus but it is true too of the
book of Ruth, which is a kind of parable. Its purpose was to awaken
God's people to their high privilege and responsibility towards the
nations around them.

In the time of Ezra and Nehemiah (450–400 B.C.) the Jewish
community had, by force of circumstances, become highly exclusive. There were rigorous, fanatical attempts to keep pure the great
revelation they had received, and to prevent its being contaminated
or diluted by the paganism of the nations around them. It was only
too easy for this religious zeal to become arrogant and hostile to the
Gentiles.

The Book of Ruth speaks directly to such a situation, reminding
the Jewish people that the revelation they have received is meant to
be *available for all*, and that Gentiles have a place in the community
of Israel. For was not a Moabite woman (Ruth) the ancestor of the
great king David (Ruth 4:17)?

'Is it conceivable that the Church should deliberately court contamination of her high moral standards and happy congregational
life by inviting her coloured neighbours or unchurched, rebellious,
and exuberant youth to use her well-kept premises? Or again, should
the Church endanger the purity of the faith once delivered to the
saints by deliberately seeking contact with Communists, agnostics,
homosexuals, or other kinds of deviationists?' (G. A. F. Knight).

New Testament Reading (Epistle)   **Acts 11: 4–18**

Peter is summoned to meet the leaders of the Jerusalem Church and
gives an account of the dramatic events which have taken place in

268

Caesarea. He tells them how God led him by a vision (Acts 10) and the arrival in Joppa of messengers from Cornelius. As Peter was speaking in Cornelius's house, the Holy Spirit came as he had come upon the apostles at Pentecost. Peter recalls that Jesus had told them: 'John baptized with water, but you shall be baptized with the Holy Spirit' (Acts 1:5). Since God has now given the same gift to the Gentiles in Caesarea as to the Jerusalem disciples when they acknowledged Jesus as Lord, Peter asserts that he could not hinder God's purpose by refusing to baptize them. Having heard his account of what has taken place the Church leaders, including those who have opposed him, now acknowledge that God has indeed acted and that 'repentance leading to Life' has been granted to Gentiles without their first having to become Jews. This chapter marks the climax to the story of the extending of the Church's mission to Gentiles.

New Testament Reading (Gospel) **Luke 10: 1–12**

One of the chief characteristics of Luke's Gospel is its conviction that *the Gospel is for all*. It is universal in its scope and its appeal. It is Luke who gives us the *Nunc dimittis* in which Simeon sees the infant Jesus as 'a light for revelation to the Gentiles'; Luke, who quotes Isaiah 40: 'All flesh shall see the salvation of God'. It is Luke who gives us the sermon of Jesus, in the Nazareth synagogue, with its examples taken from the widow of Zarephath in *Sidon*, and from Naaman the *Syrian*. Another example of Luke's universalism may be seen at the end of his Gospel when he speaks of repentance and forgiveness being 'preached in Christ's name *unto all the nations* beginning from Jerusalem'.

In today's Gospel, the sending out of the 70 (or 72) foreshadows the universal mission of the disciples which is to be extended 'to every place where Jesus was about to come' (*v.* 1) in the wider world beyond the borders of Judaism.

Can you think of practical ways in which the vision of your own local church may be enlarged to embrace all men, all nations? Is that vision reflected in your Sunday worship?

Sixth Sunday after Pentecost
The New Man

Old Testament Reading   **Micah 6: 1–8**

The people of Israel ask 'Micah' how they may atone for their sins.
What they propose is a series of offerings to God increasing in
magnitude and costliness from burnt offerings and calves, to
thousands of rams and rivers of oil, even to child sacrifice! The
prophet replies that, contrary to popular expectation, the Lord does
not demand an unending supply of sacrifices. What he does require
is the practice of justice, kindness and humility. Micah's reply has
been called 'the finest guide to practical religion to be found in the
Old Testament'.

Just as today's Epistle describes the way of life for the baptized
Christian, so this lesson from Micah is a kind of Old Testament
catechism.

It sums up the teaching of the great prophets:
'Let justice roll down like waters' (Amos 5:24);
'I desire steadfast love and not sacrifice' (Hosea 6:6);
'The meek shall obtain fresh joy in the Lord' (Isaiah 29:19).

New Testament Reading (Epistle)   **Ephesians 4: 17–end**

In the days of the early Church, when a man was baptized, he would
strip off his old clothes before entering the water, and then as he
emerged, newly baptized, he would put on white garments, sym-
bolizing the new life in Christ upon which he had now entered. This
practice may well account for the language used in this epistle about
'putting off' the old nature and 'putting on' the new. Here the
Christians are told (*v.* 22) to put off 'the old man' with his corrupt
deceits and to put away falsehood (*v.* 25) and to put on 'the new man'
created for holiness and righteousness (*v.* 24).

Each sin or weakness is to be replaced by a positive virtue.
Thus:

The old man	*The new life in Christ*
falsehood	truth
stealing	work and giving
corrupt speech	conversation to build others up
bitterness	forgiveness
drunken revelry (5:18)	exhilaration of Christian worship (5:19)
darkness (5:8)	light (5:14)

'Awake, O sleeper, and arise from the dead, and Christ shall give you light'.

New Testament Reading (Gospel)   **Mark 10: 46–end**

Here we are given a picture of blindness. 'The disciples themselves understood none of these things'—they too were blind. And by the wayside sat a blind man who reached out toward Jesus the Light, and in doing so was made whole.

In this story of the healing of blind Bartimaeus, the interest centres upon the blind man himself and his attitude and behaviour. It may well be that the early Church used this story, holding up the blind man as an example to Christian believers and to those who were on the verge of belief. The man is only too well aware of his helplessness, and when Jesus passes by, he knows that it is now or never, so he calls out urgently for help. Those around him try to silence him, but his faith is not to be quenched. As soon as Jesus calls him, he makes his eager response, and is 'saved' from his blind helplessness. At once, he begins to follow Jesus in the way of Christian discipleship (see Acts 9:2).

Father Hebert of Kelham used to teach that this Gospel comes addressed directly to ourselves. *I* am Bartimaeus, the blind man. I hear the Lord passing by on the way to the Cross. But because of the dullness of my blinded sight, I do not know what it means. The Cross is the supreme work of Love: Love in action. But I do not know what the humility and self-sacrifice of the Cross really is. So I cry to him for light. 'Lord, that I may receive my sight!' When he has opened my eyes that I may see, then I shall follow him with his faithful people in the way.

271

Seventh Sunday after Pentecost
The More Excellent Way

'What does the LORD your God require of you?' (Deuteronomy 10:12) is a profound question to which men of differing perceptions have offered different answers. Today's readings all presume that it is possible to answer this question. And they do so for one reason alone: their writers believed that the Eternal, Unknowable God had in fact revealed himself sufficiently for man to *want* to respond to him personally. They therefore expected men to make a deliberate response of obedience.

Old Testament Reading   **Deuteronomy 10: 12–11: 1**

The Book of Deuteronomy, like a massively constructed sermon, recites God's saving activity in Israelite history; lists God's known commands; and then exhorts people to obedience, reasoning, persuading, and challenging them into response. These elements, common throughout the book, are all present in today's passage. The God we are speaking of is the Creator (*vv.* 14, 17). Yet astonishingly he has 'set his heart in love upon. . . . you' (*v.* 15). The famous deliverance of Israel from Egypt (*v.* 22) left this statement beyond doubt. Such love requires and expects love in return. Hence the incredible command to love God (*v.* 12)—how can one *command* love? This love is to be expressed in utterly down-to-earth ways: by keeping 'the commandments and statutes of the LORD' (*v.* 13). These commands include such practical affairs as ensuring justice and the necessities of life for the community's disadvantaged (orphans, widows, and non-citizen inhabitants). Such people are declared to be the concern of God (*v.* 18). By loving them, we are thus in an almost sacramental way expressing our love for God.

New Testament Reading (Epistle)   **Romans 8: 1–11**

Paul takes up a similar stance. God has declared his love not only in rescuing Israel through the Exodus from Egypt, but in the New

Exodus achieved through Christ's death and resurrection, with the result that 'there is therefore now no condemnation for those who are in Christ Jesus' (*v.* 1). This joyous news, however, expects a response. Christians are expected to 'walk not according to the flesh but according to the Spirit' (*v.* 4). They are to 'set their minds' (*RSV*) on certain things and not on others (*vv.* 5–7—examples of what Christians should set their minds on are listed in detail in chapters 12 onwards). This 'setting of the mind' is a deliberate thing, involving deliberate choices. But, Paul is quick to add, we do not have to rely simply upon the strength of our own mental resolution (that would indeed be 'to walk according to the flesh'). We have available to empower us the Spirit of the God who raised Christ Jesus from the dead. He 'will give life to your mortal bodies' (*v.* 11).

New Testament Reading (Gospel) **Mark 12: 28–34**

The Gospel reading contains Jesus's so-called 'summary of the law', now built into our eucharistic liturgy. By 'first' commandment is meant not only the most important, but the one which is the foundation upon which all the others are built; the root from which all the others take life. His choice of first commandment is taken from Jewish liturgy (it is part of Jewish daily private prayer) and is a quotation of Deuteronomy 6:4. The second commandment is quoted from Leviticus 19:18. Notice that Christ is not prepared to cite the first command on its own: you cannot love God in the abstract! Conversely, notice that love of neighbour is a secondary command: its fulfilment rests upon our perception of the nature of God (cf. Deuteronomy 10:18). And 'he is your praise' (Deuteronomy 10:21).

Lord, all our doings without love are nothing worth. Send your Holy Spirit and pour into our hearts that most excellent gift.

Eighth Sunday after Pentecost
The Fruit of the Spirit

Old Testament Reading   **Ezekiel 37: 1–14**

The Old Testament reading holds a word of encouragement to those who are despondent, doubting that God can ever do anything through them. Ezekiel's fantasy-vision was recounted to the exiles in Babylon who forlornly claimed: 'Our bones are dried up, and our hope is lost; we are clean cut off' (*v.* 11)—that is 'we are bound for extinction'. But the message of the chapter is the sure hope of restoration ('I will bring you home'—*v.* 12), and this will come about through the life-giving power of God's spirit (*v.* 14). (To understand the force of this strange vision and prophecy, it is important to realise that the three English words 'spirit', 'breath', and 'wind', all translate a single Hebrew word *ruah*. So as you read the passage, bear in mind all three ideas, whichever word is used in English).

New Testament Reading (Epistle)   **1 Corinthians 12: 4–13**

'In the one Spirit we were all baptized into one body' is the great declaration made to us before we give each other The Peace at the Eucharist. That declaration lies embedded in today's Epistle (*v.* 13). The context is a particular problem which Paul saw to be afflicting the Christian community at Corinth: rivalry between individual church members had led them to spar with each other over their respective spiritual gifts (a parody of their attitudes is presented in *vv.* 14–21). Paul corrects this problem by insisting that any individual's spiritual gift (*charisma* in Greek) is not given for his own personal glory or advancement; it is given 'for the common good' (*v.* 7). It is significant that most (if not all) of the gifts which he then proceeds to cite (*vv.* 8–10) can only be used in the course of ministry to the whole Christian community. Utterances of wisdom and knowledge (*v.* 8) seem to refer to discourses given at Christian gatherings (cf. 'preaching with wisdom . . . preaching instruction'—*JB*); while gifts of healing, prophecy, distinguishing spirits, and interpreting tongues (*vv.* 9–10) obviously do not benefit the recipient of the gift, but those to whom he ministers. The essential point is that *each* member of the Christian community has a special gift (*v.* 11) which must be contributed to the community if that body is to be whole and healthy (*v.* 12).

New Testament Reading (Gospel)   Luke 6: 27–38

If the Epistle describes a Christian's relations within the community of faith, the Gospel portrays his relations with (hostile) outsiders. This famous collection of Jesus's sayings commences with the command 'Love our enemies' (*v.* 27), and then proceeds to develop what a radical application of love would mean in particular situations. The situations given all normally teem with resentments and provocations: violent abuse (*vv.* 28–29), theft (*v.* 29), deceit (*v.* 30), credit facilities (*v.* 34). Such teaching sounds more idealistic than realistic. One would be inclined to dismiss it as a counsel of perfection, were it not such an apt description of Jesus's own bearing in the face of provocation. Notice that the grounds for such teaching is the nature of God himself—'for he is kind to the ungrateful and the selfish' (*v.* 35). This corresponds closely with what we read last week.

Almighty God, who sent your Holy Spirit to be the life and light of your Church: open our hearts to the riches of his grace.

Ninth Sunday after Pentecost
The Whole Armour of God

It is a commonplace to describe the Christian life as a battle. At baptism each of us is commissioned to be 'Christ's faithful soldier' and instructed 'manfully to fight under his banner'. The warrant for such military imagery is to be found throughout Scripture, and typically in today's readings.

Old Testament Reading   **1 Samuel 17: 37–50**

Most of us first heard the Goliath story at Sunday School, and probably remember it as a story of heroic courage against a giant. But it is more than a war story. The narrator gives the story a decidedly theological moral. David's greatness lies not only in his physical courage, but also in his faith in the LORD; he certainly acts bravely, but he also provides a theological commentary upon his deed. The background to the story is the Israelite idea of the 'Holy War'. Their God, Yahweh, was a warrior God who himself fought to defend his covenant people (e.g. Exodus 15:3; Joshua 6:16; 8:18; Judges 7:15). The full title of the Israelite God was 'Yahweh of armies (LORD of hosts)' (*v.* 45). The emphasis of the story is accordingly on the belief that 'the battle is the LORD's' (*v.* 47) and upon David's total reliance upon this belief. Notice the powerful contrast between *vv.* 38–39 and *v.* 40, and the moralistic message of *v.* 50. The weapons which actually proved fatal were patently primitive; David does not even possess a weapon to despatch Goliath, and has to use the giant's own sword (*v.* 51). David's faith as earlier declared in *v.* 37 is thus seen to be justified.

New Testament Reading (Epistle)   **2 Corinthians 6: 3–10**

The great catalogue of Paul's apostolic sufferings, including references to his being flogged, imprisoned, and mobbed (*v.* 5), leaves us in no doubt as to the bitterness with which he was opposed. How easily he could have retaliated in kind—and lost the battle! Instead he is at pains to ensure that he puts 'no obstacle in anyone's way, so that no fault may be found with our ministry' (*v.*3), lest perchance the enemy may become a brother Christian. But Paul does not just stand placidly taking every blow delivered at him. He has weapons: 'the weapons of righteousness' (*v.*7). It is with these weapons that he positively commends the Gospel, even in the midst of the mêlée. He lists them in *vv.*6–7. Notice how many of them correspond to the Christian virtues, the fruits of the Spirit (Galatians 5:22f).

New Testament Reading (Gospel)   **Mark 9: 14–29**

The Gospel passage describes a battle of another kind. The story is often considered as the healing of an epileptic (from the symptoms described in *vv.*18 and 20). But that is not how Mark actually presents the incident. The boy is said to be in the control of a spirit, whom Jesus addresses (*v.*25). His word overpowers the spirit, and the boy is released. Throughout this gospel, Jesus is presented as freeing a world held in the grip of Satan's usurping power. Jesus's 'mighty works' are all signs that 'the Kingdom of God' is being restored, and the powers of evil driven out and conquered. In this case the chief weapon in the fight is said to be prayer (*v.*29).

We have no power of ourselves to help ourselves. Keep us both outwardly in our bodies and inwardly in our souls.

Tenth Sunday after Pentecost
The Mind of Christ

Christians have always stressed the need for holy living. When it comes to the problem of expressing what that means, Christian teachers have always resorted to stories of saintly people whose example is to be followed. Supremely the imitation of Christ is commended to us. Passages of Scripture are therefore often treated as 'examples to be followed'. Although this method of interpretation does not do full justice to today's readings, it would seem to be the spirit in which the lectionary requires us to use the Old Testament and Gospel reading: both exemplify the exhortations of the Epistle.

Old Testament Reading   **1 Samuel 24: 1–17**

The context of this reading is that after king Saul's attempt on his life, David has been forced to flee as an outlaw, and has taken refuge in the wild desert area on the west of the Dead Sea. The story may be read at two levels.

Most obviously it illustrates the magnanimity of David and exhibits him as utterly honourable, the reverse image of Saul's insane hatred. When presented with an apparently God-given opportunity, he will not touch the Lord's anointed. In which case the thrust of the story is: such was the innocence and generosity of the man who was to become king of all Israel (cf. *v.* 11).

At another level, however, the story is about the divinely prepared fate in store for both David and Saul. David saved himself from blood-guiltiness and the divine retribution that would surely follow assassination of the LORD's anointed. But he has nevertheless ensured that Saul will be killed—by Yahweh. The cutting off of Saul's skirt symbolises the cutting off of his life. (The garment, as it were, is the man himself, and to touch it is to lay hands on the person.) In ancient thought, such a symbol is *active*, and has the power to bring about the event it represents. This is made clear by David's call upon Yahweh to avenge him (*vv.* 12 and 15), and most remarkably by Saul's own acknowledgement that David will become king (*v.*20). Henceforth, events unavoidably move in favour of David.

New Testament Reading (Epistle) **Galatians 6: 1–10**

The Epistle contains wise advice on the tactful correction of misbehaviour in the Christian community. The task of correction is only to be undertaken by those 'who are spiritual', and is to be done in a 'spirit of gentleness'. The whole object of the exercise is that the sinner may be 'restored' (*v.*1). It is therefore essential that those Christian leaders charged with the duty of correction should not do so in any censorious or patronizing fashion. Their own special temptation will be to regard themselves as spiritually superior. Paul therefore wisely advises leaders to 'look to yourself, lest you too be tempted' (*v.*1). If a leader is to compare himself with anyone, it must be with his former self (*v.*4); if there has been spiritual progress, then there may be something to be proud about: 'his reason to boast will be in himself' (*v.*4). Paul warns leaders that they are accountable for their own behaviour: 'each man will have to bear his own load' (*v.*5). Nevertheless, the commandment of love, 'the law of Christ' (*v.*2), demands that they assist others who are struggling under their loads. This thought leads into exhortations to material giving (*vv.*6–10).

New Testament Reading (Gospel) **Luke 7: 36–end**

Jesus's own behaviour in the Gospel story perfectly exemplifies the attitude required by the Epistle. His correction of Simon is tactful, yet direct. Fundamentally, however, the story is about Jesus's authority to forgive sins (*v.*49).

Give us the same mind that was in Christ Jesus that, sharing his humility, we may come to be with him in his glory.

Eleventh Sunday after Pentecost
The Serving Community

A marked feature of the biblical record is its insistence that God has called not only individuals, but whole communities into his service. The Old Testament is the record of a *nation*'s pilgrimage; Paul in his missionary preaching aimed not merely to convert individuals, but to found *churches*; Jesus too gathered a *community* of disciples around himself. All three of today's readings hold a vision of a community called into being by God and devoted to his service.

Old Testament Reading   **1 Chronicles 29: 1–9**

This reading comes from one of the latest books of the Old Testament, written some seven centuries after David's lifetime. The Priestly author of Chronicles-Ezra-Nehemiah (originally a single work) aimed to review the ancient traditions of Judah from Adam to about 350 B.C. He drew heavily upon the books of Samuel and Kings, but in a highly selective way. He was living at a time when there were no more kings or prophets in Judah, when the Temple and its ordered round of worship to the One God was the focus of all Jewish faith. This fact controlled the Chronicler's selection of material. For instance he has no interest in David's court history. Rather, David is presented as the king who brought the ark to Jerusalem (an undisputed fact), and then made all the necessary preparations for the Temple which Solomon was later to build (chs. 21–29). Almost certainly the historical David did no such thing! The Chronicler is describing the Temple organization and worship of his own day, and seeking to give them ancient authority by claiming king David as their originator. He is thus presenting us with a vision of an ideal community, where the entire nation, led by their devoted king, give fabulous treasures for the service of God. Much emphasis is laid on their open spirit: they 'had given willingly . . . with a whole heart' (*v.*9).

New Testament Reading (Epistle)   **Philippians 1: 1–11**

The Church at Philippi seems to have been Paul's great pride and joy. Alone of all the letters he wrote, this one has no words of reproach. Primarily it is a 'thank-you letter' in response to presents the Philippians had sent him while in prison (see 4:18). Throughout the letter he constantly rejoices in the Philippian community's support of his mission 'from the first day' (*v.* 5), so vividly described in Acts 16:12–40. They seem completely to have caught Paul's vision of a world-wide community of Christian churches, bound together in fellowship, and supporting each other (cf. 4:15,16). Hence he speaks of them with unusual depth of feeling: 'I hold you in my heart' (*v.* 7); 'I yearn for you' (*v.* 8). His prayer for them (*vv.* 9–11) is a model of what intercessory prayer may be.

New Testament Reading (Gospel)   **Matthew 20: 1–16**

As with many of Jesus's parables, there is a surprise twist in the story. The point is made in the householder's final words (*vv.* 14–15), *not* in *v.* 16. The denarius (a small silver Roman coin) may be regarded as the usual wage for a day's labour (*v.* 2). We are left pondering whether in paying this same wage to the latecomers the householder is being unfair or generous! But this, implies Jesus, is precisely what happens in the 'kingdom of heaven'. We cannot choose our fellow-workers (Jesus's own community included some disreputable characters—cf. 21:31). Neither can we earn individual merit in the eyes of our Employer (as the Pharisees believed). It is sufficient that we have joined the labour force.

Give us the will to be the servant of others as Christ was the servant of all.

Twelfth Sunday after Pentecost
The Witnessing Community

God's people witness to his truth from within their life in the world. They share a vision of mankind united and at peace; they build on the insights already vouchsafed to men, but move beyond them by giving glory to God alone.

Old Testament Reading   Micah 4: 1–5

The terrible experiences of exile wrung from Israel this new vision of hope, restoration, peace, and justice. An oracle expressed in very similar terms was added, as in this passage, to several of the earlier prophetic books. The little hill of Zion will be lifted up as the highest mountain, a beacon for the rest of the world, attracting men by a general appeal for an end to war, for a life secure and without fear, and for reconciliation and healing of past wrongs. Israel here discovers a new mission in the world, no longer confined within its ancestral exclusivism, but as the guardian in a restored Jerusalem of the word and law of the eternal God, which is essentially universal in scope.

The hopes of the exile, however, were not carried through into fulfilment in the post-exilic period. The new mission had only moderate success in gathering the nations into Jerusalem: it remained for Jesus and the Apostles to inaugurate the period of the realization of these hopes.

New Testament Reading (Epistle)   Acts 17: 22–end

The address of Paul to the sophisticated audience at Athens is a model of missionary tactics and illustrates how he became 'all things to all men, that he might by every means save some'. Man's confused and misdirected religious yearnings are the starting point for the revelation of the sovereign Lord of Israel (*v.*24, cf. Isaiah 42:5) whose transcendence exceeds the bounds of human imagination. He is also the source of life and breath, already nearer to man than he supposed, and it is his immanent activity which determines the periods of history and the disposition of the nations (*v.* 26). Man's origin from him and his very existence within him are confirmed by quotations from the Greek poets (*v.* 28). However, in the Christian gospel the unrecognized presence of God breaks into open proclamation. For now God requires men to put away former ignorance, to repent and believe in the Resurrection of Jesus and his future coming as judge.

The reception at Athens was mixed, but Paul had borne faithful witness, incorporating the half-understood perceptions of men into a wider and clearer vision.

New Testament Reading (Gospel)   **Matthew 5: 13–16**

Jesus pictures the role of his disciples as witnesses in one of his double parables. The two images complement and explain each other. What salt is to the taste, light is to the eyes—a single crystalline point of brilliance enlivening and illuminating a dull and dark environment. The disciple betrays his commission if he merges into the bland neutrality of the world, or tries to hide his light among the clutter of ordinary life. He is rather to shine out with warmth and welcome, like a house with the lights ablaze. And together the whole community forms a city on a hill that cannot be hid, like the new Jerusalem whose radiance is a light to the nations. But this self-exposure is not that men may applaud the virtues of individual Christians or the Church, but that they may give the glory to the gracious God to whom they bear witness.

Thirteenth Sunday after Pentecost
The Suffering Community

The suffering of God's saints takes many forms: Jeremiah met with rejection and ridicule, the early Christians with persecution and heresy. Jesus himself sanctified this suffering by his own warning that it was inseparable from fidelity to God in a world alienated from him, and also by becoming himself the supreme example of it.

Old Testament Reading   Jeremiah 20: 7–11a

In this poem, Jeremiah plumbs the depths of his own suffering in the service of God. It is difficult for us to enter into another's experience of pain: the soul is here alone with its God and the blunt familiarity of the language the prophet uses to accuse God (v. 7) should be understood in this light. Jeremiah suffers inwardly from two opposing forces; one is the effect of ridicule and the consequent estrangement and whispered betrayal of his friends who will have nothing more to do with him. The other is the 'fire shut up in his bones' (v. 9) when, unwilling to appear foolish in the eyes of men, he tries to suppress the message. He is caught therefore in a dilemma. He feels an inexorable compulsion to preach a message that men reject as folly. But 'the foolishness of God is wiser than men, and the weakness of God is stronger than men' so that initial accusation and despair turn eventually to faith that God is with him, despite everything, as a dreadful warrior (v. 11).

New Testament Reading (Epistle)   Acts 20: 17–35

Paul's farewell speech to the presbyters at Miletus is a testament of suffering faithfully endured in the service of the Gospel, and a warning of suffering still to come for the church after his departure. The trials which befell Paul through the plots of the Jews (v. 19) are impressively listed in his own Second letter to the Corinthians (11:23–9). And although he prayed often with tears for an end to his troubles, he was taught to suffer in humility when God said

(2 Corinthians 12:9) 'My grace is sufficient for you, for my power is made perfect in weakness'. And he preached the Gospel even more insistently because of his sufferings. The Church leaders are warned (v. 29) of future troubles even more heart-rending, for after Paul has gone and is no longer able to fight their battles for them, 'fierce wolves will come in among you not sparing the flock', that is heretics arising from the community itself who will draw the disciples away from the truth. And this suffering, though inward, will be even more anguished. They will see their work being undermined from within, they will feel betrayed and frustrated. Nevertheless God's word of grace (v. 32) is able to build them up to sanctification. And suffering can be accepted, even this extreme form of spiritual suffering, if it is held together with that redemptive shedding of blood by which the Lord obtained a people for his own possession (v. 28).

New Testament Reading (Gospel)   **Matthew 10: 16–22**

The teaching of Jesus on the inevitability of suffering was not an untried theory, but a lived experience. His words here are to be seen in the light of his own self-offering in life and in death. In his controversies with opponents he was wise like a serpent; in his meekness when accused as innocent as a dove; he was delivered up to the Council, flogged, taken before pagan courts, betrayed by his own brethren, but enduring to the end he was raised from the dead and became the source of salvation to all men.

Matthew interprets the warning about wolves, like Paul in Acts, of the threat of heresy (cf. 7.15). He has also placed the prediction of persecution to come much earlier in his gospel than it is in Mark (cf. Mark 13:9–13) within the so-called mission charge, in order to show that suffering is not just a sign of the End, but even more is a present reality for the Church. In this way the community, persecuted from without, and torn apart within, imitates her Lord and remains faithful to his teaching.

Fourteenth Sunday after Pentecost
The Family

The family is the primary earthly analogue for the relations of God with the world. It is the setting in which men are taught by nature to respond to the claims of charity, to share in the creative process, and where after betrayal they learn the poignant lesson of reconciliation.

Old Testament Reading
Genesis 45: 1–15

This touching scene of reunion forms the climax of the story of the family of Jacob. His was anything but a united and happy family. In earlier sections of the story we have seen jealousy, inconsiderateness, and tactlessness driving wedges between the twelve brothers. Now at last they are reunited. The reaction to Joseph's self-disclosure is first one of fear. His brothers had seen their misfortunes as the result of divine anger at their treatment of Joseph, so are in a penitent and nervous frame of mind. However, Joseph shows himself unexpectedly forgiving, and is overcome by tears at this reconciliation.

But this story has more than human interest. For the relations of the twelve patriarchs are the model for the sacred unity of the twelve tribes of Israel. Forgiveness and reconciliation are concepts grasped first in the context of family life, but they contribute to a higher religious consciousness.

New Testament Reading (Epistle)
Ephesians 3: 14–end

Here we are told that the Fatherhood of God is that from which all human families are named. This is the reverse of what we should expect, for we tend to think of God's fatherhood as the projection of a comforting paternalism onto a universe in which we feel less than fully at home. But not so the biblical writers; for them God's fatherhood, his loving creativeness, is the fundamental reality, and human families are permitted by his grace to share a secondary creativity. The family provides the basis of love which is necessary for growth, and God has given us, through the Spirit of Christ indwelling the heart, the root and ground of love, so that we may grow to understand the unimaginable dimensions of God's grace. In response to this transcendent love the Church, which is the family of faith (cf. 5:21–33), sings a hymn of praise (*vv*. 20–21).

New Testament Reading (Gospel)   **Luke 11: 1–13**

The Lord's prayer is the family prayer of Christ's disciples: it knits them together as a group, and they address their petitions to the one who is Father of all. The two parables which follow point to two different ways the family can operate. In the first it is inward looking and exclusive—they are tucked up in bed together, impervious to the claims of charity. But even though men may be selfish and callous to others' needs, they know, as the second parable tells us, how to respond naturally to their hungry children, and they gain thereby an insight into the nature of the heavenly Father who is eager to hear our requests and quickly gives us what we most need, his Holy Spirit.

Fifteenth Sunday after Pentecost
Those in Authority

Political power places those who wield it in a position of fearful responsibility. They need the help of God's wisdom and the constant prayers of those they govern, if they are to retain their integrity and avoid the lapse into intrigue and corruption of which the murder of John the Baptist is an object-lesson.

Old Testament Reading   **1 Kings 3: 4–15**

The young Solomon is facing the formidable task of succeeding his father David as ruler of Israel. Like all good rulers, he feels keenly the immensity of the responsibility he has been given by God (*v*.9); and he is also very aware of his youth and inexperience (*v*.7). So he prays that God will continue the covenant of steadfast love that he made with David into the new reign, and that he may be granted the practical wisdom necessary for a king.

Solomon's selfless desire for the well-governing of his people is rewarded, as he is granted an insight into the generosity of God towards those who make their requests of him in humility. God promises not only to enable Solomon to rule wisely and well, but also to grant him riches and long life precisely because he has not selfishly asked for personal advancement (*vv*. 11–13). By his prayer Solomon has shown himself to be a king worthy of his calling.

New Testament Reading (Epistle)   **1 Timothy 2: 1–7**

We find the injunction to pay respect to those in authority in several of the epistles (cf. e.g. Romans 13:1–7: 1 Peter 2:13–14). The reason for this is that those in authority, whether they know it or not, hold a sacred trust from God for the maintenance of peace and justice among men. In this passage the Christian's duty is extended to include the ministry of intercession for rulers and kings. Nevertheless, obedience to the state in no way compromises the Christian's first allegiance to God. He alone is our Saviour (*v*. 3) and his salvation is mediated to us through Christ alone (*v.*5). Although the title Saviour is much used in the Old Testament, it is rare in the New, chiefly because it had been taken over by the Imperial cult. Men like Ptolemy of Egypt, Julius Caesar, and Augustus had themselves proclaimed 'universal saviour'. In reply to this the Christian worships God alone, but fulfils his duty to earthly rulers by praying for them to use their god-given authority in the proper way.

New Testament Reading (Gospel)   **Matthew 14: 1–12**

The story of the death of John the Baptist is a study in how not to use authority. Herod's decline into corruption can be traced more easily in the longer account in Mark's Gospel (6:14–29). John had made himself unpopular at court by criticizing the king's illicit marriage. To please his wife, Herod had John arrested, but he recognized the holiness of the man, and would not have him executed. He was afraid of him at the same time as being strangely attracted by his shining integrity. His wife, however, was out for revenge. By playing on his weakness—his bravado, his lust, his extravagant promises—she made him execute John despite his scruples. Little wonder that Herod was thereafter plagued by the thought that John would come back to haunt him in some form or other (*v.*2).

Sixteenth Sunday after Pentecost
The Neighbour

The neighbour in need is the sacred means through which the God who loves us brings his claim to bear upon us. To reject this claim wilfully means to reject God and to become isolated in a private hell by setting oneself at an unbridgeable distance both from God and from one's fellow men.

Old Testament Reading   **Deuteronomy 15: 7–11**

The Israelite institution of the 'sabbatical year', when debts are redeemed or even cancelled outright, has just been referred to (15:1–6). This is the Lord's way of ensuring that his people do not fall irretrievably into indigence and slavery. Even in ordinary years, compassion towards the poor is what God requires. The heart, the hand, the eye are to remain open to the needs of others. The poor man is nonetheless our brother, his prayers are heard by the heavenly Father, and to refuse his requests constitutes sin against the God of compassion. Nor is it enough to dole out charity grudgingly, nor to cut down on voluntary giving as the compulsory year of release approaches. The God who is the source of all blessing demands not cold comfort but open-handed generosity from us in return.

That poverty is an ineradicable social evil (*v.* 11) leads not to hardbitten resignation but to greater action. Jesus was saying much the same in Mark 14:7 when he defended the generosity of the woman in anointing him, for 'though he was rich, for your sake he became poor that by his poverty you might become rich' (2 Corinthians 8:9).

New Testament Reading (Epistle)   **1 John 4: 15–end**

John here links together faith and ethics in the closest possible connection. One must confess Jesus as Son of God, because this is to recognize the way God has loved us. But in order to abide in God, one must also abide in love. It is because he sees it as a failure of love that John is so hostile to heresy and unbelief in this letter. But conversely, any lack of love towards the brother in need is itself heretical. 'If a man says he loves God while hating his brother, he is a liar.' It is sometimes suggested that John's concentration on love within the Christian brotherhood constitutes a reduction of the all-embracing definition of the neighbour as anyone in need which we find in the teaching of Jesus, but this is to make a false deduction from the limited scope of the author's immediate purpose. Furthermore, the principle of love for all, even the enemy, is strongly implied when he says, 'we love, because he first loved us' (*v.* 19). For it was while we were yet sinners and enemies of God that Christ died for us.

New Testament Reading (Gospel)   **Luke 16: 19–end**

Seldom in the gospels are the consequences of lovelessness towards the neighbour so vividly or precisely detailed. Jesus re-employs a traditional story which describes the dramatic reversal in the life to come. The poor despised neighbour is acknowledged by Abraham as a true son; the rich man who failed to keep the law of love towards the neighbour finds that he is tormented in a lonely hell. The after-life in his case however is just a projection of the manner in which he lived on earth. He did not acknowledge the existence of his neighbour then, and he finds himself isolated and friendless now, cut off by an impassable gulf both from the redeemed and from his brethren who are still alive. The hellish loneliness of one whose heart and eye and hand are closed to human need is exactly mirrored in this story; for such a one not even the message of God's love in the death and resurrection of Christ could break through the self-imposed isolation.

Seventeenth Sunday after Pentecost
The Proof of Faith

Faith is not an arbitrary decision, it has its own certainty. The inner proof which convinces the believer includes the dimensions of resilient hope, the gift of the Spirit, and trust in the intrinsic authority of the message.

Old Testament Reading   **Jeremiah 32: 6–15**

What at first seems a purely commercial transaction turns out on closer inspection to be an act of faith. Jeremiah is given the right of redemption of a piece of land belonging to his uncle. The law is explained in Leviticus 25:25ff. and was presumably intended to keep property from passing out of a family's control. All the procedures of probate are carefully observed in *vv.* 10–12. The point of the incident comes in *v.* 15 taken against the background described in *vv.* 1–5. The city was at that moment in an uproar, besieged and on the point of collapse. Nevertheless, in a supreme act of hope and faith in the future, Jeremiah purchased the field at Anathoth, for he believed that the time to plant and to build would by God's mercy eventually return. Such heroic action at a time of crisis actually effects what it symbolizes, for it inspires and produces faith in a situation of despair.

New Testament Reading (Epistle)   **Galatians 2: 15–3: 9**

Paul gives here the theological reasons for rejecting the demand that circumcision should be imposed on Gentile Christians. Conformity to the law of circumcision was the outward expression of membership of the people of Israel, but it is not its inner essence. Right relationship with God is the result of God's own action in vindicating Christ and incorporating men into his body through the death of the old self, and new life with Christ (20–21). So it is hearing with faith, not outward observance of law that realizes the gift of the Spirit (3:2). Membership of the true Israel, then, is proved not outwardly in the flesh, but inwardly by the Spirit (v.3). Abraham's faith was an anticipation of the preaching of the Gospel to all men (v.8), and one becomes a true son of Abraham by sharing his faith and receiving the blessing God promised to his offspring (v.9).

New Testament Reading (Gospel)   Luke 7: 1–10

The healing of the Centurion's servant is to the detached observer the least convincing of all Jesus's miracles in terms of proof. We are not told what the boy was suffering from; only that he was at the point of death (v.2). But this may well reflect the extent of the concern felt by the Centurion rather than an objective diagnosis. Jesus was not approached directly, nor did he even come to the sickbed (v.7f), but he merely spoke the word. The Centurion however was able to recognize Jesus's intrinsic authority, and that was enough for him. The sceptic could dismiss the cure as pure coincidence. But the Centurion knew the truth intuitively; and his faith was praised by Christ as greater than any he had found in Israel. This man who had been a conspicuous benefactor of God's people had yet felt himself unworthy to receive Jesus under his roof. His faith then was not just blind credulity, it belonged essentially to the goodness and humility that made up his character.

Eighteenth Sunday after Pentecost
The Offering of Life

When at the end of the service of Holy Communion we tell God that we 'offer' him 'our souls and bodies to be a living sacrifice', what exactly do we mean? We mean total commitment to God's service, day in, day out, in terms of the gifts, responsibilities, and opportunities which he himself has given us. These vary from person to person, and today's readings give us differing patterns of response, one or more of which may find a parallel within our own circumstances. But always it is 'through Christ' and 'in the power of (his) Spirit'.

Old Testament Reading   Nehemiah 6: 1–16

Nehemiah had an important task to perform in the teeth of strong and sustained opposition, which took the form of repeated attempts to undermine his determination and faith in God. The rebuilding of the walls of Jerusalem after the Jews' return from exile was easily construed as an act of rebellion against the Persian king, when it was really nothing of the kind. It was Sanballat and his friends who felt threatened, as such people always do when anyone decides to take the Lord's work seriously in hand. By his faith, courage, and obedience, Nehemiah was able to ride out the misrepresentations, and bring the work to a successful conclusion in which even his opponents recognized the hand of God.

or   Ecclesiasticus 38: 24–end

This, the longest book in the Apocrypha, was written in Jerusalem about 200 B.C., and is one of the books of Wisdom emanating from Pharisaic and Sadducean circles. True wisdom finds its beginning in the fear of the Lord (cf. Psalm 111:10) and shows itself in all kinds of ways. Not only the scholar and the man of affairs but also the man who works with his hands shows reverence for the mysteries of God's creation by the diligence with which he sets about his daily task in field or forge or factory. He may not be able to talk articulately about spiritual realities, but he reveals his grasp of them by the quality of his workmanship, so that his work itself becomes his prayer to God (*v.* 34 margin).

New Testament Reading (Epistle) **1 Peter 4: 7–11**

The Christian lives his life on the threshold of eternity. Every moment is precious. Self-discipline, prayer, the love which heals men's souls, all these should be much in evidence. Even opening our homes to other people can be a way of dispensing the manifold grace of God. Teachers and preachers and all who perform any kind of public service are God's messengers and ministers to those who need to have their minds opened to God's wonders in creation and redemption, and to those who need a helping hand to enable them to meet life's demands and alleviate its problems. In all these ways God's glory can be shown.

New Testament Reading (Gospel) **Matthew 25: 14–30**

C. H. Dodd called this the Parable of the Money in Trust, and identified the complacent one-talent man who would take no risks with the Israel of our Lord's own day who had failed to share with the rest of the world the treasures of revealed truth. As a result, the Kingdom was taken from them and given to others (see Matthew 21:43). Stewardship of time, talents, or worldly wealth calls for adventure and courageous faith. Only those who are prepared to hazard their lives for the cause of Christ will discover what the rewards are in terms of increased opportunities of service and the Lord's 'Well done'.

Nineteenth Sunday after Pentecost
The Life of Faith

For a Christian, faith is commitment, not just assent to a number of propositions about God. To believe in God is to enter into a personal relationship with him through Christ, and this relationship immediately begins to show itself in changed attitudes towards other people and in a new set of values. This may bring us into collision with the powers that be, or it may make us do things which the world can make no sense of at all, because it does not understand the motives which underlie our actions. But if, as today's Epistle says, 'Christ died for us while we were yet sinners', then such a demonstration of God's love for us must find a similar response, whatever sacrifice or suffering that may involve on our part.

Old Testament Reading   **Daniel 6: 10–23**

'Daniel was so tough that the lions couldn't get their teeth into him at all.' This extract from a schoolboy's essay contains a great truth. Faith makes men tough—able to stand up to whatever trials and tribulations life may bring. For Daniel, his fearless trust in God brought immediate deliverance; others have been 'tortured to death, disdaining release, to win a better resurrection' (Hebrews 11:35), like the early Christian martyrs. In either case, faith won through, and the forces of evil were powerless to stifle it. One of its secrets is the keeping up of the habit of daily prayer—for Daniel, morning, noon, and night—whereby each day, whatever it may bring, is firmly committed to God, and his saving help is sought and found.

New Testament Reading (Epistle)   **Romans 5: 1–11**

Peace with God, access into his presence through the atoning work of Christ, joy in the midst of suffering, reconciliation, daily salvation through the indwelling of the living Lord, these are some of the fruits of justifying faith. For justification means a new relationship with God, made possible for us through what he himself has done for us in Christ. In Christ he accepts us as we are, in all our helplessness and sin, and brings us into contact with his healing love and grace. His Spirit works within our hearts, and we are able to look forward with eager hope to the sharing of his glory. Justification is not a subjective experience, but an objective act on God's part, sealed to us in baptism. Faith is the hand which reaches out and appropriates the new life God offers us in Christ, and lives it out within the fellowship of his Church.

New Testament Reading (Gospel)   **Luke 19: 1–10**

'To see what Jesus looked like' may not have seemed a very high ambition, but underlying it was a deep sense of need. For all his great wealth, Zacchaeus was a lonely and frustrated man. What he had heard about Jesus presented a challenge to his whole way of life, a challenge to which he had the courage to respond. To mingle with unsympathetic crowds was not easy for him, to pull his stocky little body up into a tree made him appear ridiculous, but he persisted in his quest, and his determination was rewarded. He not only saw 'what Jesus looked like' but found himself welcomed into his company as 'a true son of Abraham'. Such generous treatment sparked off a generous response, for when faith finds what it is looking for, everything one has is placed at the disposal of the One who sets us free from bondage to worldly possessions which can never satisfy the hunger of the heart. The life of faith is a life of reckless and joyous abandonment to the purpose of God.

Twentieth Sunday after Pentecost
Endurance

It is easy to be a Christian in the company of likeminded people and in an atmosphere of prayer and Christian service. It is much harder when surrounded by those who have little use for 'religion' and regard any profession of it as tantamount to hypocrisy. And we ourselves can become depressed and grow weary of well-doing. We must have a faith firmly grounded in the promises of God, a faith which helps us to come to terms with our own weakness and gives us courage to persevere against all odds. We need to know the secret of endurance.

Old Testament Reading   **Genesis 32: 22–30**

Having cheated his brother Esau of his birthright (25:29ff.) and his blessing (ch. 27), Jacob had fled for safety to his mother's cousins in Haran. Now, twenty years later, he desired to return home. Before crossing the river Jabbok, he sent gifts ahead to appease his brother's anger, but he still needed the assurance that God too had forgiven him, and would truly bless him and his descendants as he had promised. Hence this strange story of an overnight contest with an unknown assailant which may owe something to the contemporary practice of settling disputes by the 'ordeal'. In it was epitomized the long struggle Jacob had had in exile to come to terms with himself and with God. He had been brought to see himself as he really was, and was now ready to throw himself entirely on the mercy and goodness of the God who had fulfilled his promise never to leave him until he had done that of which he had spoken to him (28:15).

New Testament Reading (Epistle)   **1 Corinthians 9: 19–end**

Like the more famous Olympic Games, the Isthmian Games, held regularly in Corinth, were a notable feature of the city's life. It is not surprising that Paul draws on them for illustrations of the self-discipline and determination which should characterize every Christian. In his own case this self-discipline was exercised in relation to the longing he had to bring the gospel within reach of everybody, Jew and Gentile alike. What might appear to be inconsistency was really part of a carefully thought out plan of evangelism in which first things were put first. To achieve this aim, he had to be fully trained in order to keep himself from 'being disqualified after having called others to the contest' (v.27, TEV).

New Testament Reading (Gospel)　　　　　　　**Matthew 7: 13–27**

These verses form the closing section of the Sermon on the Mount. They tell us of four things which make for stability in the Christian life.

1. A commitment which is deliberate and total (vv. 13, 14), involving the choice of the narrow way of faith.
2. An ability drawn from observation and practical experience of discerning the counterfeits to genuine Christianity (vv. 15–20).
3. Unhesitating obedience to Christ's commands, so that our profession and our practice march as one (vv. 21–23).
4. Building up our lives on the only sure foundation, which is Christ himself (vv. 24–27, cf. 1 Corinthians 3: 11).

Twenty-first Sunday after Pentecost
The Christian Hope

Hope is a basic ingredient of all human activity. The politician, the social reformer, the parent, the teacher, the manufacturer, all need hope to spur them on towards the achievement of their aims. So does the man who wrestles with trouble or suffering. For him the hope of ultimate release shines like a bright point of light at the end of a dark tunnel. For the Christian, hope finds a place alongside faith and love as one of the three theological virtues. It is the direction of the will towards God and to the joy of everlasting union with him, a joy which we have already begun to experience in Christ.

Old Testament Reading   Ezekiel 12: 21–end

The prophet Ezekiel was with the first group of Jews deported from Jerusalem to Babylon by king Nebuchadnezzar in 598 B.C. For the next twelve years the city remained intact, and those still there carried on with their idolatry and immoral practices with apparent immunity in spite of repeated warnings sent to them by Ezekiel. 'Time runs on', they said, 'nothing is going to happen to us'. But it did, and the eventual destruction of the city (2 Kings 25, cf. Ezekiel 33:21) showed that God's warnings should always be heeded, however long their fulfilment might seem to be delayed. So too his promises of forgiveness and restoration. No situation is without hope for those who accept God's judgements and look for his mercy.

New Testament Reading (Epistle)   1 Peter 1: 13–end

1 Peter was written to Christians in Asia Minor who were faced with 'trials of many kinds' (1:7). These trials however had the effect of throwing them more completely on Christ, whose saving power had been foretold by prophets long ago. They must not grow weary of well-doing; holiness was the mark of all who professed to be children of the one Father (*v.* 17). The unseen Lord, whom they had come to love, had himself suffered persecution and outrage, and had gone to

the Cross for their salvation. His resurrection proved that the final word is not with sin and death, but with God who raises the dead. So to look to Christ is to be 'stripped for action' and 'perfectly self-controlled' now, as well as to be sure of his gracious acceptance when he comes again. For Christian hope is not wishful thinking but joyful anticipation.

New Testament Reading (Gospel)   **John 11: 17–27**

Martha shared the view of most devout Jews of her day that there would be a resurrection for the righteous at the end of this present age. But here Jesus says 'I am the resurrection!'. He claims to be a future event! It follows from this that the consolation Christ offers to those who mourn the death of a Christian brother is not that he will rise again some day, true though that is, but that in Christ he is *already* in possession of the life which is immortal. As A. M. Hunter has said: 'there is no denial of a resurrection at the last day, but an insistence that for those in fellowship with Christ the life to which resurrection leads begins now'.

Twenty-second Sunday after Pentecost
The Two Ways

From beginning to end the Bible treats us as responsible beings and offers us a clear choice between good and evil, blessing and cursing, life and death. Two ways are presented to us, and upon our choice depends not only our eternal destiny, but also the success with which we are able to cope with life's problems and opportunities here and now. This can be difficult at times, but a decision for God and the things of God means that we shall not be left to fend for ourselves, for all who entrust themselves to him find that he is with them, pledged to their support and victory.

Old Testament Reading   **Deuteronomy 11: 18–28**

A 'phylactery' is a small, rectangular leather box containing verses of Scripture (the *Shema*, Deuteronomy 6:4–9) which the pious Jew still fastens with leather bands on his forehead or arm at special times. A similar box, called a *mezuzah*, may also be noticed on the doorposts of his house. 'Phylactery' means 'safeguard', and it is intended to remind him of his obligation to remember God's mercy and to serve him in holiness of thought and action. It could however so easily become a lucky charm or means of self-advertisement, and our Lord warned against its misuse in Matthew 23:5. It is good to surround ourselves with reminders of the faith which we profess, especially when there are children about (*v.* 19), for they act as a constant challenge to our allegiance. But we must never allow them to become substitutes for the real thing. The blessing belongs to those who have the Word of God written on their hearts.

New Testament Reading (Epistle)   **1 John 2: 22–end**

A Christian is one who believes that in Christ God has acted in a unique way for the whole human race. Through him he has provided not only cleansing from sin, but also a close, personal relationship with himself which John calls living or abiding in the Son. All this is expressed, however inadequately, in the descriptions of Jesus as Messiah and Son of God. To deny it is to deny the fundamental tenet of the faith, and a failure to recognize the way in which God has chosen to reveal his Fatherhood. To acknowledge Jesus as the Son of God is to receive 'the anointing', i.e. the gift of the Holy Spirit, who integrates us into God's family and makes known to us the things of Jesus in our daily walk and conduct (see John 16:13f).

New Testament Reading (Gospel) **Luke 16: 1–9**

Although normally careless about what he did with his master's property, the unjust or dishonest steward, when faced with immediate dismissal, acted with great astuteness and even won his master's congratulations (*v.*8)! What he did may have been to remit interest on loans, so that, instead of having to write off the larger amounts owing to him, his master would at least have the chance of some reimbursement, and the reduced amounts would please his clients also and secure their goodwill towards the ousted steward. One lesson of the parable is that money or 'worldly wealth' can be used for good or ill. The Christian is under obligation to use it, not for his own aggrandisement, but for the good of others, who, thanks to his wise stewardship, will be there to welcome him into the heavenly home.

Last Sunday after Pentecost
Citizens of Heaven

The author of *The Cloud of Unknowing*, that marvellous English devotional classic which has come down to us from the fourteenth century, has some good advice to give about spiritual meditation. We should think deeply, he says, about three things—our own wretchedness, the sufferings of Christ, and the joys of heaven. The last one forms the theme of this Sunday's readings. Perhaps we rather fight shy of such a theme nowadays for fear of being thought escapist ('pie in the sky' and all that) and of failing to come to terms with our life here and now. But it is well to reflect that the joys of heaven figure in some of the greatest of our hymns (e.g. 'Jerusalem the golden') and that the Lord himself 'for the joy that was set before him endured the cross, despising the shame'.

Old Testament Reading   Isaiah 33: 17–end

This passage points a contrast between the present state of Jerusalem, overrun and hemmed in by foreign invaders who exact harsh tribute, and Jerusalem set free from her enemies and surrounded once again by quiet countryside, and not needing for its protection broad rivers and naval armament such as Egypt relied upon, once more a centre of pilgrimage (Zion) for the whole earth. A splendid vision which must have brought encouragement to the Jews in exile in Babylon. For us too it speaks of a divine intervention (*v.*22) working itself out in the processes of history, and finding its focus in the figure of a 'king in his beauty' who is not only judge and ruler, but also the one who 'will save us'.

New Testament Reading (Epistle)   Revelation 7: 2–4, 9–end

In this wonderful vision the Seer of the Apocalypse follows up his description in the previous chapter of God's judgements upon earth with a twofold picture of God's people, the true Israel. First he sees them protected by God during their present troubles. The 'sealing' secures immunity, not from physical suffering or even martyrdom, but from spiritual apostasy. The precise number, twelve by twelve multiplied by a thousand, indicates the completeness and individuality of God's saving grace (cf. John 10:28). Then he sees the same people, now past all counting, gathered around the throne of God at the Last Day when suffering and sorrow are no more and the Good Shepherd himself, who shed his blood for the sheep, will be in their midst to share with them life at a deeper level than they have yet experienced. Their song of praise (*v.* 12) is anticipated in the acclamation at the end of the Prayer of Thanksgiving in the new Eucharist.

New Testament Reading (Gospel)   **Matthew 25: 1–13**

In this parable the lamps, i.e. torches, may be said to represent a profession of purpose, the outward marks of the Christian life, while the oil stands for inward spiritual power which alone can impart light, warmth, and value to the externals of religion. *All* the girls 'dozed off' but when the crisis came, it showed who were really ready for the bridegroom's coming and who were not. We shall not be able to rely on other people's experience when Jesus comes. 'I do not know you' implies an already existing relationship. If we would be present at the Marriage Supper of the Lamb (Revelation 19:9), then something more is required of us than outward religious observance or reliance on being born and brought up within a Christian tradition. 'Spiritual preparedness is an individual matter' (F. V. Filson).

Index of Readings in biblical order

307